Lidia Guzy

# Marginalised Music

# KlangKulturStudien
# SoundCultureStudies

herausgegeben von

Lars-Christian Koch
und
Raimund Vogels

Band 8

LIT

Lidia Guzy

# MARGINALISED MUSIC

Music, Religion and Politics
from Western Odisha/India

LIT

*... to all musicians of the Bora Sambar region of western Odisha*

Cover Picture: Ganda Baja, Padampur 2005, Lidia Guzy

Published with the generous support of the National University of Ireland Grant in Aid of Publication

This book is printed on acid-free paper.

**Bibliographic information published by the Deutsche Nationalbibliothek**
The Deutsche Nationalbibliothek lists this publication in the Deutsche Nationalbibliografie; detailed bibliographic data are available in the Internet at http://dnb.d-nb.de.

ISBN 978-3-643-90272-6
Zugl.: Berlin, FU, Habil.schrift, 2011

**A catalogue record for this book is available from the British Library**


Klosbachstr. 107
CH-8032 Zürich
Tel. +41 (0) 44-251 75 05
Fax +41 (0) 44-251 75 06
E-Mail: zuerich@lit-verlag.ch
http://www.lit-verlag.ch

LIT VERLAG Dr. W. Hopf
Berlin 2013
Fresnostr. 2
D-48159 Münster
Tel. +49 (0) 2 51-62 03 20
Fax +49 (0) 2 51-23 19 72
E-Mail: lit@lit-verlag.de
http://www.lit-verlag.de

**Distribution:**
In Germany: LIT Verlag Fresnostr. 2, D-48159 Münster
Tel. +49 (0) 2 51-620 32 22, Fax +49 (0) 2 51-922 60 99, E-mail: vertrieb@lit-verlag.de
In Austria: Medienlogistik Pichler-ÖBZ, e-mail: mlo@medien-logistik.at
In Switzerland: B + M Buch- und Medienvertrieb, e-mail: order@buch-medien.ch
In the UK: Global Book Marketing, e-mail: mo@centralbooks.com
In North America: International Specialized Book Services, e-mail: orders@isbs.com

## *Acknowledgement*

This publication has been possible due to a generous *Grant in Aid of Publication* provided by the National University of Ireland in 2012. I would also like to thank the Volkswagen Foundation and the German Research Council for their generous research grants supports from 2002 to 2010 enabling me to conduct continuous basic research into the musical and social traditions of the Bora Sambar region of western Odisha (until 2011 Orissa). I thank Prof. Dr. Georg Pfeffer for inspiring me to start with this research. I am grateful to Prof. Dr. Deepak Kumar Behera for giving me the necessary help in Sambalpur to embark on my fieldwork. For the ethno-musicological advice and contextualisation I thank Prof. Dr. Lars-Christian Koch, the Director of the Ethno-musicological Department of the Museum of Arts and Cultures in Berlin. I owe special thanks and gratitude to Nikolaos Papandreou for his invaluable support in sound and video documentation. I also thank Andreas Fliedner for his English lectorate and Daniela Weber for her support in layout.

Without the friendship of and professional cooperation with Surendra Kumar Sahu and with all local musicians, the writing of this book would not have been possible. It is the result of the great cooperative and communal spirit of the local musicians in the region. To all of them this book is dedicated.

Lidia Guzy

## *Content*

# Introduction

## Music as Culture, Medium and Religion

How to grasp culture? How to define religion? Both concepts are as universally used as they are difficult to pin down. It seems impossible to come to a general, exhaustive and unambiguous definition of culture, a term that covers notions such as "tradition", "cultural heritage" or "custom".[1] The same applies for the concept of religion as

> *"without recourse to the self-understanding of a religion's adherents and the recognition of this self-understanding by the historical and social surroundings, it is usually impossible to decide whether actions are religious or not."* (Zinser 1997: 162).[2]

Academic attempts to clarify the both terms have either led to a multitude of definitions and academic disciplines or to a "methodological nationalism" (Hann 2007: 127). It seems that, in order to avoid a substantialist representation of culture and religion, new perspectives on social ideas, values and behaviour have to be explored.

> *"Music is an appropriate medium with which to begin such a project. It is certainly a medium which can cement the sense of belonging to a community, and it can be put to serve the causes of nationalists and other power-holders (Stokes 1994), but it also opens up a quintessential field of human creativity for anthropological comparison."* (Hann 2003: 234)

In the present study, a local society in an ongoing process of transformation is approached through an ethnological exploration of its musical culture. The following chapters focus on various ritual musical traditions in the East Indian region of western Odisha (until 2011 Orissa). especially on those of marginalised village musicians and non-Brahmin priests, and on their alterations under the influence of ethnic and regional political movements.

---

[1] On the problem of definitions and concepts of culture see Kroeber / Kluckhohn 1952 and Lévi- Strauss 1952; on the difficulties of a definition of religion see also Zinser (2010: 35-81).

[2] „Ohne Rekurs auf das Selbstverständnis der Anhänger einer Religion und der Anerkennung dieses Selbstverständnisses durch das geschichtliche und soziale Umfeld wird aber meist nicht entscheidbar sein, ob es sich um eine religiöse oder andere Handlungen handelt.“ (Zinser 1997: 162).

The Bora Sambar region of western Odisha is famous for its rich musical heritage. Its inhabitants consider music a major cultural factor, expressing and transmitting a consciousness of a strong regional and cultural identity. The village music of the Bora Sambar region is linked to the worship of local gods and goddesses, as well as to life and death rituals like marriages and commemoration ceremonies. Priest-musicians communicate with the ancestors and the deceased by means of special musical instruments. Trance mediums embodying local goddesses and gods act in consonance with the beats and rhythms of drums in order to heal and mediate between the human and the otherworldly sphere. Local dance and drama traditions re-stage a divine play on earth, where the scene is manifested in and mediated through the body of the human artist, while the sounds of musical instruments represent local notions of the utterances of different goddesses. To borrow the well known words of Marshall Mc Luhan, in the Bora Sambar region music indeed operates simultaneously as medium and message (Mc Luhan 1994). Not least, this holds true for the complex interrelations between music and the socio-cultural hierarchy of the caste system, where certain musical activities are restricted to members of marginalised castes and associated with the polyvalent stigma of "untouchability" and "pollution".

The present study is situated in-between disciplines: between the anthropology of music and the anthropology of religions, between ritual studies, anthropology of the senses and media anthropology. It attempts to understand a local society and its religion through its specific music and seeks to analyse music as a crucial medium of cultural continuum, creativity and social expression. Music and sound interlink with other media, such as body movement, dance, visual and performing arts. In this study, I would like to underline the intermediality of music as a crucial and powerful cultural mechanism of creating meaning and transmitting local values.

The study is intended as an extension of the still rudimentary bridge between anthropology and music – a bridge whose importance has been underlined in recent anthropological discussions, as for example in the 2004 issue *Musique et Anthropologie* of the French anthropological revue *l'Homme.* I attempt to decode music as a cultural and religious language which operates without words, but expresses complex, fluid and ambivalent value configurations such as the social construction of "untouchability", or ideas about life after death and the social fact of trance mediumship or embodiment.

On the following pages, sounds, music and rhythmic structures are taken as practical expressions of indigenous media theories, transmitting concepts of the Sublime, the Self and an otherworldly Other. Rhythmic structures or forms of dance are analysed as media techniques revealing indigenous forms of meaning and its transmission. The sound of music is understood as a medium of multisensory experiences (Howes 1991; Quereshi 2000: 805-838), embodying cultural emotions, memories (Feld 1990; 1994) and ambiguities.

## *State of Discussion*

In recent discussions about the "anthropology of the senses", music as sensory experience (Howes 1991), sound and auditory culture (Bull/Back 2003; Wulf 1993) has emerged as a central issue. The power of sound and what Walter Ong has termed "aurality" (Ong 1969: 634-647; Ong 1991) has been explored in order to challenge the "logocentricity" of modern occidental science and culture and, in a next step, to "*turn the tables and recover a full bodied understanding of culture and experience*" (Howes 2005: 1). Such an understanding seeks to describe culture as a multi-sensory symbolic system (Classen 2005: 147-163) but also takes into account the social constructedness of sensorial perceptions and of the sensorial dimensions of culture.

In the same vein, the discourse on the "aesthetics of religion" within the German Studies of Religions (Cancik / Mohr 1988; Münster 2001) stresses the sensorial and aesthetic dimensions of religion.[3] The sensual and sensorial side of religion is discussed either on the basis of its iconographic (Lanwerd 2003; Koch 2004: 330-342), museological (Bräunlein 2004; Pantke 2004: 195-222; Kamel 2004) or kinaesthetic (Mohr 2004) expressions. The sensual dimension of individual European religiosity has especially been outlined in the context of the European reception of Buddhism (Prohl 2003: 259-276; 2004: 291-299). However, music up till now has been a rather neglected field in the German discourse on the aesthetics of religion. Exceptions are Isabel Laack's analysis of the identificatory role of music in relation to religion in the context of the Glastonbury Festival of Performing Arts (2005: 123-153; 2007: 114-133; 2009: 32-35) and the indological work of Annette Wilke (2008: 15-60) and Moebus (Wilke/Moebus 2012). The latter focus their attention on the sensual role of sound as a crucial element of aesthetic perception in Sanskrit Hinduism, taking into view the sonic rather than the textual characteristics of Hinduism.

In attempting to describe music and rhythmical structures as media and expressions of a *theoretical* conception of the world or the hereafter, my work aims at contributing to such an "anthropology of the senses", overcoming the

---

[3] For a systematic theoretical overview see Lanwerd 2002.

traditional hegemony of script which has long marginalised or excluded from scholarly attention techniques of knowledge and meaning transmission which are not put down in writing.

The lack of script has become a socio-cultural pattern in the sociological and ideological marginalisation of societies dominated by orality and aurality. In short: societies and cultures relying on non-scriptual systems of meaning tend to be considered as inferior, devoid of possibilities to gain a complex intellectual – theoretical – hold of the world. In order to challenge this perspective, I would like to call to mind that the Greek term *theoria* originally denoted the physical act of regarding a ritual procession or performance as well as the ritual performance itself. It signified both: the act of looking upon as well as the action looked upon. In using the term 'indigenous theories', I attempt to revive this second, performative aspect of *theoria*. A theory is not only a systematized worldview but, at the same time, also a performance of the world.

Indigenous theories stand for local systems of meaning or understanding. A system of meaning is a subjective, culturally specific, locally designed and transmitted rationality (Weber 1980). Meaning systems create sense by means of the diverse senses: seeing, hearing, touching and the olfactory senses. Local meaning is generated and transmitted through techniques of acoustic and visual, oral or literal representation. Local or indigenous theories and meaning systems[4] consist of ideas and values that are sensually communicated. They use language in the form of ritual speech, the body as ritual embodiment (trance), music and dance. Mythological narratives or healing ceremonies, oracles or liturgies, dances or specific patterns of behaviour can be the media of indigenous theories. Due to script-centred scholarly perspectives, many of these indigenous theories were for a long time overlooked. India possesses an overwhelming richness of oral (Champion 1996) and performative forms (Vatsyayan 1980) of indigenous theories, which for

[4] What I have termed "meaning system" is in anthropological literature sometimes referred to as "local" or "indigenous knowledge". In anthropological discussion local or indigenous knowledge describes the "traditional knowledge" of a group in a particular environmental and social situation. According to Roy Ellen and Holly Harris "indigenous knowledge" relates to an "'epistemic community which permits a sufficient degree of common sense engagement to allow that they [the members of the particular community] refer to the same focal semantic source" (Ellen / Harris 2000: 2). Indigenous knowledge is described as local, orally-transmitted, practical and empirical (ibid: 4), thus context-bound and community-specific. For the Indian context the notions of local or indigenous knowledge are commonly used to designate the traditional ecological (Choudhury 1980; Chakraborty 1986) or medical knowledge (Shukla /Gardner 2006) of local communities.

the most part still wait to be discovered. These indigenous theories often have a religious character or are at least expressed in religious narratives or rituals. They create meaning by establishing a relation between human lives, the cosmos and notions of the hereafter, thus constructing particular rationalities of individual and collective action. In my study of diverse musical traditions of the Bora Sambar region of western Odisha it is my aim to explore the emic, indigenous concepts of music and sound linked to diverse religious ideas, rituals and performances of the region. I will attempt to describe music, dance and ritual such as possessions and healing séances and drama traditions as indigenous theories with their own internal rationalities, based, in the first place, not on the value and meaning of texts but on the value and meaning of the sounds of human voices and musical instruments as well as on a sophisticated body-culture.

### *Indian village music*

Even if almost no ritual in rural India is performed without music, in the context, ritual village music is not a popular topic in ethnographic ritual studies on village India.[5] The long-term ethno-musical researches by Ulrich Wegner (1986 a/b; 1987, 1988) and by Mireille Helffer (1969a/b) on Nepal, the recent works by Nicolas Prévôt on musicians in Chhattisgarh (Prévôt 2008: 75-88; ibid 2005), the overview on Asian "Tribal Music" by Stephan Slawek (2001/2002) and the study by Christine Guillebaud (2008) on itinerant musicians in Kerala and by Rolf Killius on Kerala's percussion temple music (2006) as well as Georg Pfeffer's ethnologic account on the music of the Dombo in Koraput in southern Odisha (Pfeffer 1994: 14–20), are notable exceptions. In contrast, there are numerous ethno-musicological works on the so called "classical" Indian music, namely North Indian *raga*-music and the south-Indian carnatic music.[6]

With the present book on the living musical traditions of the rural Bora Sambar region, I deliberately try to focus on marginalised village music traditions, which have for the most part not been recognised as valuable cultural expressions and have in consequence remained over- and unheard until now. But it is not my aim to incorporate these indigenous musical traditions

---

[5] To mention only few: Carrin 1997; 2006; Mallebrein 2000; 2001; Mallebrein / Stietencron 2008, Otten 2006.

[6] For an overview see Daniélou 1979; 2004; Ray 1985; Arnold 2000; Vir 1999; Wade 1979; for a study on the raga music see Koch 1995; Widdess 1995; Moutal 1991; for the courtly musical culture of North India see Bor / Bruguière 2003.

into the canon of "classical" Indian music theories and practices. I think that they harbour their own complexities and theories – and are thus equally valuable. Furthermore, to "make classical" a musical tradition, which has its local and regional colour, means to run the risk of destroying or at least overlooking its specificity through systematization and classification under hegemonial categories and hierarchies.

### *Music as culture and sound*

Music, in the context of this study, is conceived as "humanly organised sound" (Blacking 1973: 3-31) and body movement.[7] It represents, as John Blacking has put it, a "dance-music-verbal" language which is innate and universal. There is no such thing as an unmusical human being. Music thus can be described as a universal code, a system of signs that can be decoded in reference to its social context (Blacking 1973: XIX). According to the definition of Artur Simon, Music is a universal human phenomenon which incorporates song, play of musical instruments and rhythmic body touch. Music is a "sonic order" which, as a cultural phenomenon, must be approached in relation to aesthetic, communicative, social, psychological and religious culture-specific categories (Simon 2000: 162-63). Music can thus be understood as a "total cultural language" (Feld / Fox 1994: 25-53) that seeks to express something where words end. Every contribution to the "anthropology of sound" is indebted to the groundbreaking work of Steven Feld. Feld's ethnographic study of the Kaluli of the Southern Highlands province of Papua New Guinea (1990) has shown, how their aural-oral culture reveals a specific sound system echoing an "acultural" symbolic system of ecology of the rainforest. In recent studies Feld has extended his ethnography of sound towards an acoustemology (2003: 223-240; 2005: 179-192), a system of knowing and perceiving the world through the oral-aural experience of "*placing sound*" in a "*sounding place*" (2005:188). While Murray Schaffer introduced the notion of soundscapes (1977) in order to describe the individual and collective perception of cultural and imagined acoustic spaces, Feld develops upon this the idea of "sound worlds" and "embodied memories" (2003: 223-241; 2005:179-191) describing a cultural symbolism of sound which transports ideas, historical and biographical memories, collective identities and emotions through specific sounds and instruments. Music thus

[7] Defined as a general communicative practice of sound production, music would include songs of birds and the language of dolphins (Stokes 1996: 383). Such an approach would be too broad for the present study but it hints at the dimensions of communication through sounds.

operates as an embodied and communicating system which resonates a local history and a culturally specific emotional memory – a perspective which I attempt to explore in the course of the following study on the basis of examples from my fieldwork in Bora Sambar.

As it is culturally created, music touches the "cultural self" of individuals and societies. Music is a vital medium of personal perception and thus especially significant for the emotional transmission of ideas and values. Being culturally shaped but personally experienced, music takes its place at the interface between society and the empirical individual.[8] On the following pages, I will assume that music is a social form of non-verbal communication, taking over functions of consolation, commemoration, remembrance and the representation of ideas and values (Coppet / Zemp 1979: 117-119). Music is also a significant cultural form of marking personal, cultural, sociopolitical and ethnic identity. As a supra-personal medium music provides a means of collective response to both individual and collective crisis. Music expresses cultural memories and emotions through the creation and re-creation of culture-specific sound spaces which in moments of crisis help to re-establish a feeling of a sociality. Through music, which can transmit values, ideas and models of behaviour by means of its patterns, a personally experienced feeling of social continuity may be created. This feeling of continuity through music seems to be especially effective and discernible in mourning and funeral rites, as I attempt to show in this study in the musical traditions of non-Brahmin priests of western Odisha.[9] Universally, music is not only used in religious worship and mourning and funeral rites but as well in other rituals of personal and collective crisis and reintegration, especially in rituals of healing. The use of music in healing performances is emotionally, sensually and imaginatively engaging and thus can be sensually and culturally effective. On the following pages, healing performances, as they appear in the diverse forms of the *boil* trance-medium tradition of the Bora Sambar region, will be a central object of investigation[10].

Music, in the form of religious chants and the sacred, ritual and liturgical music of diverse societies, seems nearly everywhere in the world to work as

---

[8] The term empirical individual refers to Dumont's (1983: 304) distinction between western ideological notions of the individual and the physical fact of a human being which can be empirically experienced.

[9] Compare the Kalulis' identification between the sound of the dead and the sound of the birds described by Steven Feld (1990: 45).

[10] For trans-cultural comparison of healing performances see Laderman / Roseman 1996.

a privileged expression of religious identity. Why is music universally considered so suitable for the communication or evocation of messages and sentiments associated with the realm of the religious?

The sound of music is intangible, thus abstract. But the tonality and immateriality of music implies its physicality – the material production and reception or recording of sounds –, manifest in the musical instruments, in the human singer and listener. Sound is a presence of something which can not be grasped but which can be perceived and felt.[11] Sound as an intangible medium has the capacity to transgress space. Music therefore is, on the one hand, an epitome of the transcendent (*transcendere* (lat.) = to exceed) and immaterial side of "culture." On the other hand music can only be mediated through physical objects like instruments or the vocal cords. The paradoxical character of music as a cultural artefact that is both immaterial and material at the same time seems to symbolise precisely its social and religious function. It makes music a suitable cultural metaphor for a non-empirical world.

## *The Empirical Context*

The data for the present study has been collected during a long term ethnomusicological fieldwork in rural and urban western Odisha, undertaken from 2002 to 2005 in the context of the Orissa Research Project overseen by the German Science Foundation.[12] From 2006 to 2010 this research was followed by a project on local museums and music documentation funded by the Volkswagen Foundation (Guzy/Hatoum/Kamel 2009; 2010)[13]. The aim of my investigations was to document and analyse the unknown and vulnerable musical and artistic traditions of marginalised musicians of the Bora Sambar region of western Odisha, especially of the "untouchable" Ganda

---

[11] Viktor Zuckerkandl (1958: 53-63) has already hinted at the paradoxical character of the experience of sound and musical perception which he describes as intangible and tangible, invisible and visual at the same time.

[12] The research was conducted from Mai 2002 to April 2005 in western Orissa. I would like to thank the German Research Council (Deutsche Forschungsgemeinschaft) for the generous grant without which the research could not have been undertaken. I would also like to express my gratitude to Prof. Dr. Georg Pfeffer and Prof. Dr. Deepak Kumar Behera for their constant and unfailing practical help and intellectual guidance.

[13] I would like to thank the Volkswagen Foundation (Volkswagenstiftung) for the generous grant without which the research could not have been undertaken. I would also like to express my gratitude to Prof. Dr. Hartmut Zinser, who hosted the research project at the Institute for Scientific Studies of Religions (Institut für Religionswissenschaft) at the Freie Universität Berlin, for his constant and unfailing support and his thoroughgoing and challenging intellectual advice.

village musicians and of various non-Brahmin priest-musicians of ambivalent social status.

## *Methodology*

The data on which I rely in this study are: observed rituals, recorded musical settings, dialogues, conversations and discussions with musicians and other interlocutors, and not least my own perception of the metaphoric levels of cultural allusions and expressions transmitted through music. I am indebted to the continuous and enthusiastic cooperation of local musicians such as Surendra Kumar Sahu, musical director and master folk singer, who during my years of research became my official research assistant. I rather would like to term Surendra K. Sahu a research partner than a assistant – as we mutually assisted each other in our intercultural understanding. Together with his music group (*baja* party) *sanskuritkaa,* whose members often accompanied me on my travels, I discovered the cultural expressions and meanings of the manifold musical traditions of the Bora Sambar region. What we encountered, recorded and observed I continuously discussed with Surendra K. Sahu and the musicians of the *sanskrutikaa baja* party, Rasul Kumbhar (*mohuri* master), Ladu Mohanand (*nissan* master), Ramesh Gurla (*mandal* master), Sartika Sunna (*tasa* master) and Aswini Patel (*dhol* master) and with many others, whom we met on the road during our discovering tours in the Bora Sambar region. Their views and the information and criticism I received from them have deeply shaped the present study.

For my research, I used qualitative methods such as the classical ethnographic method of "participant observation"[14], a dialogic approach and the systematic cooperation with local musicians. My basis became the town of Padampur from where we travelled by jeep to the villages of the Bora Sambar region, in order to record music, to document rituals and to speak to local performers. Naveen Sethi, our driver, became over time a vital part of our group, leading us with his courage and considerateness to the remotest villages. I remember many night travels to far-off villages in order to grasp the sounds of nightly healing rituals or of local theatre performances. The news spread quickly in the Bora Sambar region: a European lady came – alone - to research and record local music! No one had been interested in village music before! Why she? Who could she be? Curiosity spread. Many local musicians came to the house I had rented on the outskirts of Padampur on their

[14] For a detailed discussion of the methodological problems of participant observation, see Spradley (1979).

own initiative, in order to let me record their music. As a local and a famous musician, Surendra K. Sahu acted incessantly as mediator: during the times of my absence he kept contact to the musicians and untiringly explained my endeavour:

> *"Madam records our old music. Old musicians are dying, who gives the knowledge about our music to our children? Madam does this".*

The reaction of villagers and musicians was in general extremely friendly and welcoming. Locals embraced my enterprise and invited me to their rituals, processions, healing - and drama performances. Many times we met itinerant musicians on the road. Then our jeep stopped. We talked. We explained. We recorded. We followed the musicians to the villages they visited. We tried to keep track of them in their wanderings, an attempt that often turned out to be extremely difficult. My knowledge of Oriya, the local language, as well as the repeated audio-visual documentation of rituals, musical events and settings and discussions since 2002 enabled me to acquire an insight into the local musical traditions and to gain, in the long term, a certain familiarity with the emic – the culturally internal – perspectives. In the present study, I have attempted to combine a rendition of this emic perspective with an external – etic – socio-cultural analysis. However, I have always tried to hold on to my conviction that scientific theory should be guided by empiricism. In the first place, therefore, my ethnography of music and its ritual and performative culture has the aim to give a voice to indigenous theories and local worldviews.

### *Sustainable documentation*

My ethnographic endeavour in the Bora Sambar region had a twofold objective. On the one hand, it was my aim to describe and understand the musical and performative culture of the region; on the other hand, I wanted to establish a documentation of this culture by means of audio-visual recordings. The classical long term ethnography itself already represents a form of documentation, as socio-cultural change is continuously observed and recorded by various means. But in the special case of the musical traditions of the Bora Sambar region, it was my aim to develop a *sustainabledocumentation*, in other words: to establish sound archives, which documented the vulnerable local musical traditions and thus contributed to preserving the intangible heritage[15] of the region.

In my endeavour of *sustainable documentation*, I relied on the approach of dialogical ethnography (Tedlock / Mannheim 1995; Bakhtin 1973; 1981). In the first place, this meant the establishment of long-term relations with local musicians. Recorded data was documented in collaboration with the musicians and later mutually discussed and interpreted. The local musicians were introduced to the techniques of audio-visual recording in order to pursue the documentation of their musical culture on their own. Music was not regarded as stable or "authentic", but as a transformative expression of culture. Thus, musical and socio-cultural changes could be grasped throughout the years.

At the heart of a *sustainable documentation* lies the participation of local representatives in the establishment of sound archives and a mutual exchange of knowledge: what is important to document in the eyes of local musicians and what for me? The appreciation, marginalised musicians and their music experienced in becoming an object of scholarly attention and as worthy of international documentation, has also changed their cultural self-awareness. Groups of marginalised musicians develop new, symbolically empowered socio-political identities and strongly identify with the created sound archives. When the musicians themselves become conscious of being the creators of valuable meaning systems transmitted through music, the preservation of important immaterial cultural heritage can rely on a basis of self-conscious commitment. Thus, a sustainability of documentation and culture can be achieved.

In my case, *sustainable documentation* not only meant a long-term dialogic cooperation with local agents in India but also a long-term cooperation with the Berlin Phonogramm-Archive. From my first up to my recent recordings in 2009, I have brought my sound findings under the custodianship of this institution. As it was my aim to treat and preserve the valuable sound recordings in an appropriate manner – in a secure place, in a moderate temperature and with professional data digitalisation – I decided to share my recordings with this renowned European institution[16]. Nevertheless, I would like to dis-

---

[15] The UNESCO defines „Intangible Heritage" as „...practices, representations, expressions, knowledge, skills – as well as the instruments, objects, artefacts and cultural spaces associated therewith – that communities, groups and, in some cases, individuals recognize as part of their cultural heritage." (ICOM 2004: 10).

[16] I would like to thank Prof. Dr. Lars-Christian Koch, Director of the ethnomusicological department 'Musikethnologie, Medien-Technik und Berliner Phonogramm Archiv' of the Ethno-

tinguish my approach from the historical sound documentations aiming at psychological and physical sound analysis, which informed the beginnings of the Berlin Phonogramm-Archive (Koch/Mengel 2007: 114-124). The main goal of my sustainable documentation is not the storage and scientific analysis of recorded materials in a European institution, but the establishment of a participatory sound archive of western Odisha, which contributes to a socio-cultural empowerment of the source communities. To achieve this, further digitalisation and expansion of recorded materials into a globally accessible virtual archive (open-source repository) is envisaged for the near future.

## *Music in the Bora Sambar region*

In the following chapters I investigate diverse aspects of the symbiotic relationship between religion, rituals and music in the Bora Sambar region. In exploring the role of the music of *ganda baja* village orchestras in the context of trance and possession rituals of goddess embodiment (*boil*), I will try to point out, how a local meaning and belief system is transmitted by the sounds of specific instruments. Music is thus understood as the practical expression of a local media theory and an indigenous theory of the sublime and the sacred. In the course of the study, special attention will be paid to the relationship between music, marginalisation and ritual specialisation. Music in the Bora Sambar region has both: a polluting, marginalizing as well as a purifying, sacred character. Music as sound is impossible to grasp and thus ambivalent. This ambivalence is reflected in the precarious social status of the priest-musicians coming from different local communities administratively labelled Scheduled Castes (SC) or Scheduled Tribes (ST). The Ganda musicians (SC) are considered of a low social status due to the materials of their musical instruments. The diverse subaltern categories of non-Brahmin priest-musicians (SC and ST) are of an ambivalent social status as they handle both the inauspiciousness and purification of death and the commemoration of the deceased through musical dialogues with them. The complex interrelationship between music, social structure and transition between life and death is expressed in the Bora Sambar region through music and sound as crucial media of the performance of social and spiritual order and values.

---

logical Museum in Berlin, for his year-long cooperation – which led to the publication of a CD Par e Sur - Sounds of the Goddess (Guzy 2008) – and for his invaluable ethnomusicological advice.

Besides, local concepts of music and the market as well local dance and theatre traditions will be described as important meaning systems and instruments of cultural value transmission as well as important instruments of socio-cultural and political expression. Finally, recent transformation processes of ritual music in the context of regional politics and social movements will be investigated.

### *Working assumptions*

As a starting point, I would like to propose five working assumptions on the music of the Bora Sambar region which indicate some of the directions the following investigation shall take.

1) Music can function as a *thea-phony.* A local meaning and belief system based upon the belief in local goddesses (greek: *thea*) is transmitted through a system of sounds (greek*: phonē*). The concept of *thea-phony* may be understood as an antithesis or addition to the concept of *theo-logy* which rests upon the idea of a *theos* (greek: god) expressed through a system of words, theories and discourses (*logos*= greek: speech; system of words).

2) In the Bora Sambar region, a strong relationship exists between music and social structure: Music, musical instruments and musicians from the subaltern strata of society are parts and at the same time mediators of a complex socio-cosmic vision and morphology. The subaltern status of musicians has a systemic logic within the local socio-cultural hierarchies.

3) Music as such is a paradoxical medium. It is intangible and elusive and thus predisposed to express cultural specific notions of ritual transgression and transformation as well as local concepts of transcendence. At the same time, music is produced physically through instruments or the voices of human beings.

4) Music is intermedial in so far as it is inseparably interconnected with other performing arts like dance, theatre or poetry.

5) Through its intangibility and physicality alike, music has a power of bundling up diffuse feelings of togetherness, crucial for the expression of cultural, religious and socio-political identities.

But finally – and this question might as well have opened this introductory remarks – how to write about music, about sounds and rhythms? How to grasp in written words a culture of orality which is perceived and transmitted through sensual and sensorial mediums such as acoustics, movements and evoked emotions? Is it even appropriate to use the medium of text in order to describe non-textual, performative, aural and oral cultural expressions?

In the course of writing this study, I have often painfully experienced the limits of language in my endeavour to describe an aural and visual culture. Practically, I have tried to face this problem by attempting a panoramic ethnographic description of social key actions where sound occurs as a vital power for the local people. My ethnography concentrates thus on the description of ritual performances where music and the sound of specific instruments is fundamental for cultural constructions of the after life, the sacred and the handling of critical life situations. I have further given ample space to local narratives, stories, explanations and opinions, to capture at least some "sound bites" of a local worldview. But most of all I hope that on the following pages the reader too will sometimes experience the limits of the written word, because these very limits are a reflection of the immense richness which lies beyond.

### *Orthographic notes*

As the collected data deal with oral traditions of a particular local culture that have not yet been standardised in scriptual form, I have deliberately abstained from diacritical characters. Instead, I use a phonetic transcription of indiginous terms oriented on English pronounciation. Long a = aa; aspirated vowels are indicated by an "h". Local terms are marked in italics; names of gods, persons, groups and places however are not.

### *Music recordings*

This work is the continuation of the published CD and booklet: Lidia Guzy 2008, *Par e Sur – Sounds of the Goddess, Bora Sambar Region / Eastern India.* ©2008 WERGO, SCHOTT MUSIC & MEDIA GmbH, Mainz, Germany. Museum Collection Berlin, ed. Lars-Christian Koch. All recordings can be found there.

# First Chapter: The Region

## The Bora Sambar Region

The *Bora Sambar* region belongs to the Bargarh district, a western part of the Indian State of Orissa, bordering on the province of Chhattisgarh.[17] Surrounded by the mountains of the *Gandhamardan* to the north and south, the

Map: The Bora Sambar region within Orissa / Odisha and India

[17] The Bargarh district, one of the most western districts of Odisha, was established on April 1, 1993. To the north, it borders on the State of Chhatisgarh, to the east on the district of Sambalpur; to the south lies the district of Balangir and Subarnapur and to the west the district of Nawapara. The Bargarh district can be divided into 3 natural partitions, (1) Bargarh Plain (2) Bora Sambar (3) Ambabhona & Lakhanpur (see http://orissadiary.com/orissa_profile/district/Baragarh.asp, retrieved on 12.02.2010).

Bora Sambar region extends around the town of Padampur (Padmapur), on a plain watered by the river Ong (Ang), *"which rises in the south west, describes a great semi-circle to the north and then runs eastward in a widening valley"* (O'Malley 2007: 3). Literally, Bora Sambar means *"the region of the deer swallowed up by the cobra"*. The language of the region is Sambalpuri.

Historically, the *Raj Bora Sambar* can first be traced as an autonomous little kingdom or rather chiefdom of the indigenous Binjhal population, bordering on the tributary Princely State of Patna. However, due to the "*inaccessible forest tracts*" (Sahoo 2007: 1) which covered large parts of the area and owing to the lack of written sources, a reconstruction of the structure and boundaries of the historical Bora Sambar kingdom remains difficult.

Bora Sambar, according to the Bengal District Gazetters on Sambalpur of 1909, belonged to the Maharajas of Patna, *"who where the head of a cluster of States known as the Athara Garhjat (the 18 forts)"* (O'Malley 2007: 21). Bora Sombar presumably was one of the Athara Garjhats, whose chiefs were indigenous Binjhal. Recent research on Princely States in Orissa has shown the important role of indigenous (tribal) communities in establishing a regional autonomy of the local sovereigns, which were called "little kings" (Schnepel 2002).

Under the British colonial rule, the status of Bora Sambar changed from Raj Bora Sambar (Bora Sambar kingdom) to Bora Sambar zamindari.[18]

With the establishment of the zamindari system by the British colonial Empire in the Bengal Permanent Settlement Act in 1793, many indigenousterritories were conferred to feudal lords for the purpose of revenue collection (Bijoi 2007: 15-27; Munda 2002). During the British Raj (1858-1947), with its feudal Princely States headed by local governors such as Maharaja (great king), Raja (king) or Nawab (governor)[19] as well as holders of land domaines (zamindar) for land tenure and tax collection, the Bora Sambar region was the largest among the sixteen zaminari of the Sambalpur district[20]

---

[18] *Zamindari* is the historical term for a land tenure and patronage system introduced in rural India by the Mughal dynasty (1526-1858) and adopted by the British colonial rule in the course of its politics of Princely States and distribution of land domains. The *zamindari* system was based on the collection of taxes by landholders (*zamindar*) possessing proprietary rights in the collection of revenues but not in the land itself. The *zamindar* acted as an intermediary between the government and the inferior revenue farmers. The term *zamindar* generally denoted a person who had landholdings, proprietary rights and tax collection responsibilities, ranging from autonomous or semi-independent chieftains to peasant-proprietors.

[19] For the history of the Princely States see Ramusack 2004; Coplan 2002; Kulke 2005.

[20] At this time the Barghar district, to which Bora Sambar belongs today, was a subdivision of

(O'Malley 2007: 21; 164). The traditional relationship between the Bora Sambar chiefs and the Maharaja of Patna remained. During the British Raj it is reported that

> *"the Binjhal zamindar of Borasambar still affixes the tika [the royal sign on the forehead of the king] to the Maharaja of Patna at the time of his accession"* (ibid: 76).

While the *zamindari*-system as such was abolished with the independence 1947, the independent India adopted the administrative and regional divisions shaped by the *zamindari* system. The Sambalpur Gazetteer of 1971 estimated the expanse of the Bora Sambar *zamindari* at 2178 square kilometres (841 sq. miles), containing 476 villages (Senapati/Mohanti 1971: 516). Today, the regional administration is organized on the basis of the former *zamindari* around the sub-divisional headquarters in Padampur.[21] The region is divided into three *tahsil* (administrative divisions whose centre is mostly a city or town): 1) Padampur; 2) Paikmal; 3) Sohela; and into six administrative blocks: 1) Padampur; 2) Paikmal; 3) Jharband; 4) Gaiselet; 5) Bijeipur and 6) Sohela. The Cenus of India 2001 counted 3035 households and 15442 people in the town of Padampur.[22]

## *Oral History*

### *Bora Sambar: a name and a legend*

Mythologically, the name Bora Sambar is linked to the small village of Bora Sambar and to its inhabitants from the local Adivasi community of the Binjhal. In India, the Adivasi (Sanskrit *adi* - the first; *vasi* - dweller) number ca. 100.000 million people, forming more than six hundred socio-culturally autochthonous language and kinship groups, administratively labelled as "Schedule Tribes". These diverse small-scale pre-industrial communities mostly live in remote areas as forest dwellers, hunter-gatherers, shifting cultivators, agriculturalists or on urban margins. Their socio-cultural systems and religious worldviews generally differ strongly from the hierarchical logic of the Indian caste system (see Pfeffer 1997a: 3-27). Due to the historic

---

the Sambalpur district (O'Malley 2007: 200).

[21] The area consists of 17 revenue inspection circles and includes 8 police stations: 1) Bijeipur; 2) Sohela; 3) Melchamunda; 4) Gaiselet; 5) Padampur; 6) Paikmal; 7) Jahrband; 8) Buren.

[22] http://www.censusindia.gov.in/Population_Finder/View_Village_Population.aspx?pcaid=2030&category=N.A.C.

and sociological impact of hegemonic Hindu ideas, Adivasi societies have been constantly changing in many Indian regions. The process of cultural adjustment, amalgamation or resistance has created a continuum between their indigenous worldviews and the hegemonic trans-regional Hindu concepts. The same situation can be observed in the Bora Sambar region.

Literally, Binjhal means "without sweat" and the Binjhal have a local reputation as hard fighters and labourers. The Binjhal consider themselves as the most ancient people of the region, as the local *purkha lok,* who cleared the jungle (*safo koriba*), and invented agriculture (*chas bas*), thus creating culture out of nature. Up to now, even if the Binjhal besides their traditional occupation as agriculturalists have to hire themselves out as daily workers (*buti*), they still have a proud self-perception of being peasants and owners of their land. In former times, the Binjhal had their own language, called *Binjhal basa*, which however has fallen into oblivion and cannot be remembered even by the oldest living members of the community. Only some fragments have survived in the oral tradition of certain songs. Binjhal music thus represents a kind of cultural archaeological artefact, fragments of the sound vessel of a cultural memory.

Legends tell that from the Binjhal village of Bora Sambar, the Bora Sambar kingdom (*Raj* Bora Sambar) emerged. Old Binjhal men tell the following story about the village and the region:

> *"Once upon a time a big snake (bora) attacked a deer (sambar). At the moment when the big snake tried to kill the deer, the Binjhal saved it."*

From this time on, the legend concludes, the Binjhal became the safeguards and representatives of the region.

Another version of the legend runs as follows:

> *"Once a deer came from the Gandhamardan Mountains to the village Bora Sambar. Suddenly the deer jumped into the village pond and died immediately. At that time the founders of the Bora Sambar kingdom, the Baro Bhai Bendkar (the twelve Bendkar brothers) decided to create their capital (rajdani) in the village of Bora Sambar."*

Another old Binjhal adds:

> *"the Binjhal kings loved music and dance. They engaged many baja partys for their rituals".*

The Binjhal kings are reported to have been ardent propagators of local dance and theatre groups, supporting any kind of artistic expression in the region.

During the time of the British Raj in the 19th century, as a consequence of the status change from *Raj* Bora Sambar (Bora Sambar kingdom) to Bora Sambar *zamindari*, the centre of the local Binjhal kingdom shifted from the village Bora Sambar to Padampur town (*Padam*= the center of the hand; *pur*= the place). In Padampur, a prominently located palace was erected for the Binjhal king, which still plays a crucial role during rituals associated with the former kingdom, such as *dusshara*. Up to now, the impoverished descendants of the petty king reside in Padampur.[23] The current informal king Raja Pratab Kesari Singh still lives in the palace constructed by his father Rajendra Singh Boria, who was the 49th king of the Bora Sambar region and the last king in the time of the British. Even though Raja Pratab Kesari Singh is today without any real political influence connected to his title, he still retains his power on a symbolic level. This becomes manifest especially during the time of the annual festival Durga *puja,* when the petty kingdom is symbolically renewed through the worship of the goddess Durga in *dusshara* ceremonies. On this occasion, the inhabitants of the whole town of Padampur as well as of the surrounding villages come together in order to participate in the ritual of the symbolic renewal of the former kingdom. Until today, the private celebrations for the family of the king take place in the altar (*kutti*) of the goddess Pathneshwari in a hidden part of the former palace. However, in present times, the former authority of the king over the organisation of the Durga *puja* has been transferred to a Durga *puja* committee, consisting of representatives of the town.

It is narrated that in the 19th century the king of Padampur, Rajendra Singh, had four legitimate wives, each inhabiting a separate palace in Padampur – of which today only some ruins have remained – and a number of concu-

---

[23] After the Independence, all Princely States and land holder domains were abolished, and the feudal elite lost their ruling rights, keeping however their hereditary titles and residences as well as some landed property. In 1971 however, with the constitutional reforms introduced by Indira Gandhi, the Princely States ceased to exist as political entities, titles lost their significance and land was expropriated from the royal families. The abolition of the traditional feudal structure has remarkably impoverished the former ruling elite.

bines (*rokini*) with separate small palace-like houses, dispersed over the nearby villages. The socio-biological result was a widely ramified family and hence a high conflict potential. The polygamic structure of the *Raja*'s family as well as the right of primogeniture – the reign of the firstborn – caused severe arguments and permanent controversies about the legitimacy of the ruler. Until today, the question of who is entitled to the special rights of the first born remains disputed and while without any political power, the descendants of the former king Rajendra Sing still quarrel about the legitimacy of their symbolical kingship.[24]

### *Population of the Bora Sambar region*

The population of the Bora Sambar region is an ethnic tapestry of Adivasi communities and different categories of Hindu settlers. Today, the Adivasi communities have mostly assumed a peasant Hindu identity, while retaining a high self-esteem of being culturally distinct from other regions. Bora Sambar is still mostly an agrarian area, not yet transformed by industrialisation as some of the neighbouring districts.[25]

Besides the Binjhal, local Adivasi communities of Gond, Dumal, Soara and Khond are the dominant groups in the area. Beyond these communities other local categories and groups such as Mali, Telli, Luhar, Gour, Kulta, Ganda (Harijan[26]) and Brahmin populate the Bora Sambar region. A strong intercommunal exchange is emphasized by many people. A Kulta man expresses this by remembering the following local myth:

> *"...The Binjhal did not take any water from any other community (sammaj) except from the Gond and the Soara. Once, a group of Binjhal brothers went for hunting. Suddenly the younger brother felt extremely thirsty. There was no drinking water in the forest. Unexpectedly the iron maker from the Luhar (iron maker) community offered him water but only under the condition that the Binjhal in exchange gave him a daughter for marriage.*

[24] As the quality of the firstborn is contested due to the king's many wives and concubines from different social origins, no ritual can be performed without disputes. Especially during funeral fire rituals for the firstborn, disputes over the legitimacy of symbolic power become manifest.

[25] Such as, for example, Sambalpur, the urban centre of western Odisha (see chapter eight).

[26] Harijan is a euphemism introduced by Mahatma Gandhi to re-designate the "untouchable" castes as "God's children". It embraces a multitude of subcategories of marginalised castes and is often used in order to avoid the pejorative notions of indigenous categories.

*The thirsty Binjhal agreed and thus, from that time on, the Binjhal married the Luhar and shared their meal with them."*

## *The Binjhal*

The local community of the Binjhal plays an outstanding role for the cultural memory and identity of the region. Oral narrations relate the history of the Binjhal to the mythical twelve Binjhal brothers (*Baro Bhai Bendkar*) who are believed to have migrated from Rajasthan to the Bora Sambar region and who are connected to the Jagannath[27] cult of Puri. The imagined migration from Rajasthan and the narrative link to the religious tradition of the Jagannath worship establish a connection topan-Indian royal and religious traditions, thus including hegemonic historical traits into an indigenous perspective. A Binjhal man relates:

> *".... when the Baro Bhai Bendkar moved in to the Gandhmardan hills, they only used their arrows. Once, they saw a bore. They shot the animal but did not hit it. Instead the arrow flew a very long way and hit the Jagannath temple in Puri of coastal Orissa. The arrow had such power that no one was able to pull it out. The king of Puri made a state-wide announcement that the one who will be able to pull out the arrow will be awarded with a kingdom. The twelve brothers thus went to Puri and pulled out the arrow. The king then wanted to make one of the brothers a king of the kingdom. But all the brothers refused. They did not accept that only one of them should be awarded in a special way, so the king made them all equally chiefs (Path Boria) of the Bora Sambar region."*

Another Binjhal man further explains that:

> *"[. . .] the Binjhal, as descendants of the Baro Bhai Bendkar, then started to live in the forests and to hunt animals."*

Many narrations recall the important role of the Binjhal community during the Indian resistance struggle against the British colonial rule. In the end of the 19th and beginning of the 20th century, the British rulers tried to gain control over the last autonomous indigenous petty principality of *Raj* Bora Sambar. In the orally narrated local history, as it is delivered by intellectuals

---

[27] The god Jagannath is the most popular incarnation of Vishnu in Odisha. His main temple is located in Puri. The Jagannath cult may be seen as the prototype of a regional cult that bundles up indigenous and hegemonic Brahmanic traditions. For a detailed ethnography on the Jagannath cult see Hardenberg (1998; 2008).

from Padampur and from the neighbouring village of Ges, it is reported that *Raj* Bora Sambar was regarded by the British as a "Garden of Eden" because of its natural beauty and supposed wealth. The fierce resistance of the Binjhal fighters and the struggle of the indigenous population against the intruders however posed serious problems to the British forces. The Binjhal are orally reported to have been the first group of the region who attacked the British, joining forces with the legendary insurgent Surendra Sai from Sambalpur who was a leader of the 1857 pan-Indian mutiny In many local narratives, this famous freedom fighter and martyr of western Odisha is related to the Binjhal community, and it is reported that he was married to a Binjhal woman. It is narrated that together with his Binjhal Adivasi allies, Surendra Sai fought against the Sepoy (local army) of the British. It is told that the Binjhal fighters were of outstanding braveness and never surrendered before the British.

The local narratives of indigenous resistance, going back as far as the 1847 mutiny, can be seen as important identity markers for the Bora Sambar region. Even a local story about the origin of the folk dance *dalkhai* is connected to the history of Binjhal resistance.

> *"Dalkhai", a school master from the village of Ges tells, "was supposed to be a dance danced by naked girls and young women in front of the British. When the Britishers looked fascinated at the naked girls dancing, the Binjhal killed them. They hanged the Britishers "uchki chungri" during the dalkhai dance. The Binjhal thus defeated the British through their weakness, like the goddess Durga who killed the demon Moisasur by displaying him her naked beauty."*

In 1862, the British finally defeated the mutiny and Surendra Sai's fighters. In the aftermath of this defeat, the rebellious Bora Sambar region was degraded from the status of kingdom (*Raj* Bora Sambar) to the lower administrative category of *zamindari*. Even if the region of western Odisha had to succumb to the British rule, the nimbus of the rebellious freedom fighters remained. Until today, the people of the former kingdom of Bora Sambar describe their place as autonomous and resistant in character.

## *The Binjhal pantheon today*

The most important deity of the Binjhal is the goddess Vindyabasani. According to cultural constructions of a mythical migration, the goddess is sometimes believed to have come from the Narmada River in central India to Chhattisgarh and then to Bora Sambar. Yearly, during the summer month *choit maso* a big feast for the goddess Vindhyabasani takes place. During the time of her worship, trance rituals (*boil)* take place and it is believed that the goddess comes upon small girls, who during their trance embody the goddess while dancing the local dance *dalkhai*. The goddess Vindhyabasini is often represented in the shape of a girl carved in stone. Besides, the goddesses Bhima Burhi ("the old lady farmer goddess"), Patneshwari ("the goddess of Patna"), Samley ("the goddess of the samaley (cotton) tree"), a main goddess of the town Sambalpur), Burhi Ma ("the old mother goddess") and the god Dungar Burha ("the old mountain god") are venerated at this festival.

Next to Vindyabasani, the god Burha Raja ("the old king god") has a special importance for the Binjhal community and for the Bora Sambar region. The god Burha Raja is related to the mythical seven divine sisters (*sato bhani*) who are each linked to a village of the Binjhal community, forming thus a union of seven villages: Koira village, the Bora Sombar village, Bengrajpur, Temri, Polsada, Jhengnadi and the village Sura. An old Binjhal lady tells the following myth (*katani*) about the god Burha Raja and his villages:

> *"...Burha Raja lived in the village of Khoira. There, his temple is still located. Bura Raja married the goddess Rakam Devi (Rakhya Ma = "save me, Mother"). However, after some days a quarrel between the newly married couple occurred and Bura Raja divorced his new wife. After this incident he was about to flee to the village of Bengrajpur, where he soon got amorously involved with another goddess named Brahmani Patri Devi. Shorty after, he married his new beloved and returned to Khaira with his new goddess-spouse. However, after some days only, Bura Raja again quarrelled with his second wife. He even lost his mental balance and as a result of his anger gave his wife to a Brahmin from Polsada.*
>
> *But things happened not to resolve easily, as both, the goddess as well as the Brahmin, had a short temper and could not tolerate each other for long. In his anger about the unwanted new wife, the Brahmin threw the goddess into a pond, where she died.*
>
> *After some years a fisherman threw his net into the pond in order to catch some fishes. But instead of fish, he found a stone statue (murti).*
>
> *First, he threw the stone statue back into the pond, disappointed that he was not successful while fishing. Again he threw his net into the pond with new hope. But again, only the stone statue emerged. The fisherman became angry but he finally kept the stone statue in his fish-*

*ing bamboo basket (kholei). To his surprise, shortly after this event a huge amount of fish arrived in his net! The fisherman immediately put the stone statue on the earth recognising it as the goddess Brahmani Patar Devi earlier thrown into the pond. He started to worship the goddess and later constructed a bigger stone statue of her, which he also worshipped. Since then, the stone statue is worshipped as Brahmani Patri Devi [literally, the Brahmin goddess out of stone].*

*After the construction of the second stone statue (murti) of the goddess Brahmani Patri Devi, finally the king Burha Raja remarried (punor biba hod) the statue of his former divorced and dead wife, who was thus miraculously revived from the statue."*

This myth is retold by the Binjhal every three years, when the *tin sali yatra* (the three years festival) is held, celebrating the remarriage of Burha Raja and his revived wife Brahmani Patri Devi.[28] In this myth it becomes visible, how a region is conceptualized as a unity: myths connect gods and goddesses with specific localities, thus forming a regional unity of ritual exchange. The ritual and the mythological narrative surrounding it create elements of a social bond and a local identity.

## *Yearly celebrations in the region*

The yearly celebrations in the region are orchestrated by the natural seasons. The Durga *puja* which takes place during the month of *dusshara* (September/October), after the rainy season, has a crucial importance for the symbolic renewal of the former Bora Sambar kingdom as well as for the veneration of local goddesses. Besides the goddess Durga, a multitude of local goddesses and gods is celebrated during this festive time. Goddess worship is always connected with trance rituals (*boil*) and animal sacrifices (*boili*).

As a harvesting festival, the celebration of *Maren Yatra* is performed in the month of *kartiko* and *margosiro* (November/December). At the time of harvesting, the population of the Bora Sambar region worships all their gods and goddesses.

During the rainy season in the month *suro* or *srabana* (August) the *Kadu Yatra* or *Mod yatra*, the veneration of planted seeds and of the muddy earth

[28] See chapter 3.

takes place. At this time, especially village goddesses such as Burhi Ma and Mauli Ma are honoured.

*Dungar Burha Yatra* is the celebration of the god Dungar Burha (the old hill/mountain), held during the full moon of the month *pous* (*pous purnima*) in April/Mai. Dungar Burha is identified with and worshipped as the Gandhamardan Mountains. He is believed to manifest himself in the form of stones and quarries. In the indigenous conceptualization a quarry is considered a divine expression:

> "*How could water and earth coming from the mountain disappear?*" people ask, "*There was no flood! How could the earth move?*" "*God came*", they answer.

The geological phenomena are interpreted as divine intrusions into the world of the humans. In consequence, the movements and forms of the earth have to be worshipped, which is usually done by positioning three stones in a line on the earth. This form signifies the divine presence, which ought to be respected. During the annual *Dungar Burha Yatra* an inter-communal exchange takes place in the region: local communities of the Binjhal, Soara and Dhol Kond come together in order to worship the god of the mountains. During this time, god Dungar Burha possesses his priest who transforms into *boil* - the dancing manifestation of the god, represented in his ecstatic human body. In a big procession, the trance medium *boil* descends from the mountains, symbolising the descending god who visits the dwellings of the humans in order to cure their ailments.

The worship of Dungar Burha as the god of mountains symbolises a strong identification of the people of the Bora Sambar region with their natural environment. In this sense, even when they intend to climb the mountains, the local people ask all gods and goddesses of mountains, stones, waterfalls and caves for their permission to do so. For them, the ensemble of natural sites of the Bora Sambar region represents a sacred landscape which is to be worshipped, communicated with and granted respect.

## *The Sacred Landscape of the Bora Sambar Region and the Memory of Resistance*

### *The Gandhamardan hills*

The Gandhamardan hills which surround the region, forming a natural boundary, are themselves considered to be of sacred and mythological importance. The hills, which stretch out for a length of approximately 90 km, are surrounded by 22 perennial water streams, forming a biotope for more than 225 medical plants.[29] According to legends and to local Ramayana versions

> "*the god Hanuman was sent to the Gandhamardan hills in order to collect medicine* (Gandha) *for the wounded Lakshmana, the younger Brother of god Rama who, due to an arrow, was in danger. God Aswini Kumar then came to earth and advised a herbal plant for the curing of Lakshmana.*"

Besides the mythological narratives, the Gandhamardan hills have a symbolic socio-political importance for the region and its population. The hills are linked to a civic resistance movement against state-sponsored industrialisation projects in the region, named *Gandhamardan Surekhya Andulan* - the Gandhamardan protection movement. Originating from the village Paikmal, it became in the years between 1980 and 1990 the only successful example of local resistance against the industrial exploitation of the region. During the Gandhamardan movement the Binjhal as a local majority group played a key role in the struggle against environmental destruction.

Since 1980 the London based company Vedanta Resources had been proposing to mine bauxite from the Gandhamardan Mountains at Paikmal/Paikamal in Bargarh district. Vedanta Resources filed an application with the Paikmal *tehsildar* (revenue administrative officer) for lease of 1,150 acres for bauxite mining and the establishment of a refinery. Meanwhile, the central-sector Balco Aluminium Company had taken land from the government on lease for bauxite mining in the area in 1980, and in 1983 started the exploitation of the ground. In 1984, activists fearing disastrous consequences for the life of the people lanced an agitation campaign against Balco. From 1985 on, the peaceful resistance (*satya graha*) of the local population, supported by intellectuals and activists,[30] started under the leadership of Pradib Purohit. The population completely refused to cooperate with the company in its endeavour: roads were blocked, especially by women, who were often arrested and put to jail by the police; neither food nor housing were provided to the company's employees, nor other daily life services delivered. The lo-

---

[29] According to the list of medicinal plants deposited in various herbaria of the Botanical Survey of India (1960: 180-273).

[30] Amongst others, Professor Artabandu Mishra of the Life Science Department of Sambalpur University, Mr Lingaraj, leader of the western Odishan farmers resistance and self-help organisation Paschim Orissa Krushak Sangathan Samanwaya Samiti (POKSS).

cal resistance movement maintained its struggle for five years, to be finally recognised officially as a grassroots political movement with a national relevance. In 1986, a cycle rally was organized to Sambalpur and to Bhubaneshwar in order to underline the significance of the Gandhamardan movement for the whole of western Odisha. The Gandhamardan movement became an issue of election campaigns, and finally in 1991 the Balco project was cancelled. Until today however the danger of state-infused industrialisation projects and of the renewal of Vedanta's plans persists. In 2007, the Central-sector company Nalco once more applied for the bauxite reserve in Gandhamardan. The awareness of the industrial menace to the life of the people of Bora Sambar has led to the determination of many locals to ensure that "*till we die, there will be no bauxite mining*". Today, the local resistance is still organised as the *Gandhamardan Surakhya Yuba Parisad* led by Pradip Purohit and Dhiren Mohanty, while Vedanta Resources has not given up its bauxite refinery plans. As *The Financial Express* from January 18th, 2010 reports from Bhubaneshwar:

> *"After the tribals in Southern Orissa, the tribals in Western Orissa are now gearing up to launch an agitation against the Vedanta Resources. (...) Vedanta's proposal has triggered sharp reactions among the locals. The Gandhamardan Surakhya Yuba Parisad, which had spearheaded the agitation in 1980, has warned the government as well as the private company against taking the mines on lease. "The government would be responsible for the consequences," cautioned the Parisad leaders Pradeep Purohit and Dhiren Mohanty.*
>
> *The Congress Legislative Party chief whip, Satya Bhusan Sahu, who is also the local MLA* [Member of the Legislative Assembly], *has written a letter to the chief minister, Naveen Patnaik, urging him not to allow Vedanta to mine bauxite from the Gandhamardan hill range. Since the Nrusinghanath and Hari Sankar temples are on the hill tops, the mining activity will hurt the religious sentiment of the local people, he has stated. He also mentioned that the bio-diversity of the region would be destroyed."*

On January 1, 2010, the Silver Jubilee Year of the Gandhamardan movement was celebrated among the activists, displaying the strength of local resistance and identity of the Bora Sambar region today.

## *Nursingnath and Hari Sankar - two waterfalls and two temples*

The waterfalls and hill temples of Nursingnath (Nrsinganath) and Hari Sankar (Harishankar) represent the heart of the sacred landscape of the Bora Sambar region. The legend of the *satya amba* (the true mango tree) tells that on the top of the Gandhamardan hills there is a bifurcating spring: one of its streams leading to Nursingnath, the other to Hari Sankar. Seven mythological hills are supposed to be located between the streams, at the same time separating and binding the holy places.

Nursingnath *mandir*, which was erected by the Patna king Baijal Dev, in the 12th century, is the temple of Nursinghnath, an aniconic god, who is conceived as a local incarnation of the god Vishnu. In the Hari Sankar temple, which was also erected by the king Baijal Dev, the divine couple Shiva and Parvati is venerated. Besides these two important Hindu gods, the temple also lodges Saptapeni Brahma, the seven headed god cobra, Buddha and the god Jagannath. Whereas in the Hari Sankar Tempel the religious service is organised by a genealogical line of Dhol Khond priests (*pujari*), the Nursingnath temple is managed by a temple trust and the religious service is performed by Brahmin child priests (*balio pujak*). The customs of the temple prescribe that the child priest has to be a celibate boy or young man between 10 to 20 years of age from the Jharua Brahmin or Ananyak Brahmin cast, who is allowed to marry after leaving the service of the temple.

Both temple locations are considered holy mountains and are worshipped as divine natural sites, thus combining indigenous deities and local concepts of the sacred with influences of hegemonic Hindu and ascetic traditions.

## *Boj Pur Godh*

Boj Pur Godh is another important natural site regarded as a holy place by the inhabitants of the Bora Sambar region. It is related to the village of Bora Sambar of the Binjhal, whose religious specialists (*jhankar*) take care of the altars of local goddesses and gods scattered in the holy landscape. Amid the Gandhamardan hills, Bhoj Pur Godh is the site of a jungle altar of Mahadev, the god Shiva. Here, the god Shiva is venerated especially on Shiv *ratri* in the month of *falguna* (February/March). Bhoj Pur Godh is a big waterfall, where, on a step of the cascade, a natural basin is formed. In this basin, small bronze figurines of god Shiva in his appearance as a snake are kept. In a mountain cleft above the sacred basin, a statue of the god Bhairava in his anthropomorphic form is venerated.

When approaching Boj Pur Godh through the jungle, one passes the altar of Patneshwari, the clan goddess (*kulta devta*) of the Bora Sambar king's lineage. The altar of the goddess is represented through three stones in the mids of the jungle. Used incense sticks (*agerbatti*) near the stones and a red spot (*tikka*) of ritual paste on the upper side of each stone indicate a regular worship at the sacred abode. Only the *jhankar*, the ritual specialist of the Binjhal, visits this place regularly, for his daily worship. Otherwise, no human sound is heard at the jungle altar, surrounded merely by the noises of the tropical forest, birds and animals. Only twice a year the loneliness of the forest is intruded: During the month *dusshara* (September/October) and during the month *choit* (June /July) a local feast (*porba*) and veneration of the goddess are celebrated. Then the whole village of Bora Sambar gathers loudly at the jungle altar and participates in goddess possession rituals (*boil*) and goat sacrifices (*boili*).[31]

The name Bhoj Pur Godh also refers to another sacred site in the mountainous landscape: a large mountain cave, situated slightly above the waterfall, which is a focal point for the cultural memory of local resistance. Here, the "jungle fort" was situated, where the Binjhal *raja* of the Bora Sambar kingdom is supposed to have taken refuge during the 1847 mutiny against the British.

### *Durgeikhol - The valley of the goddess Durgei*

Deep in the Gandhamardan hills, the holy valley of the goddess Durgei, called Dugeikhol, is located. It is a natural sanctuary of the community of Adhi Khond living in the Bora Sambar region. The altar of Durgeikhol integrates itself into the surrounding landscape. A straw house shelters a stone sculpture of Durgei. The stones symbolise the rocks and mountains (*pahar*). Rests of ancient walls are visible on the way to the natural altar. Local people tell that they represent the border land of the former king of Patna. The altar of Durgeikhol is attended by a priest (*pujari*) of the Khond group. On full moon of the month *maxir* (*maxirpuni*) (December) the most important religious festival of the location is celebrated.[32]

---

[31] Oral narrations tell that some decades ago not only a goat but a seven years old Brahmin boy was sacrificed, who was given to the local king by a special Brahmin family in Puri.

[32] On this occasion diverse status groups of the Khond community meet: The Adi Kondh are considered as the Boro Khond (eB), the most senior in status, also called Dhol Khond; the Gouria Kondh represent the middle category (mB) and the Putia Kondh, also called Kolahan, represent the most junior category. For sophisticated ethnographies on the Khond in Odisha

Besides the goddess Durgei, the gods Shiva and Bhairava are worshipped at Durgeikhol. The Bhairava feast (Bhairava *jatra*) takes place during the *dusshara* celebrations and is mainly celebrated by members of the Binjhal and Gond communities.

## *Dev Dhora – god's depth*

Dev Dhora, god's depth, also called *devta kudan* (the place were all gods and goddesses live), is situated in a lake on the outskirts of the Gandhamardan mountains. It also signifies the deepest point of the lake. Above the lake, a temple of Mahadev/Shiva (Mahadev *mandir*) is situated. Opposite to the temple dedicated to Mahadev, a smaller temple of the god Bhairava is to be found. It is decorated with 17 cut-off heads and figures of surrendering persons.[33] The two temples at Dev Dhora were constructed 1929 by the local king Rajendra Singh Boria from Padampur. A mythical story recalled by the priest of the temple tells:

> "*Once a watchman saw seven honda* [a *honda* is a big pot where rich people store their wealth] *croaking and searching for water. The big honda* (baro honda) *asked the watchman: "Where do I get some water? Please, tell me." The watchman answered, "go a bit ahead, where the water is deep* (dhora)*".*
>
> *In reality, in the seven pots the seven sisters resided* [*sato bhani,* locally the most important mythological figures]. *The big pot was very happy about the watchmen's hint and thus she told her six sisters to open her pots in order to take the holy waters from the river. Since that time, the seven sisters reside in the Dev Dhora place".*

Another myth tells that Dev Dhora was the hunting place of the former king *raja* of Bora Sambar, Rajendra Singh Boria, and recounts the reason for the construction of the temple. The priest of the temple continues to explain:

> *"Once, when the king Rajendra Singh Boria hunted near the river, he needed some rest and fell asleep. While sleeping he had a dream. During that dream, Shiva accused him of being a big murderer, who had*

see Hardenberg (2005) and Nayak (1989).

[33] The symbol of cut-off heads may be interpreted as alluding to the value of sacrifice, or specifically self-sacrifice. A possible association with human sacrifice was always denied by my interlocutors. However, the iconographic sign of the loss of human life enshrined in a temple indicates the value of sacrificial human death, a cultural idiom common in Khond communities in India. The history of human sacrifice in Odisha is described by Barbara Boal (1997).

*to be punished for killing so many animals. Shiva then advised the Raja to build a temple at the place of his favourite hunting ground, in order to expiate himself. The day after the dream, the king became seriously ill. Phulmati, his first wife prayed to the god Shiva and made a vow (manosik): If you rescue my husband, I will start ardently worshipping you. The next day, the kingrecovered and his wife started to worship Shiva."*

Thus, in 1929, the temple (*mandir*) was constructed as a manifestation of the newly introduced continuous worship of the god Shiva in the region. Throughout India, the worship of Shiva is an indicator of the hinduization of Adivasi regions (Eschmann 1986: 79-98) as the following narrative, also told by the priest of the temple, underlines:

"*Once, a rusi* [wise man] *stayed at the place where now the temple is situated. Hundreds of people came to see and meet the rusi. During the rainy season, the rusi performed jagia* [a sacrificial fire] *to prevent the region from drought.*

*God Mahadev* (Shiva) *once gave a dream to Rajendra Singh Raja to go to the rusi and to build a temple were the rusi lived. The king and his wife went to the place and called the village gontia* [*gontia*= is a local village chief and land holder] *from a nearby Khond village. They told him about their dream and about their intention to build a temple for the grace of Lord Shiva. This temple should be more beautiful than the Nursingnath temple. The village gontia (local chief) agreed to help the king. After the construction of the temple the Khol Kond gontia became its priest* (pujari). *He was the only one who was not afraid to worship in the jungle.*

*The Khond served for some time at the temple, but then the king introduced the Tanapati caste from Padampur as the priests of Shiva. The king considered the Tanapati as fitter to digest the food of Shiva. Then, the king gave land to the Tanapati as a gift for their ritual services.*"

This narrative describes the phases of the local hinduization process: first, a local Adivasi priest takes over the newly introduced ritual specialisation. In due course of time however, the indigenous specialists are replaced by a specialised Hindu caste which receives land for its ritual services from the local king, indicating the land tenure and patronage system, focused around the petty king of the region.

Another local narrative tells of a female ascetic – a *mata* – living at the same holy place. The story is remembered by an old lady who weekly worships at the Dev Dhora temple:

> *"... Once a mata came to Dhev Dhora and stayed there in one of the caves (gumpa) around the lake. In the depth of Dev Dhora a big fish (boro macho) and a crocodile (mogar) lived. The mata pierced the crocodile and the fish and painted them gold. From that moment on the fish and the crocodile listened to the orders of the mata who stayed there 50 years long."*

The story of the hermit *mata* points out the importance of the fact that the natural sanctuaries of the Bora Sambar region are venerated by local devotees as expressions and manifestations of the local divine. The trans-regional impact of Hindu ascetic practices in the Bora Sambar region is visible in the hermitage of the female ascetic. Even if in the traditional discourse of classical Hinduism[34] women were excluded from the cultural institution of asceticism - which was reserved for men and Brahmins - both the religious history of the Indian subcontinent as well as the popular practices of Hinduism today show that again and again there have been and continue to be female ascetics.[35]

## *Politics of indigenization*

Today, Padampur, the urban centre of the Bora Sambar region, is prominently represented in regional politics. Bijaya Singh Bariha, a local descendant from the Binjhal kings, has since 1990 been working as a MLA (Member of the Legislative Assembly) from 1990-2000 for the Janata Dal[36] Party (JD) and from 2000 until now for the Biju Janata Dal (BJD) Party.[37] After the regional success of the BJD Party in Orissa in the general polls of 2009, Bijaya Singh Bariha has become the Cabinet Minister for Scheduled Tribes

---

[34] "Classical Hinduism" here refers to the Brahmanic tradition, which is based on the authority of the Vedas and of the Brahmin priests (see Michaels 1998:55).

[35] On female asceticism in India see Clémentin-Ohja 1981: ibid 1990; Poggendorf / Guzy / Zinser 2000; Babb 1982: 49-66; Guzy 1998: 56-74.

[36] The JD was a regional political party, led by V. P. Singh, which split from the Indian National Congress, in 1989.

[37] The Biju Janta Dal is a right-wing regional Party of Orissa which split from the hindu-right BJP (Bharatrya Janata Party). Under the leadership of Naveen Patnaik it has in recent years experienced a considerable success in rural India.

(ST) & Scheduled Castes (SC) Development, Minorities & Backward Classes Welfare of the Orissa government.[38]

His political influence has contributed to a re-traditionalisation of the region: In 2002, a memorial and temple for the Baro Bhai Bendkar has been built in the Binjhal village of Molda, where the twelve mythological Binjhal brothers are supposed to have settled. In 2004, Bijaya Singh Bariha for the first time instituted the worship of the goddess Vidhyabasani, traditionally only performed in the jungle, in Padampur town. The reinvented ritual has since become a forceful tool for the transmission of the BJD's political agenda. For the worship of Shiva in Boj Pur Godh on Shivrati, a temporary accessible track for jeeps and hikers has been established. Today's political programmes of regional parties such as the BJD use the cultural re-traditionalisation and the re-invention of local identities to enhance their political powers. The consciousness of the region's cultural distinctiveness has been discovered as a political tool. But vice versa the politicisation of local religious symbols is often put forward by members of the indigenous communities. Thus, from both sides, in the context of today's local politics, the cultural memory seems to be channelled into an indigenization of regional politics, local mythologies becoming the basis for the invention of new political strategies.

Let us resume: The oral history of the Bora Sambar region mediates the memory of the small indigenous kingdom of the Binjhal. Natural sanctuaries and temples demarcate a sacred landscape and outline the former territory of the Raj Bora Sambar in terms of a socio-religious, cultural and natural unit. On the one hand, local narratives characterise the Bora Sambar region as locally autonomous and resistant against the British intruders. On the other hand, they recall how indigenous concepts amalgamated with trans-local hegemonic Hindu ideas, values and narratives to establish a socio-cultural continuum. The Bora Sambar region is thus moving in-between two worlds: between the memory of the local ancestors and the memory of external hegemonic cultural, religious and political influences. The fusion of multi-faceted cultures and religions indicates a cultural and religious conjuncture, creating a unique regional pattern of indigenous traditions, expressing itself amongst others in a multitude of vital musical traditions.

[38] http://ws.ori.nic.in/ola/mlaprofile/assembly.asp, retrieved 20.03.1010.

# Second Chapter: Religion – Rituals - Music

## A Boil Ritual in Sargival Village

In Sargival, one of the villages of the Bora Sambar region, the Goddess Durga is worshipped weekly in a spirit possession ritual – *boil.* But during *sula puja*, the 16 days worship of the goddess Durga taking place before the tenth day of *dusshara*, *boil* performances take on a particularly intensity, and are ascribed a special efficacy to cure the ailments of attending patients.

To start the *boil* ritual during d*usshara*, the *dhunkel* instrument, an earthen pot (*handi matire*), is played by the *dhunkel*-player (*dhunkelya*) at the altar of the *dhunkel*, called the *dunkhel kutti, Durga kutti* or *sula kutti*. The altar is a separate square room with mud walls, located inside the house of the village priest (*pujari*). Here, the *dhunkel* instrument is kept and the local gods and goddesses are venerated. The *dhunkelya* begins the ritual with a sung meditation, accompanied by the *dhunkel* to call the goddesses and gods into the altar. The *dhunkel* is placed on a straw crown (*dhora/oira*) and topped by a straw mat (*kula*). It is rubbed with an iron rod (*jumka bari*) fixed on a bamboo bow (*dhun*). A straw string, which is fixed on the bow, is simultaneously plucked in order to create a dull, low sound. The sounds of the *dhunkel* are considered to be the sounds of the goddesses Durga and Lakshmi. They are also held to attract or call all other gods and goddesses into the place of the ritual and thus to prepare the following manifestation of the goddesses. The *dhunkel* player, who also is called *dhunkel gayako* ("the singer of the *dhunkel* instrument"), sings mythical stories (*katani*) about the seven sisters (*sato bhani*) Rohela, Tulsa, Krishtei, Subokeshi, Nila Rani, Onjona Rani, Dohona Rani. The names of the mythical sisters may vary from village to village, but they are mostly known under the names given here. During this ritual prelude for the *boil* ritual, the *dhunkel* player sings the story of the origin of the *dhunkel* instrument. With this song together with the sound of the *dhunkel* instrument, the microcosmic character of the instrument is put in relation with the macrocosm of the local worldview, as the following narrative fragment illustrates:

> *"When the 7 sisters did the puja for Shiva, Shiva told them: If you want to satisfy me, you should meditate. You should meditate with the dhunkel.*
>
> *The 7 sisters got the dhunkel from the Adi Khond village. There lived a female singer (gauni) who played the dhunkel.*

*The 7 sisters took the Khond gauni to their kingdom. Brahma then told the 7 sisters about the making and playing of the dhunkel.*

*Brahma told the 7 sisters to take a straw mat (kula) from the Mahar (bamboo maker) and then he told them to take a pot (handi) from the khumbar (potter).*

*Brahma himself gave a bamboo, for the bow (dhun) to the 7 sisters. For the bow, the 7 sisters made the string (sitalpot) and the straw crown (oira) by themselves.*

*From the blacksmiths (luhar) the 7 sisters took the iron for making the iron rod (dhunbari)."*

According to the accounts of *dhunkel* artists, the *dhunkel* is made for meditation as well as for the worship of all gods and goddesses. No kind of trance or goddess spirit possession occurs during the *dhunkel* performance ("*boil ne ase*"). Singing accompanied by the *dhunkel* (*dhunkel gana*) has merely the function of narrative story telling, ritual preparation and ritual accompaniment. The sound of the *dhunkel* only calls and attracts the goddesses and gods, but it does not transform the musician itself.

Photograph 1: Dhunkel player, at the *dhunkel kutti*, village Sargivahal, 2009, L.G.

Photograph 2: *Dhunkel kutti*, the altar of the *dhunkel*, village of Romedega, 2006, L.G.

When the persistent, monotonous sound of the *dhunkel* is heard by the villagers, people start to gather in the *dhunkel kutti*. The local priest (*pujari*), who some moments later will transform to *boil*, the trance medium of the local goddesses, is a middle aged man with long hair who belongs to the Mali community. Some years ago, after an apparition of the Goddess Durga in a dream, he became her priest.

While the *dhunkel* is played, he performs the worship (*puja*) for the goddess Durga. Coconuts, flowers, and incense-sticks (*agerbati*) are sacrificed in the *sula* or *Durga kutti* to please the goddess. Finally, the priest meditates without moving. For this part of the ceremony, he is wearing white clothes. After the end of his "white *puja*" (*dhola puja*) and his meditation, the music of the *ganda baja* village orchestra starts outside the *Durga/dhunkel kutti* but it can clearly be heard inside. While the monotonous sounds of the *dhunkel* instrument are held to recall the divine local narratives, the wild sound of the *borua par*, the holy rhythms of *ganda baja,* leads to an escalation of the ritual atmosphere and incites the following eruption of the divine power embodied by *boil*, the trance-medium. Inside the small and crowded altar the tension rises. The rhythm and the volume of the *ganda baja* orchestra rise and fuel the nervousness and excitement of the crowd.

A villager acting as assistant priest *(pujari)* helps the main priest to change from his white clothes into a red female sari skirt. Slowly, the main priest (*pujari*) starts to lose control over his body. His eyes close and his limbs become heavy and powerless. Finally, the assistant priest touches his head with a small lamp of melted butter *(ghi)*. Touched by the light, the almost unconscious priest starts to tremble. He is moving his head as if he is weeping. "*Boil asila*!" ("*Boil* has come"), the people whisper. "*Ma asila"* ("the mother (goddess) has come"), they tell each other. Now the mother goddess has taken possession of her priest, and the priest himself has become "*boil"*. *Boil,*

Photograph 3: Trance medium *boil* as the possessed priest and embododied goddess, Sargivahal village, 2009, L. G.

the priest turned trance medium, then takes an iron chain - a symbol of the local goddess – from the ground with his right hand. He grunts and falls into a wild ecstatic dance. During the dance *boil* – the possessed priest – starts to silently sing a melody.

Immediately after the priest has transformed himself into *boil*, the trance medium, physically and psychologically suffering patients (*kosti*) approach him from out of the crowd and wind garlands of flowers around his neck. The trance medium *boil* trembles and starts to utter predictions and incantations. In a repetitive tune he is chanting different names of goddesses:

> *"Mother is with you – Mother is with you - Mother will save you – Mother will save you – Durga Ma (mother) - Durga Ma - Maha Kali Ma- Maha Kali Ma- Mangala Ma – Mangala Ma - Tarini Ma - Tarini Ma - Oila Ma - Oila Ma- Subakesi Ma - Subakesi Ma Tulsa Ma - Tulsa Ma- Bontei Ma - Bontei Ma- Chandraseni Ma- Chandraseni Ma - Ganga Ma- Ganga Ma - Parvati Ma - Parvati Ma- Lakshmi Ma - Lakshmi Ma - Buri Ma - Buri Ma - Patneshwari Ma - Patneshwari Ma- Samleshwari Ma- Samleshwari Ma - Mother is with you – Mother is with you – Mother will save you – Mother will save you – Mother will save you"*

While *boil* chants to the patients, the music from outside, which up to now has driven on the ceremony, stops. For a time, the tension level of the priest's ecstasy is moderated. But as the *ganda baja* music sets in anew, the priest's – *boil*'s body starts to tremble again and he commences to move in a circular movement. After moving around for some time with closed eyes, *boil* steps outside the altar. Here, he meets the *ganda baja* musicians, playing their instruments: *dhol, nissan, tassa, mohuri*, and *jumka*. The *dhol* player (*dholya*) takes a leading function in the following trance performance. He visibly interacts with *boil* and drives forward an ecstatic communication process. A provocative dialogue between the sound, beat and rhythm and the dance of the trance medium sets in. The *dhol* drum seems to offend *boil*. The *baja*, which means "music", but also signifies "bite", literally "bites" (*baja*) the goddess. An aggressive communication unfolds between the beats of the *dhol* and the dance of the trance medium, who expresses the answers and reactions of the goddess through its wild ecstatic movements, which are derived from the *dalkhai* folkdance.

The music, the rhythms, the dance and the cries of the crowd touch everyone gathered around the sacred space of the dance of *boil*. There is a thrill about the ritual escalation, about the sudden appearance of *boil*, the goddess embodied in her trance medium. But the crowd is also excited about the power and effectiveness of the ritual performance. The *boil* ritual and the consultation of the *boil* trance medium are particularly believed to make fertile those who attend the performance – both men and women. The dance and the wild music are held to manifest a curative and procreative energy which flows from the goddess personalised in *boil* to the participants of the ritual. The iron chain and the iron sword that *boil*, the trance medium, carries, are symbols of the power of the goddess. In *boil*'s body the goddess dances for her believers. She is wild and she can give fertility. But it is also the feminised male priest transformed into a divine woman, who is held to have obtained healing and transformative powers. The creative and procreative power of the goddess, according to the belief of her worshippers, is not only manifested in *boil* as a medium, but transferred from the Goddess to the possessed priest.

## *Thea-phony - Music and the Goddess*

The *boil* ritual reveals an indigenous multi sensory and intermedial theory of the sacred and of healing transmitted through the cultural idiom of trance and possession of the trance medium *boil.* In cross-cultural perspective, music is often a crucial medium which accompanies, enables and guides trance mediumship in trance and possession cults (Rouget 1990: 87-91; 134-238). Trance mediumship implies a specific relationship between a ritual agent and his or her deity, overreaching the boundaries between the individual and the environment (Boddy 1994: 407-434). It is in most cases expressed through embodiment, understood as a non-dualistic perception and lived experience (Csordas 1990: 5-47). While possession refers rather to external influences in terms of the notion of a subject being possessed by something exterior to her or him, trance according to Gilbert Rouget, denotes a sounding, agitated, unusual state of transitory consciousness in a social context (1990: 47, 55), induced through music. However, in academic discussion, the concepts of trance, possession or ecstasy (Lewis 1971) are often used arbitrarily and interchangeably to describe various kinds of ritual techniques which are connected to an "altered state of consiousness" (Bourguignon 1973).[39]

[39] For a discussion of the definition of concepts such as trance, ecstasy or possession and the problem of their exchangeability, see Zinser 1990, 253–258. For a comparison with ecstatic cults of classical antiquity, see Schlesier / Schwarzmaier 2008. For a comparison with ecstatic and possession cults in contemporary Southern Europe, see Hauschild 2002. For a general discussion on the performative turn in anthropology and ritual studies, see Köpping/Rao 2000.

It is also a common feature that trance and possession are acted out in a performance which may be termed "theatrical" (Leiris 1958). Transculturally, trance and possession performances seem to be intrinsically related to ritual efficacy and healing (Laderman / Roseman 1996; Csordas/Lewton 1998: 435-512) and are central elements of initiations.[40] In South Asia possession and trance are generally widespread as idioms for ritual communication and expression.[41]

During the trance mediumship ritual *boil* a central indigenous meaning and belief system of the Bora Sambar region becomes visible, which I have tentatively termed *thea-phony*. The term *thea-phony* is intended to express the idea that a local goddess (*thea*) is manifested in a system of sounds (*phony*) related to ecstatic body expressions. In the Bora Sambar region, social values, ideas and morals are associated with the idea of a feminine sacred power personified by diverse local goddesses and ritually mediated through musical and trance performances. The belief in local goddesses, such as the *sato bhani* (the seven sister goddesses), Durga, Maha Kali, Mangala, Tarani, Nissani Oila Devi, Subakesi, Tulsa Devi, Bontei Devi, Parvati, Lakshmi, Boiravi, Burhi Ma, Patneshwari and Samleshwari/Samley Ma is predominant throughout the region. This belief must be seen in the larger context of the widespread religious notion of the feminine sacred (Tambs-Lyche 2004), which can be traced all over India, manifesting itself in local cults of diverse goddesses.[42] The pan-Indian idea of the feminine sacred embraces manifold indigenous notions of power which are often referred to as *shakti* (Tambs-Lyche 2004: 15-16; Wadley 1975). In the Bora Sambar region, these indigenous conceptions of divine powers are particularly associated with the sound of the *ganda baja* music and the concept of *par*, the rhythm. Ritual polyrhythmic music is believed to effect transformation, consolation and healing. Local goddesses are assumed to manifest themselves in the sounds and

---

[40] Especially the studies on Korean shamanism by Laurel Kendall reveal the crucial role of initiations for effective and successful ritual specialisation and healing (Kendall 1988; 1996: 17-59).

[41] For an overview on studies on possesion cults and trance see Assayag/Tarabout 1999 and Schoembucher 1993: 239-267; 2006; for an exemple of female possessions see Obeysekere 1981. In contrast to the mentioned broad ethnographic literature on lived traditions of religious possession in South Asia, Frederick M. Smith (2007) explores diachronically the multifaceted and multi-vocal forms of possession from ancient Sanskrit literature to vernacular living traditions, giving an exhaustive overview of the cultural and religious phenomena of deity and spirit possession in South Asia.

[42] For extensive studies of goddess worship in India, see Kinsley 1985; Wilke / Michaels / Vogelsanger 1994; Fischer / Goswamy / Pathy 2005.

rhythms of the village orchestra *ganda baja* as well as in a variety of drums played in various contexts, such as *nissan* symbolising the goddess Nissani and *sarmangalia* symbolising the Goddess Mangala. The local goddesses are venerated through the sound and rhythms of these drums, while at the same time being identified with them. Sounds, rhythms and instruments are simultaneously the medium and message (see Mc Luhan 1964) of a goddess.

## *The Village Orchestra - Ganda Baja*

*Ganda Baja* is maybe the most prominent musical and ritual feature of the Bora Sambar region. It is an instrumental orchestral[43] music, performed exclusively by musicians originating from the marginalised Harijan caste Ganda (also called Pano). The instruments forming the *ganda baja* village orchestra can be divided into three categories: membranophones (*dhol*, *nissan*, *tasa*, also called *timkiri*), an aerophone (*mohuri*) and idiophones (*kastal/jhang* or *jumka*). Membranophones are musical instruments that produce sound by a stretched membrane (animal skin). Aerophones are musical instruments which produce sound only by using air without any string or membrane and idiophones are musical instruments which resound in themselves, without any strings, air or membranes.[44]

---

[43] An instrumental orchestra is understood as an ensemble of instruments, where the interplay of the diverse instruments has a choral character but which does not contain any form of human vocals. The instrumental orchestral tradition of South Asia differs fundamentally from the traditional (classical) form of Indian modal music. The classical Indian modal music is characterised by individual solo performers and solo compositions (Daniélou 2004:10-11). It lacks the choral character of instruments playing together as "voices". The South Asian orchestral tradition could rather be compared to the tradition of European orchestral performance (chamber orchestra, opera orchestra etc.), except for the facts a) that musicians belong to special social groups or ethnic categories, b) that the music is restricted to special occasions (Sachs 1923: 2-3) and c) that it represents specific regional traditions of ensembles of regional instruments (see Sachs 1923: 3-11), as for example the *Naykhibaja* of the Newar (Wegner 1988 ) or the *Damai baja* (Helffer 1969a/b), also known as *Pancai baja* of the Damai (Tingey 1994 ), in Nepal.

[44] The classification refers to the Hornbostel-Sachs scheme of a universal fourfold division of musical instruments: membranophones, aerophones, idiophones and chordophones (strings) (Hornbostel / Sachs 1914: 553-590).

### *Dhol*

The *dhol*, which is the village orchestra's leading instrument, is a large membranophone. This large, long drum (90 cm to 1.5 metres in length) is made from the trunk of a tree and strung with cowhide (gai chomora) on two sides. Along the length of the *dhol* run strips of cowhide (*badi*) which are attached to the instrument by rings (*kol kola*). The skin of the right-hand side, named tali, is made from calf's skin; the left-hand skin *dhaaya* is made from cowhide. The tali is slightly smaller (37 cm in diameter) than the *dhaaya* (38 cm in diameter). The *dhaaya* is beaten with a rubber stick (khanda/nara) of about 40 cm in length; the tali side is played with the right hand. The *dhol* player, known as the *dholya*, directs the changes of the rhythms of the ganda baja orchestra. Rhythms usually emerge spontaneously with the *dholya* giving the lead. Musicians gain knowledge of the rhythmic and melodic patterns by listening to various rhythms from early childhood on. It is said that the voices of the goddesses appear first in the *dhol* drum and express their moods by changing the rhythms.

Photograph 4: *Ganda baja* orchestra met on a road to Padampur town, from the left: *nissan, mohuri, tassa, jumka, dhol*, L.G.

## *Nissan*

The *nissan* drum, another membranophone, has a tapered form, resembling a melon cut in half. It is reported to be the most ancient instrument of the village orchestra. A *nissan* is made of wooden and iron sheets and is played with two rubber sticks (*chimta*). The leather (*chipra*) of the drumhead is made of cowhide or goatskin and often covered with colourful paintings. In the Bora Sambar region and Sambalpur area *nissan* drums were traditionally decorated with deer antlers, but as hunting deer has been forbidden, today this form of embellishment has nearly disappeared.

The *nissan* is always played with maximum strength, thus producing a deep and penetrating sound which is compared to the "*sound of the thunderstorm*" and identified with the horrifying strength of Goddess Nissani.

## *Tasa*

The *tasa* (also called *timkri*), a small membranophone, is a drum made from clay (*matul*) and strung with cowhide (*gai chomra*). The drumhead is attached with leather strips to the tapered body of the instrument (*mola*). It is played with two thin bamboo sticks. The *tasa* produces a high and thin sound. Even if the sound of the *tasa* drum is not associated with a specific goddess, it contributes to the divine drum chorus.

## *Mohuri*

The *mohuri* is an oboe-like instrument. According to the Ganda musicians, its sound plays a crucial role in changing the character of the music and rhythm. It is often compared to the "*seductive voice of a capricious woman*", as the musicians explain, but can also be associated with the "*desperate wailing of a mother crying for her dead son*". Those poetic sound, de-

Photograph 5: *Mohuri* player, village of Cherchela, 2006, L.G.

scriptions refer to the arbitrary character of the mohuri's which is considered the most difficult instrument to play in the orchestra. The sound of the *mohuri* is identified with the expression of the specific goddess which enters the musical scene during a *ganda baja* performance.

## *Kastal*

The *kastal* or *jhang* are iron cymbals; they may be replaced by a kind of rattle called the *jumka*. Their sound is associated with the goddess Gantheshwari ("the goddess of bells" (*gantha*=bell).

Ideally an orchestra consists of five instruments and might include five to seven players. Sometimes, it is also called *panchabadya* referring to the five instruments assembled. Similarities can be traced between *ganda baja* and other orchestral traditions like those of Chhattisgarh (Prévôt 2008: 75-88) or Nepal (Helffer 1969a/b, Tingey 1994, Wegner 1988).

All *ganda baja* instruments play together in tune and rhythm. It is central for the formation of a Ganda musician to listen to the play of other musicians and to learn to play together with them. Besides the command of one's instrument, playing *ganda baja* thus implies a sophisticated culture of listening. The beat of the right-hand *tali* side of the *dhol* provides orientation for the *tasa*, which in response beats a double rhythm. The beat of the left-hand *dhaaya* side of the *dhol* provides orientation for the *nissan*, which answers with a counter-rhythm to the beat of the *dhaaya*. As the sound of the *mohuri* is intended to resemble the flirting of a women's voice, it is played in an extremely alluring way. All the instruments in the inter-village orchestra are worshipped before being played. Notably, they are used for the worship of gods and goddesses, but at the same time require worship themselves. The instruments are usually only touched by the musicians, but there is no ritual prohibition to touch the instruments. However, no one should step over them as this is considered disrespectful and is supposed to cause a curse by the goddesses. The instruments are stored in a secular context: they are kept by the particular musician who plays an instrument. The sacredness of the instruments evolves mainly through the ritual context and the sound vibrations transforming the instrument to the mediator as well as to the corpus of a particular goddess.

Photograph 6: The worship of the instruments of the *ganda baja* orchestra, village of Banjen Munda 2004, L.G.

In the performances of *ganda baja* notions of an identity between music and goddesses come to light. Various goddesses are assumed to appear through the sound of specific instruments and their rhythms (*par*), while the polyrhythmic structure of the orchestra is understood as the manifestation of their voices.[45] In the rural regions of Bora Sambar no socio-religious ceremony, such as marriage or *puja*, the ritual service for gods and goddesses, may be celebrated without *ganda baja* music, played exclusively by the Ganda musicians. A village orchestra, usually formed by inhabitants of one

[45] Rhythms are recognised as the specific language of a goddess and accordingly named: Durga Par (the rhythm of Durga); Maha Kali Par (the rhythm of Maha Kali); Ma Mangala Par (the rhythm of Mother Mangala) ; Ma Tarani Par (the rhythm of Mother Tarani) ; Oila Devi Par (the rhythm of goddess Oila); Subakesi Par (the rhythm of Subakesi); Tulsa Devi Par (the rhythm of goddess Tulsa); Bontei Devi Par (the rhythm of goddess Bontei); Chandraseni Par (the rhythm of Chandraseni); Ganga Devi Par (the rhythm of goddess Ganga); Parvati Par (the rhythm of Parvati); Lakshmi Par (the rhythm of Lakshmi) ; Boiravi Par (the rhythm of Boiravai); Buri Ma Par (the rhythm of Mother Buri ); Patneshwari Par (the rhythm of Patneshwari); Samleshwari Par (the rhythm of Samleshwari).

and the same village, is called to the neighbouring villages for the celebration of such musical-religious events. The musicians are invited though turmeric powder by the different local communities of Binjhal, Gouro, Dhol Khond, Mali or Kulta in order to perform in their villages. Thus, the music of the Ganda musicians connects local communities, places and religious concepts. The *ganda baja* can be considered as an inter-village orchestra, representing a force of relatedness, connection and communication between different villages and communities. The Ganda musicians play the role of ritual and social mediators[46], linking tribal and semi-tribal local groups and mediating local values as well as local power configurations. The *ganda baja* orchestra thus plays a double role: On the one hand the *baja* transcends local communities in its function as a ritual inter-village orchestra. On the other hand, through its musical expression of transcendence, the *baja* creates a sensual experience of the local community in terms of communication with a holy sphere and the manifestation of the powers of local goddesses.

In former times, musicians were engaged and patronised by local *raja*s or landowners (*zamindar*) of the Raj Bora Sambar kingdom (later Padampur). Local power holders employed village musicians for the performance of politico-religious rituals, legitimating their social and symbolic power during such events as *dusshara*, the festival of the goddess Durga, and of the clan goddess Patneshwari. A proverb describes the ritual relationship between musicians and the local king: "*ager baja, poche raja*" – in front of the local king, there should always march the village orchestra. While performing in front of the *raja* or the *zamindar* the musicians had to wear colourful and extravagant clothes, a tradition that can still be traced today in the multi-coloured clothes and longer than usual hair of village musicians. The performance of the politico-symbolic powers of the power holder was designed to be a cheerful event, associated with public entertainment and joyful festivities.

## *Ganda baja music and goddess-embodiment: the boil ritual*

The instrumental orchestras of the Ganda musicians play a central role in the *boil* rituals of goddess embodiment and ritual healing. Every Monday during the worship of the Goddess Durga, the Goddess will appear in the body of her priest: "*boil*" comes upon the *pujari*. The *ganda baja* orchestrates the act of possession with specific rhythms. The goddess manifests herself in the dance and speech of the priest. This weekly *boil* tradition is an

[46] For comparison with the Pano in Koraput, see Pfeffer 1994: 14–20.

artistic ritual healing performance which integrates dance, music, and ritual speech in order to heal patients (*kosti*). Once a year, during the festival of *dusshara* or Durga *puja* in honour of the goddess Durga, which takes place during the month of *dusshara* (October), *boil* rituals gain a special intensity. At this time, the spirit of the goddess comes with a particular power and efficaciousness upon her priest (*pujari*), who becomes her trance medium - *boil*.

Photograph 7: A *ganda baja* orchestra from village Kalenda in its festive costumes for *dusshara*, 2004, L.G.

## *Goddess embodiment and the sixteen rhythms*

The goddess spirit possession *boil* is musically symbolised by a specific sequence of rhythms, the *sulapar*, or 16 holy rhythms. These rhythms are named after 16 different goddesses and are said to express their speeches and characters. As different rhythms (*par*) are beaten, different goddesses manifest themselves in the body of the possessed trance medium. The concept of *bol,* the rhythm, plays a crucial role both in structuring the ritual performance of the trance medium *boil*, as in the healing of patients (*kosti*). *Sulapar,* the sixteen possession rhythms, represent the polyrhythmic and polyglot interacting of the different goddesses with each other. The musicians aurally recognise the identity of the specific goddesses and rhythms.[47] As the structure of 16 rhythms is a core element in all *boil* rituals, I would tentatively describe it as a rhythmic sound liturgy within the ritual of goddess embodiment.

Photograph 8: *Dusshara* at Padampur town, 2005, L.G.

[47] Locally, the identifications of rhythms and goddesses can vary.

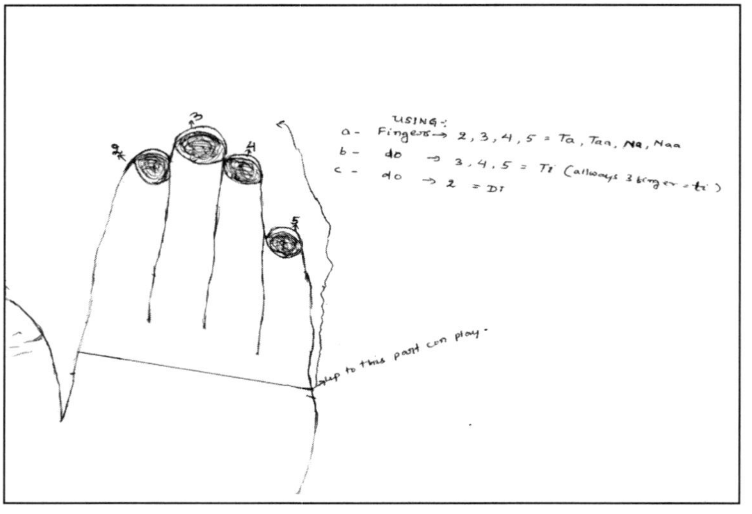


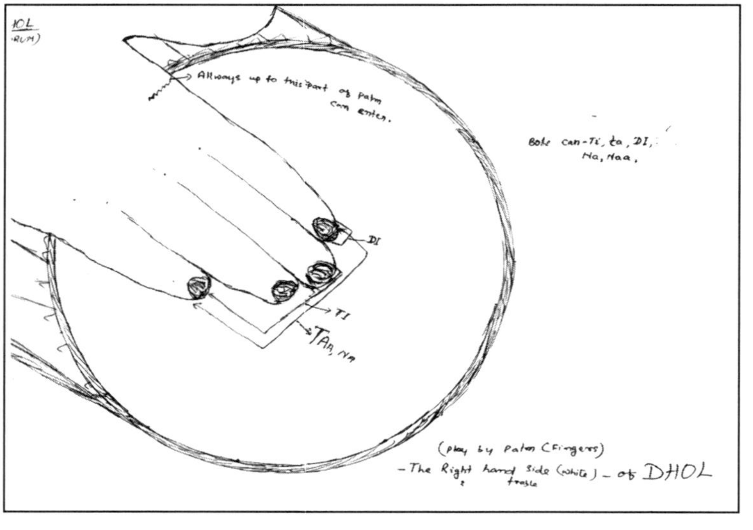


Illustrations 1-4: Schematically sketched basics for play of dhol, by Surendra Kumar Sahu

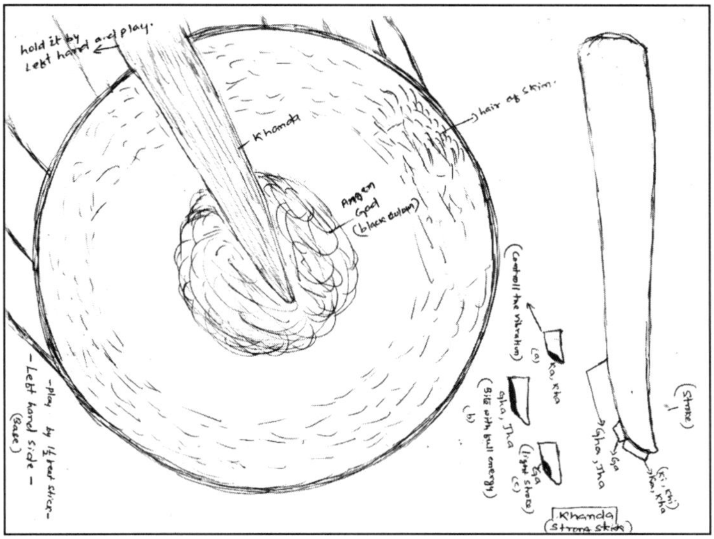


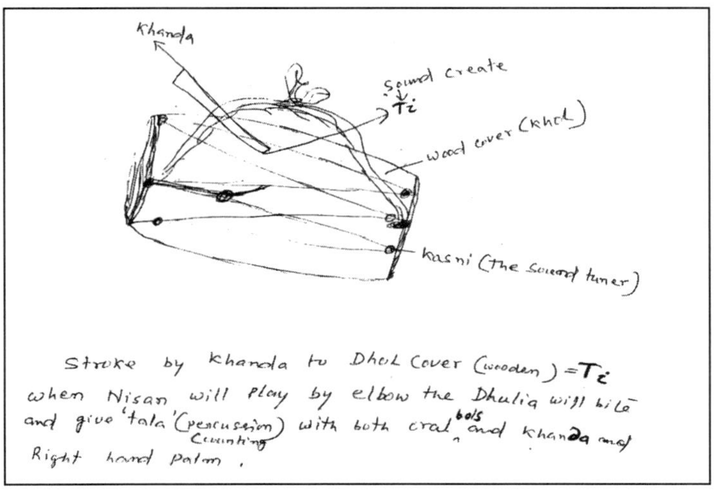


The local syllabic sound transcriptions are indicated in the location of the fingers of the dhol player's right hand as well as in the positions of the khanda stick, played by the left hand. The transcriptions indicate the creation of the specific sound nuances.

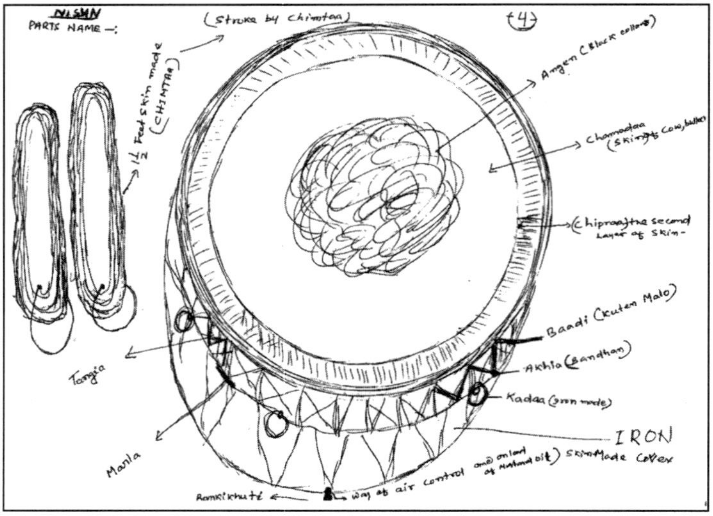


Illustration 5-6: Schematically sketched basics for play of *nissan* and *mohuri*, by Surendra Kumar Sahu

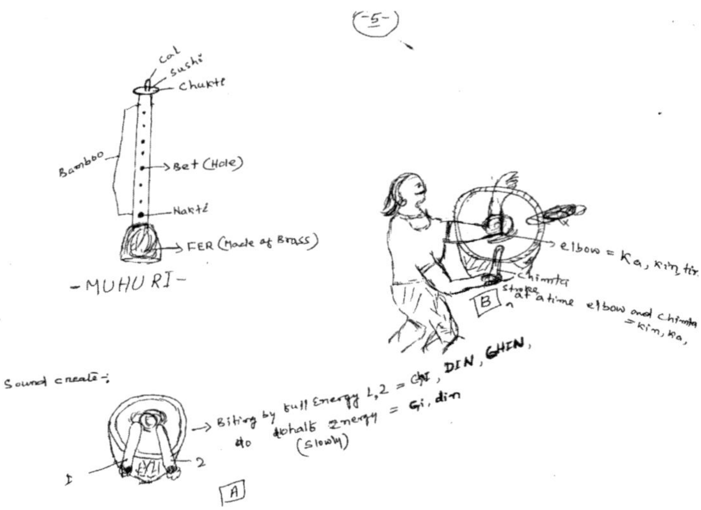

**The Orchestra *par***

For example 8 matras = it means that for one second you take 8 *matras* (rhythmical strokes)

Tal – Kaharaba

Symbols x = Clapping

0 = Empty

_/s = 1 matra

_ _/ss = 2 matras

= unit of matra

(per second you take 8 *matras* like 1 second= dha ge na ka dhi na)

| Matra = | 1 | 2 | 3 | 4 | 5 | 6 | 7 | 8 |
|---|---|---|---|---|---|---|---|---|
| Kaharaba Tal Theka = | Dha<br>X | ge | na | ti | Na<br>O | ka | Dhi | na |

Ilustration 7: Musical trasciptions by Surendra Kumar Sahu

***Musical transcriptions***

**8 Matras** (Stroke)

1 2 3 4 / 1 2 3 4

Gidi Gidi Gidi Gidi / Gidi Gidi Gidi Gidi

1 2

Natural tempos-Gidi Gidi Gidi Gidi / Gidi Gidi Gidi Gidi of to four count.

x x

1) Adighat The first - prelude preparation rhythm (8 matras = strokes)

**Dhol (Drum):-**

| 1 | 2 | 3 | 4 | / | 1 | 2 | 3 | 4 |
|---|---|---|---|---|---|---|---|---|
| Ta | Ghi | Ta | S | / | Ghi | Ta | Ghi | S |
| Jhan | S | S | S | / | Ta | S | S | S |

**Nisania:-**

| 1 | 2 | 3 | 4 | / | 1 | 2 | 3 | 4 |
|---|---|---|---|---|---|---|---|---|
| Gi | Di | Gi | Di | / | Gi | Din | Din | S |
| Din | S | S | S | / | S | S | S | S |

**Tasa:-**

| 1 | 2 | 3 | 4 | / | 1 | 2 | 3 | 4 |
|---|---|---|---|---|---|---|---|---|
| Ti | Ra | Ka | Na | / | Ti | Ra | Ka | Da |

**Orchestra /Sec :-** 1 time (Stroke) for one Matra

| 1 | 2 | 3 | 4 | 5 | 6 | 7 | 8 | 9 | 10 | 11 | 12 | 13 |
|---|---|---|---|---|---|---|---|---|---|---|---|---|
| Ta | Ghi | Ti | Gi | Gi | Jha | Ki | Ti | Jhan | S | Ki | Ti | Ta |
| x | | | | x | * | | | | | | | |

| 14 | 15 | 16 |
|---|---|---|
| S | S | S |

('x' = claping)

**By the recorded tempo** (Speed):-

| 1(clap) * | 2 * | 3 * | 4 * |
|---|---|---|---|
| Taghitigi Gijagini | JahakititaSSS | Taghitigi Gijagini | JahakititaSSS |
| x | x | x | x |

(Tempo may be this to speed tempo)

2) *Maileshri par* - Rhythm of goddess Maileshri (8 matras)

**Dhol:-**

| (1 clap) | | | (2 clap) | | | | (3 clap) | | | (4 clap) | | |
|---|---|---|---|---|---|---|---|---|---|---|---|---|
| 1 | 2 | 3 | 4 | 5 | 6 | / | 1 | 2 | 3 | 4 | 5 | 6 |
| Gi | Jhan | S | Ghi | Ta | S | / | Gi | Jhan | S | Ghi | Ta | S |

**Nisan:-**

| (1 clap) | | | (2 clap) | | | | (3 clap) | | | (4 clap) | | |
|---|---|---|---|---|---|---|---|---|---|---|---|---|
| 1 | 2 | 3 | 4 | 5 | 6 | / | 1 | 2 | 3 | 4 | 5 | 6 |
| Gi | Di | S | Gi | Di | S | / | Gi | Di | S | Gi | Di | S |

**Tasa:-**

| (1 clap) | | | (2 clap) | | | | (3 clap) | | | (4 clap) | | |
|---|---|---|---|---|---|---|---|---|---|---|---|---|
| 1 | 2 | 3 | 4 | 5 | 6 | / | 1 | 2 | 3 | 4 | 5 | 6 |
| Ta | Ti | Ti | Ta | Ti | Ti | / | Ta | Ti | Ti | Ta | Ti | Ti |

**Totally orchestra beat by 1 stroke/second:-**

**Jhum-:**

| (1 clap/ Sec. ) | | | (2 clap/ Sec.) | | | | (3 clap/ Sec.) | | | (4 clap/ Sec.) | | |
|---|---|---|---|---|---|---|---|---|---|---|---|---|
| 1 | 2 | 3 | 4 | 5 | 6 | / | 1 | 2 | 3 | 4 | 5 | 6 |
| Gi | Jha | Na | Ghi | Nda | Ka | / | Gi | Jha | Na | Ghi | Nda | Ka |

**The natural orchestra tempo may be :8-(From slow to speed tempo)**
**Starting tem:-**

**Jhumka:-**

| (1 clap/ Sec. ) | (2 clap/ Sec.) | (3 clap/ Sec.) | (4 clap/ Sec.) |
|---|---|---|---|
| Gijhana Ghindak | Gijhana Ghindak | Gijhana Ghindak | Gijhana Ghindak |

3) *Bharni par* – The rhythm of trance (6 *matra*s)4) *Samley par* – the rhythm of Samley (10 *matra*s)

**Dhol:-**
**Jhumka:-**

| | (1 clap) | | (2 clap) | | | | (3 clap) | | (4 clap) | | |
|---|---|---|---|---|---|---|---|---|---|---|---|
| | 1 | 2 | 3 | 4 | 5 | / | 6 | 7 | 8 | 9 | 10 |
| DHOL -: | Dhi | Ghita | Ghi | Ghita | Ta | / | Dhi | Ghita | Ghi | Ghita | Ta |

**NiSan:-**

| (1 clap) | | (2 clap) | | | | (3 clap) | | (4 clap) | | |
|---|---|---|---|---|---|---|---|---|---|---|
| 1 | 2 | 3 | 4 | 5 | / | 6 | 7 | 8 | 9 | 10 |
| Gi | Gidi | Gi | Gidi | Di | / | Gi | Gidi | Gi | Gidi | Di |

**Tasa:-**

| (1 clap) | | (2 clap) | | | | (3 clap) | | (4 clap) | | |
|---|---|---|---|---|---|---|---|---|---|---|
| 1 | 2 | 3 | 4 | 5 | / | 6 | 7 | 8 | 9 | 10 |
| Ti | Titi | Ti | Titi | Kiti | / | Ti | Titi | Ti | Titi | Kiti |

**Orchestra Paar:-**

| (1 clap) | | (2 clap) | | | | (3 clap) | | (4 clap) | | |
|---|---|---|---|---|---|---|---|---|---|---|
| 1 | 2 | 3 | 4 | 5 | / | 6 | 7 | 8 | 9 | 10 |
| Ghi | S | Jhi | Ni | Ghi | / | S | Jhi | Ni | Ki | Ti |

**Natural tempo:-**

| (1 clap) | (2 clap) | (3 clap) | (4 clap) |
|---|---|---|---|
| Ghijhini | Ghijhinikiti | Ghijhini | Ghijhinikiti |

4) *Samley par* – the rhythm of Samley (*10 matras*)

**Dhol:-**
(1 Matra/ Second)

| 1 | 2 | 3 | 4 | 1 | 2 | 3 | 4 | 1 | 2 | 3 | 4 |
|---|---|---|---|---|---|---|---|---|---|---|---|
| Jhan | Ghi | Ti | Jhan | S | Ghi | Ti | Jhan | Ghi | Ta | Jhan | S |

**Nisan:-**
(1 Matra/ Second)

| 1 | 2 | 3 | 4 | 1 | 2 | 3 | 4 | 1 | 2 | 3 | 4 |
|---|---|---|---|---|---|---|---|---|---|---|---|
| Gidi | Gi | Di | Gin | SDi | Gi | Di | Gin | Gi | Din | Gin | S |

**Tasa:-**
(1 Matra/ Second)

| 1 | 2 | 3 | 4 | 1 | 2 | 3 | 4 | 1 | 2 | 3 | 4 |
|---|---|---|---|---|---|---|---|---|---|---|---|
| Tar | Ka | Da | Kada | Tar | SKa | DaS | Kada | Ta | Kada | Ta | Kada |

**Orchestra / sec./ beat:-**

| 1 | 2 | 3 | 4 | 1 | 2 | 3 | 4 | 1 | 2 | 3 | 4 |
|---|---|---|---|---|---|---|---|---|---|---|---|
| Jhan | Ghin | Ni | Jhan | S | Ghi | Ni | Jhan | Ghi | Nak | Jhan | S |
| x | | | | | | | | | | | |

**Natural:-**

| 1 | 2 | 3 | 4 | 5 | 6 |
|---|---|---|---|---|---|
| JhanGhinijhan | SGhinijhan | Ghinakjhan | JhanGhinijhan | SGhinijhan | GhinktaS |
| x | x | x | x | x | x |

5) *Samley Julen par* – The rhythm of goddess Samley (6 *matra*s)

**Dhol:-**

| 1 | 2 | 3 | 4 | / | 1 | 2 | 3 | 4 | |
|---|---|---|---|---|---|---|---|---|---|
| SSGhi | Tighiti | JhanSS | JhanSS | / | TaSGhi | | Tighiti | TaSk | TaSk |

**Nisan:-**

| 1 | 2 | 3 | 4 | / | 1 | 2 | 3 | 4 |
|---|---|---|---|---|---|---|---|---|
| SSGi | Digidi | GhinS | GhinS | / | S | off | S | S |

**Tasa:-**

| 1 | 2 | 3 | 4 | / | 1 | 2 | 3 | 4 |
|---|---|---|---|---|---|---|---|---|
| Taraka | Dakada | TaSS | TaSS | / | Taraka | SS | SS | SS |

**Orchestra Paar/ Sec.:-**

| 1 | 2 | 3 | 4 | / | 1 | 2 | 3 | 4 |
|---|---|---|---|---|---|---|---|---|
| SSGhi | Nighini | JhanSka | JhanSka | / | Targhi | Tighiti | TaSka | TaSka |
| x | | x | | | x | | x | |

**Natural tempo:-**

| 1 | 2 | / | 3 | 4 |
|---|---|---|---|---|
| SSGhiniGhini | JhanSk JhanSk | / | Targhinighini | TaSka TaSka |
| x | x | | x | x |

**(Cotinue)**

6) Path kondha par (*6 matras*)

**Dhol:-**

| 1 | 2 | 3 | 4 | 5 | 6 | / | 1 | 2 | 3 | 4 | 5 | 6 |
|---|---|---|---|---|---|---|---|---|---|---|---|---|
| S | S | Ghi | Ti | Jhan | S | / | Ghi | Ta | S | Jhan | S | S |

| 1 | 2 | 3 | 4 | 5 | 6 | / | 1 | 2 | 3 | 4 | 5 | 6 |
|---|---|---|---|---|---|---|---|---|---|---|---|---|
| Ta | S | Ghi | Ti | Jhan | S | / | Ghi | Ta | S | Jhan | S | S |

**Nisan:-**

| 1 | 2 | 3 | 4 | 5 | 6 | / | 1 | 2 | 3 | 4 | 5 | 6 |
|---|---|---|---|---|---|---|---|---|---|---|---|---|
| S | S | Gi | Di | Gi | S | / | Gi | Di | S | Ghi | S | S |

| 1 | 2 | 3 | 4 | 5 | 6 | / | 1 | 2 | 3 | 4 | 5 | 6 |
|---|---|---|---|---|---|---|---|---|---|---|---|---|
| S | S | Gi | Di | Gi | S | / | Gi | Di | S | Ghi | S | S |

**Tasa:-**

| 1 | 2 | 3 | 4 | 5 | 6 | / | 1 | 2 | 3 | 4 | 5 | 6 |
|---|---|---|---|---|---|---|---|---|---|---|---|---|
| Ta | Ra | Ka | Da | Ka | Da | / | Ta | Ka | Da | Ta | S | S |

(Continue)

**Orchestra:-**

| 1 | 2 | 3 | 4 | / | 1 | 2 | 3 | 4 |
|---|---|---|---|---|---|---|---|---|
| SSGhi | NiJhanS | Ghinaka | JhanSS | / | TarGhi | Nijhan | Ghinak | Jhan— |

**Natural tempo:-**

| 1 | 2 | / | 3 | 4 |
|---|---|---|---|---|
| SS GhniJhan | Ghinakjhan SS | / | Taghinjhan | Ghinakjhan |

7) Mangala Julen par (*6 matras*)

**Dhol:-**

| 1 | 2 | 3 | 4 | 5 | 6 | / | 1 | 2 | 3 | 4 | 5 | 6 |
|---|---|---|---|---|---|---|---|---|---|---|---|---|
| Jhan | S | Ti | Ghi | Ta | S | / | S | S | Ti | Ghi | Ta | S |

| 1 | 2 | 3 | 4 | 5 | 6 | / |
|---|---|---|---|---|---|---|
| Ghi | Ta | S | Jhan | S | S | / |

| 1 | 2 | 3 | 4 | 5 | 6 | / | 1 | 2 | 3 | 4 | 5 | 6 |
|---|---|---|---|---|---|---|---|---|---|---|---|---|
| Jhan | S | Ti | Ghi | Ta | S | / | S | S | Ti | Ghi | Ta | S |

| 1 | 2 | 3 | 4 | 5 | 6 | / |
|---|---|---|---|---|---|---|
| Ti | Ta | S | Ta | S | S | / |

**Nisan:-**

| 1 | 2 | 3 | 4 | 5 | 6 | / | 1 | 2 | 3 | 4 | 5 | 6 |
|---|---|---|---|---|---|---|---|---|---|---|---|---|
| Gi | S | Di | Gi | Di | S | / | S | S | Di | Gi | Di | S |

| 1 | 2 | 3 | 4 | 5 | 6 | / |
|---|---|---|---|---|---|---|
| Gi | Di | S | Gi | S | S | / |

| 1 | 2 | 3 | 4 | 5 | 6 | / | 1 | 2 | 3 | 4 | 5 | 6 |
|---|---|---|---|---|---|---|---|---|---|---|---|---|
| Gi | S | Di | Gi | Di | S | / | S | S | Di | Gi | Di | S |

S S S / S S S

**Tasa:-**

| 1 | 2 | 3 | 4 | 5 | 6 | / | 1 | 2 | 3 | 4 | 5 | 6 |
|---|---|---|---|---|---|---|---|---|---|---|---|---|
| Ta | Ra | Ka | Da | Ka | Da | / | Ta | Ra | Ka | Da | Ka | Da |

**Orchestra :-**

| 1 | 2 | 3 | 4 | 5 | 6 |
|---|---|---|---|---|---|
| Giniki | Ginak | SS Gi | Nijhan | Ghinak | JhanSS |
| Giniki | Ginak | SS Gi | Nijhan | Titak | TaSS |

**Natural Tempo:-**

| 1 | 2 | 3 | / | 1 | 2 | 3 |
|---|---|---|---|---|---|---|
| GinikiGinak | SS Ginijhan | GhinakJhanSS | / | GinikiGinak | SS Ginijhan | Titak Ta SS |

8) Kali par – the Kali rhythm (*6 matras*)

**Dhol:-**

| 1 | 2 | 3 | 4 | / | 1 | 2 | 3 | 4 |
|---|---|---|---|---|---|---|---|---|
| Ghi | S | Jhan | S | / | Ti | S | Ta | S |

**NiSan:-**

| 1 | 2 | 3 | 4 | / | 1 | 2 | 3 | 4 |
|---|---|---|---|---|---|---|---|---|
| Gi | S | Gi | Di | / | S | S | S | S |

**Tasa:-**

| 1 | 2 | 3 | 4 | / | 1 | 2 | 3 | 4 |
|---|---|---|---|---|---|---|---|---|
| Ti | Ra | Ka | Da | / | Ti | Ra | Ka | Da |

**Orchestra:-**

| 1 | 2 | 3 | 4 | / | 1 | 2 | 3 | 4 |
|---|---|---|---|---|---|---|---|---|
| Gan | S | Jhe | Ne | / | Tik | S | Te | Ne |
| x | | | | | o | | | |

**Natural tempo:-**

| 1 | 2 | |
|---|---|---|
| Genjene Tiktene | Genjene Tiktene | (Repeat) |
| x o | x o | |

9) Khelati *par* (*8 matras*)

**Dhol:-**

| 1 | 2 | 3 | / | 4 | 5 | 6 |
|---|---|---|---|---|---|---|
| Gi | Jhan | S | / | Ghi | Ta | S |

**Nisan:-**

| 1 | 2 | 3 | / | 4 | 5 | 6 |
|---|---|---|---|---|---|---|
| Gi | Din | S | / | Gi | Din | S |

**Tasa:-**

| 1 | 2 | 3 | / | 4 | 5 | 6 |
|---|---|---|---|---|---|---|
| Ti | Ta | Da | / | Ti | Ta | Da |

**Orchestra:-**

| 1 | 2 | 3 | / | 4 | 5 | 6 |
|---|---|---|---|---|---|---|
| Gi | Jhan | Na | / | Ghi | Nda | K |

**Natural tempo:-**

| 1 | 2 | / | |
|---|---|---|---|
| Gijhan S Ghindak | Gijhan S Ghindak | / | (Continue ……….) |
| x | x | | |

10) Devta Chali *par* (*6 matras*)

**Dhol:-**

| 1 | 2 | 3 | / | 4 | 5 | 6 |
|---|---|---|---|---|---|---|
| Gi | Jhan | S | / | Ghi | Ta | S |

**Nisan:-**

| 1 | 2 | 3 | / | 4 | 5 | 6 |
|---|---|---|---|---|---|---|
| Gi | Din | S | / | Gi | Din | S |

**Tasa:-**

| 1 | 2 | 3 | / | 4 | 5 | 6 |
|---|---|---|---|---|---|---|
| Ti | Ta | Da | / | Ti | Ta | Da |

**Orchestra:-**

| 1 | 2 | 3 | / | 4 | 5 | 6 |
|---|---|---|---|---|---|---|
| Gi | Jhan | Na | / | Ghi | Nda | K |

**Natural tempo:-**

| 1 | 2 | / | |
|---|---|---|---|
| Gijhan S Ghindak | Gijhan S Ghindak | / | (Continue ..........) |
| × | × | | |

**Dhol:-**

| 1 | 2 | 3 | 4 | 5 | 6 | / | 1 | 2 | 3 | 4 | 5 | 6 |
|---|---|---|---|---|---|---|---|---|---|---|---|---|
| Ta | S | Ghi | Ti | Jhan | S | / | Gi | Jhan | S | Jhan | S | S |
| Ghi | Ta | Gi | Ni | Jhan | S | / | Ti | Ta | S | Ta | S | S |

**Nisan:-**

| 1 | 2 | 3 | 4 | 5 | 6 | / | 1 | 2 | 3 | 4 | 5 | 6 |
|---|---|---|---|---|---|---|---|---|---|---|---|---|
| S | S | Gi | Di | Gi | S | / | Gi | Di | S | Gi | S | S |
| Gi | Di | Gi | Di | Gi | S | / | S | S | S | S | S | S |

**Tasa:-**

| 1 | 2 | 3 | 4 | 5 | 6 | / | 1 | 2 | 3 | 4 | 5 | 6 |
|---|---|---|---|---|---|---|---|---|---|---|---|---|
| Ta | Ka | Da | Ta | Ka | Da | / | Ta | Ka | Da | Ta | Ka | Da |
| Ta | Ka | Da | Ta | Ka | Da | / | Ta | Ka | Da | Ta | Ka | Da |

**Orchestra:-**

| 1 | 2 | 3 | 4 | 5 | 6 | / | 1 | 2 | 3 | 4 | 5 | 6 |
|---|---|---|---|---|---|---|---|---|---|---|---|---|
| Ta<br>x | S | Gi | Ni | Jhan | S | / | Gi | Jhan | S | Jhan | S | S |
| Gi | Ja | Gi | Ni | Jhan | S | / | Ti | Ta | Sk | Ta | S | Sk |

**Natural tempo:-**

| 1 | / | 2 |
|---|---|---|
| Ta S Gi Ni Jhan S<br>x | / | Gi Jhan S Jhan S S<br>x |
| 3 | / | 4 |
| Gi Ja Gi Ni Jhan<br>x | / | Ti Ta Sk Ta S Sk<br>x |

12) Mangala *par* (*6 matras*)13) Hanumana *par* (*6 matras*)

**Dhol:-**

| 1 | 2 | 3 | 4 | 5 | 6 | / | 1 | 2 | 3 | 4 | 5 | 6 |
|---|---|---|---|---|---|---|---|---|---|---|---|---|
| Ta | S | Ghi | Ti | Ghi | S | / | Ta | S | S | Ta | S | S |

**Nisan:-**

| 1 | 2 | 3 | 4 | 5 | 6 | / | 1 | 2 | 3 | 4 | 5 | 6 |
|---|---|---|---|---|---|---|---|---|---|---|---|---|
| S | S | Gi | Di | Gi | Di | / | S | S | S | S | S | S |

**Tasa:-**

| 1 | 2 | 3 | 4 | 5 | 6 | / | 1 | 2 | 3 | 4 | 5 | 6 |
|---|---|---|---|---|---|---|---|---|---|---|---|---|
| Ta | Ra | Ka | Ta | Ka | Da | / | Ta | Ra | Ka | Ta | Ka | Da |

**Orchestra:-**

| 1 | 2 | 3 | 4 | 5 | 6 | / | 1 | 2 | 3 | 4 | 5 | 6 |
|---|---|---|---|---|---|---|---|---|---|---|---|---|
| Ta | Sr | Ghi | Ni | Ghi | Ni | / | Ta | S | K | Ta | S | K |

**Natural tempo:-**

| 1 | 2 | / | 1 | 2 | |
|---|---|---|---|---|---|
| Ta Sr Ghi<br>x | Ni Ghi Ni<br>x | / | Ta S K<br>x | Ta S K<br>x | (Repeat) |

| 1 | 2 |
|---|---|
| Ta Sr Ghi Ni Ghi Ni<br>x | Ta S K Ta S K<br>x |

13) Hanumana *par* (*6 matras*)

**Dhol:-**

| 1 | 2 | 3 | 4 | 5 | 6 | / | 1 | 2 | 3 | 4 | 5 | 6 |
|---|---|---|---|---|---|---|---|---|---|---|---|---|
| S | Ghi | Ta | Ghi | Ta | S | / | Ghi | Ta | S | Ta | S | S |
| 1 | 2 | 3 | 4 | 5 | 6 | | | | | | | |
| Ghi | Ta | S | Ta | S | S | | | | | | | |
| 1 | 2 | 3 | 4 | 5 | 6 | / | 1 | 2 | 3 | 4 | 5 | 6 |
| Ta | Ghi | Ta | Ghi | Ta | S | / | Ti | Ta | S | Ta | S | S |

**Nisan:-**

| 1 | 2 | 3 | 4 | 5 | 6 | / | 1 | 2 | 3 | 4 | 5 | 6 |
|---|---|---|---|---|---|---|---|---|---|---|---|---|
| S | Gi | Di | Gi | Di | S | / | Gi | Di | S | Gi | S | S |
| 1 | 2 | 3 | 4 | 5 | 6 | | | | | | | |
| Gi | Di | S | Gi | S | S | | | | | | | |
| 1 | 2 | 3 | 4 | 5 | 6 | / | 1 | 2 | 3 | 4 | 5 | 6 |
| S | Gi | Di | Gi | Di | S | / | S | S | S | S | S | S |

**Tasa:-**

| 1 | 2 | 3 | 4 | 5 | 6 | / | 1 | 2 | 3 | 4 | 5 | 6 |
|---|---|---|---|---|---|---|---|---|---|---|---|---|
| Ta | Ka | Da | Ta | Ka | Da | / | Ta | Ka | Da | Ta | Ka | Da |
| | (Repeat) | | | | | | | | | | | |

**Orchestra:-**

| 1 | 2 | 3 | 4 | 5 | 6 | / | 1 | 2 | 3 | 4 | 5 | 6 |
|---|---|---|---|---|---|---|---|---|---|---|---|---|
| S | Ghi | Nda | Ghi | Jhan | S | / | Ghi | Jhan | S | Ta | S | S |
| 1 | 2 | 3 | 4 | 5 | 6 | | | | | | | |
| Ghi | Jhan | S | Ta | S | S | | | | | | | |
| 1 | 2 | 3 | 4 | 5 | 6 | / | 1 | 2 | 3 | 4 | 5 | 6 |
| Ta | Ghi | Nda | Gi | Jhan | S | / | Ti | Ta | Ka | Ti | Ta | Ka |

**Natural tempo:-**

| 1 | 2 | / | 3 | 4 |
|---|---|---|---|---|
| S Ghi Nda | Ghi Jhan S | / | Ghi Jhan S | Ta S S |
| x | x | | x | x |
| 5 | 6 | | | |
| Ghi Jhan S | Ta S S | | | |
| x | x | | | |
| 1 | 2 | / | 3 | 4 |
| Ta Ghi Nda | Gi Jhan S | / | Ti Ta Ka | Ti Ta Ka |
| x | | | x | |

14) Bauli par (*6 matras*)

**Dhol:-**

| 1 | 2 | 3 | 4 | 5 | 6 | / | 1 | 2 | 3 | 4 | 5 | 6 |
|---|---|---|---|---|---|---|---|---|---|---|---|---|
| Ta | S | Ghi | S | Ghi | S | / | Ta | S | Khi | Ta | S | S |

**Nisan:-**

| 1 | 2 | 3 | 4 | 5 | 6 | / | 1 | 2 | 3 | 4 | 5 | 6 |
|---|---|---|---|---|---|---|---|---|---|---|---|---|
| S | Di | Gi | S | Ghi | S | / | S | S | S | S | S | S |

**Tasa:-**

| 1 | 2 | 3 | 4 | 5 | 6 | / | 1 | 2 | 3 | 4 | 5 | 6 |
|---|---|---|---|---|---|---|---|---|---|---|---|---|
| Ti | Ki | Da | Ti | Ki | Da | / | Ti | Ki | Da | Ti | Ki | Da |

**Orchestra:-**

| 1 | 2 | 3 | 4 | 5 | 6 | / | 1 | 2 | 3 | 4 | 5 | 6 |
|---|---|---|---|---|---|---|---|---|---|---|---|---|
| Tak | Ghin | Ghin | TaS | khita | khiti | / | Tak | Ghin | Ghin | Ta S | khita | Khiti |

**Natural tempo:-**

| 1 | 2 | / | 3 | 4 |
|---|---|---|---|---|
| Tak Ghin Ghin | TaS khita khiti | / | Tak Ghin Ghin | Ta S Khita Khiti |
| x | x | | x | x |

15) Mauli Par (*6 matras*)

**Dhol:-**

| 1 | 2 | 3 | / | 4 | 5 | 6 | 7 |
|---|---|---|---|---|---|---|---|
| Ghi | Ti | S | / | Ghi | Ti | Jhan | S |

| 1 | 2 | 3 | / | 4 | 5 | 6 | 7 |
|---|---|---|---|---|---|---|---|
| Ghi | Ti | S | / | Ti | S | Ta | S |

Nisan:-

| 1 | 2 | 3 | / | 4 | 5 | 6 | 7 |
|---|---|---|---|---|---|---|---|
| Gi | Di | S | / | Gi | Di | Gin | S |

| 1 | 2 | 3 | / | 4 | 5 | 6 | 7 |
|---|---|---|---|---|---|---|---|
| Gi | Di | S | / | S | S | S | S |

Tasa:-

| 1 | 2 | 3 | / | 4 | 5 | 6 | 7 | |
|---|---|---|---|---|---|---|---|---|
| Ta | Ra | Ka | / | Ta | Ra | Ka | Da | (Repeat) |

Orchestra:-

| 1 | 2 | 3 | / | 4 | 5 | 6 | 7 |
|---|---|---|---|---|---|---|---|
| Ghi | Di | Ri | / | Gi | Ni | Jhan | S |

| 1 | 2 | 3 | / | 4 | 5 | 6 | 7 |
|---|---|---|---|---|---|---|---|
| Ghi | Di | Ri | / | Ti | Ki | Ta | S |
| × | | | | | | | |

Natural tempo:-

| 1 | 2 |
|---|---|
| Ghi Di Ri Gi Ni Jhan S | Ghi Di Ri Ti Ki Ta S (Repeat) |
| × | × |

16) Khelati par (*7 matras*) [48]

[48] All musical transcriptions are accomplished by Surendra Kumar Sahu are based on the basis of Hindustani Bhat Khande system.

## *Drums and the goddess*

Rodney Needham has pointed out that "*there is a connection between percussion and transition*" (Needham 1967: 613) and that "*practically everywhere it is found that percussion is resorted to in order to communicate with the other world* ..." (ibid: 610). In the Bora Sambar region, the drums *dhol*, *nissan*, and *tasa* are directive for inducing trance. These membranophones are identified with local goddesses and they are simultaneously equated with goddess embodiment. The *dhol* drum plays a crucial role in communicating with the goddess. By means of the *dhol*, a musician proves his strength (*shakti*) in order to detract the goddess' power of embodiment from himself and to direct it towards the priest. On multiple layers of meaning the drum is instrumental for mediating and transferring and directing the power of the goddess as well as itself identified with the divine entity.

## *Boil and dance*

As well as the percussion centred sound of the ganda baja orchestra, the dance of the trance medium boil signifies the appearance of the goddess. She dances in the body of the possessed priest, who hence becomes a dancing goddess himself. In the dance patterns of the boil ritual the traditional elements of dalkhai, the most popular folk dance style in the Sambalpur district of western Odisha, are integrated into the performance of goddess worship. The *dalkhai* dance is tradi-

Photograph 9: Trance medium *boil* dancing, Sargivahal village, 2009, L.G.

tionally associated with puberty rituals for unmarried girls preparing young women and girls for their social and biological maturity.[49] It is generally conceived as an expression of sensuality and a symbol of erotic attraction. Integrated into *boil* performances, *dalkhai* patterns indicate the intimate dialogue of the trance medium and the goddess. The trance medium *boil* is conceived as the "divine dancer" – the sacred dancer of the goddess Durga - referring both to his ritual activity and power. The erotic power of the dance symbolizes the power of fertility ascribed to all *boil* rituals and its trance mediums.

### *Boil and ritual speech*

A third element of the *boil* ritual besides the rhythms of *ganda baja* and the priest's dance is the ritual speech of *boil.* For the most part, it consists of spontaneously created poetries sung by the trance medium. The rhythmic and repetitive uttering of the names of gods and goddesses intertwines with a specific melody only known to the trance medium *boil.* The melody of the ritual speech whispered by *boil* is a personal characteristic of the trance medium. It may express the affiliation to his guru or *boil's* own personal note. Here, the medium of dance interconnects with the medium of music and rhythmic speech to form an intermedial ritual. The ritual incantations of *boil* show a repetitive linguistic and melodic structure that can be described as a balancing of pairs of successive syntactic unities. This is the kind of "parallelism" highlighted in the ethno-linguistic discussion about "*talking in pairs*" (Fox 1988). A parallelism, according to Roman Jakobson, is an elementary operation of oral communication that consists of a

> *"coming together of two elements. (...).By this definition, parallelism is an extension of the binary principle of opposition to the phonetic, syntactic, and semantic levels of expression"* (Jakobson, cited by Fox 1988: 3).

For Jakobson, even the rhetoric figures of comparison and metaphor were semantic variations of parallelism. Fox collects observations attesting to the dual structure of ritual language in many cultures, which he calls "dyadic language". The parallelism of sentences is considered by Fox to be a characteristic of poetic language, understood as a special vocabulary that is rarely used in other contexts. Parallel sentences and word constructions, the ordering of words and sentences in an alternating, repetitive form are characteris-

---

[49] see chapter 3.

tic for the ritual language of oral societies (Fox: 1-3; 6-11)[50]. *Boil*'s trance song[51] with its parallelism of sentences and alternating repetitions seems thus a pertinent example of ritual poetry

Photograph 10: Trance medium *boil* speaking in pairs, village Romedega, 2005,L.G.

## *Practices of asceticism*

*Boil* rituals are embedded in cycles of interconnected micro-rituals including temporal ascetic practices. The boil ritual on *dusshara/durga puja* is preceded by a preparatory phase of sixteen days. During the *sula puja* which starts from the celebration of *puojuntya* - the festival of mothers who celebrate their sons, the local priest (*pujari*) fasts for 16 days until the day of *nowomi*, the ninth day and the day before the day of *dusshara*. During this

---

[50] For comparative ethnographic studies on ritual language see Demmer / Ganszle 2007.
[51] See the transcription on page 45 above.

time the priest may not rest on any wooden bed (*kotha*) but has to sleep on the ground. He is supposed to take a bath three times a day as well as to perform the worship of the sixteen goddesses three times daily: in the morning hours (*sokale*), at 12 a clock (*bar baje*) and in the evening (*sondhya bele*) hours. With these ascetic practices of cleansing and control of body and mind, the priest prepares himself for the contact with the goddesses during the *boil* performance on *durga puja*.

### *Marginalized musicians*

The *ganda baja* musicians who are orchestrating the *boil* performances are without exception male and originate from a subaltern impoverished Harijan caste, called Ganda or Pano. Besides their activity as musicians, the traditional trade of the landless Ganda was the weaving of simple cotton clothes used as underwear. With the emergence of a cotton industry in Orissa / Odisha over the last 50 years, this trade fell in decline and today many Ganda earn their living as agricultural day-labourers. The indigenous term "*Ganda*" which literally means "*the bad smelling*" refers to the activity of tanning the leather for drums but also expresses the socio-cultural concept of "untouchability" or "pollution" of the Ganda musicians. From the perspective of the local culture, Ganda musicians are considered to be "untouchable" (*achua*) for two reasons. First, because their drums are made from cowhide and second, because by playing the oboe *mohuri,* they touch their own saliva while creating sounds. The direct physical contact with cowhide and saliva classifies them as extremely impure and thus "untouchable". But it is exactly this "untouchability" that qualifies the *ganda baja* musicians for contact and communication with the divine sphere of the local goddesses. Here, the paradoxical character of the Indian category of "untouchability" or "pollution" becomes visible in the shape of a ritual inversion. In the ritual performance, the socially marginalised become spiritually powerful by communicating with the sacred powers of the goddesses. The ideological notion of being "untouchable" is, so to say, prerequisite for successful contact with the "untouchable" – the intangible, immaterial, prohibited sphere of the sacred. The power of performance of the goddess is thus transferred to the socially most powerless performers who, during the ritual performance, take in and transmit the divine powers of the goddesses. That the socially powerless have physical and spiritual power inverse to their social status is a widespread notion all over India. Thus, by their marginal status they are qualified for ritual specialisation and the handling of strong, uncontrolled, divine powers feared by others.[52]

In the *boil*-performances of the Bora Sambar region, the symbolic and musical powers of the orchestral instruments, their sounds and rhythms, unite with the ritual strength of the socially marginalised musicians. Thus an indigenous theory of power takes shape, based on the empowering effects of music in a ritual context. The ritual effectiveness of music furthermore hints to an indigenous media theory where polyrhythmic music is socially and culturally considered as a crucial vehicle and message of the otherwordly. The marginalised status of the musicians directing the *boil* performance plays a substantial role in the inner logic of the ritual. The polyrhythmic music of the village orchestra musicians is generally understood as an "untouchable" sacred entity, expressing notions of the divine as a wild, uncontrolled power, manifesting itself in the rhythms of the instruments and in the dance of the possessed priest. The instruments mediate and manifest the other world of the goddesses, while the subaltern social status of the musicians, as we have seen, paradoxically qualifies them for communication with the divine world. But although it is the musician alone, who has the capacity to control the goddess, he remains socially marginalised even while interacting with her: in contrast to the ritual priest and trance medium, Ganda musicians are not allowed to enter the inner sanctum of the *dhunkel kutti* altar, where the goddess embodiment takes place.

## *Boil as a healing performance*

A central aspect of the *boil* ritual is that of a multi-sensory and inter-medial healing performance. The ritual dynamism of goddess embodiment in *boil*-ritual reveals a strong healing power of music for the ritual participants and patients who seek spiritual cure for a psychological ailment. Music induces an enormous sensorial experience with a strong affective and psychological effectiveness.

---

[52] Another example of the cultural idiom of social marginalisation and spiritual specialisation are the subaltern Sidhis in Gujarat (Basu 1994). Ritual ambivalence is also found in other regions and religions of South Asia as for example among the Korean Shamans, where the shaman – mudang, mansin - is a stigmatised unfortunate who has a story of social suffering before becoming a legitimised shaman (Kandell 1988: 31-46; 1996: 21), or in Japanese Shinto rites, where *burakumin,* the Japanese untouchables perform the ritual butchering of animals and tanning of leather for drums used in the most sacred Shinto rites (Alldritt 2000).

> *"For healing to take place in this manner, aesthetic distance must be achieved (...). The healing effects of performance are on one level caused by the catharsis that can occur when a patient's unresolved emotional distress is reawakened and confronted in a dramatic context",* Laderman and Roseman (1996: 7)

point out. This aesthetic distance occurs in *boil* performances through the dramatically ecstatic rhythms which change a priest into a dancing goddess, embodied by her trance medium *boil*. The loud sound vibrations of the *ganda baja* drums create an exceptional atmosphere and tension perceived by all participants. The dynamic and dominant sounds incite the pulsating healing powers of the ritual (Stoller 1996: 165-184).

The movements of *boil*, the trance medium, combine artistic patterns with an immediate physical, muscular presence. The *boil* ritual as a whole follows a dramaturgy of preparation, escalation and relief. The performance starts with a worship (*puja*) continued by the meditation and narrative accompanied by the *dhunkel* instrument. The music of *ganda baja* then incites a phase of escalation during which the goddess takes possession of her priest. A tensed atmosphere of hope, fear and common excitement is evoked by the orchestra's play. This escalation culminates in the ecstatic dance of the priest interacting with the beat of the *dhol* drum. Finally, the voice of *boil* whispering in the ears of the participants brings consolation and relief. In the course of the ritual, the visual experience of the trembling, rhythmic body movements of the trance medium blends with the sensual experience of the touch of *boil* and of his body covered with sweat, while the aural experience of the escalating music of *ganda baja* reinforces these impressions. This multisensual perception, in terms of Howes' "*intersensorality*" as the "*multidirectional interaction of the senses and of sensory ideologies"* (2005: 9), seems to bring about psychological relief for the patients.

The ecstatic *boil* performance provides a possibility to touch the wilderness, which is considered to be the goddess. Everyone who has touched or was touched by the wild goddess returns consoled to his or her local and social context. Satisfied about the concrete, sensual communication with the goddess, participants return re-integrated into their community. Many of those who attended *boil* rituals confirmed that questioning the embodied goddess gave them psychological comfort. They considered the words of the trance medium as a consolation and as expressions of a divine truth: "*Be quiet, Ma is with you*", thus *boil* spoke to them. With these simple words the suffering and the barren were assured and strengthened in their hope and belief that their afflictions will be cured, that the children they desire, will soon be born.

Photograph 11: Trance medium *boil*, Sargivahal village, 2009, L. G.

While the ecstasy of the trance medium boil and the collective excitement during the ritual of goddess spirit possession can be conceived as the manifestation of a wild and to a certain extent uncontrolled power both without and within the community, the *boil* ritual as a whole has a reconfirming, integrative function. This becomes especially visible in the role of the *dhunkel* instrument and the narrative songs performed to its sounds. The *dhunkel* singer remembers and repeats collective metaphors, values, ideas and stories.[53] The meditative recollection of the local world view reconfirms the collective ideas and values of the local community, thus ensuring a cultural continuity.

---

[53] For a transcription of a *dhunkel* song and narration presented during a *boil* ritual, see Appendix.

## *Music as transformation*

In the *boil* performance it can be observed that the media music, dance, and language interweave effectively for healing. This intermediality illustrates how music opens a human for transformation into a divine being. The ritual music which is embodied in the playing of the *dhunkel* and in the music of the *ganda baja* orchestra touches the priest and his body. While dancing, the priest becomes *boil*, the manifestation of the Goddess. Finally, *boil* touches the suffering patients whose hope will be strengthened and whose pain will be eased. Performing arts in rituals operate as media of transformation on a theological, psychological and sociological level. They integrate a distraught member of a local community and console him or her through sensuality. It may be assumed that the healing power of *boil* rituals lies in the sensual and transformational power of the aesthetics of ritual music, dance, and speech.

## *Thea-phony in Bora Sambar against the background of pan - Indian goddess worship*

Manifold correspondences can be traced between the thea-phonic structures in the Bora Sambar region, which I have outlined in this chapter and pan-Indian phenomena of goddess worship in rural contexts. Besides the powerful male gods of the Indian religious traditions – for example Vishnu or Shiva - multiple local goddesses are worshipped all over India.[54] They are generally called *Devi* (goddess) or *Ma* (mother). The *devi* or *ma* is considered to be the creator as well as the destroyer of the world and the cosmos. She is omnipotent and associated with the idea of *shakti*.[55] This Indian concept of religious power has an extremely ambivalent character as the goddess at the same time embodies a creative and destructive power: She can kill and she can create. In rural as well as in urban regions of India cults of goddesses are often powerful. The worship of the goddess has an important impact on the life of her believers manifest for instance in pilgrimages, although personal devotion levels differ between rural or urban contexts.[56] Altars of local goddesses are scattered everywhere: at crossroads, under trees or in plain fields on the earth. To her believers, the local goddesses manifest themselves in aniconic form: as stones, as quarries, as eruptions of the earth, as waterfalls, rivers or other natural phenomena (Stietencron 1972). Goddesses are

---

[54] See: Kinsley 1985; Wilke / Michaels / Vogelsanger (eds.) 1994; Fischer / Goswamy / Dinanath Pathy 2005.
[55] For the concept of *shakti* see especially Wadley 1975.
[56] On the differences between urban and rural goddess worship see Bakker/Entwistle 1983.

often worshipped under a number of different names. Frequently, local cults of goddesses are integrated into the pan-Indian worship of goddesses like Kali or Durga (Mallebrein 2004: 273-299). The goddess is held to exert an enormous influence on the life of her believers: In her manifold manifestations she is responsible for one's fate: she gives and takes life; she can change its course benevolently through advices given in dreams or she can change it through destructive intrusions in the form of dangerous illness, as for example chicken pox. The live-giving and life-taking power and energy of the goddess is conceived as an uncontrollable, wild force but it can nonetheless be appeased and positively influenced by means of the correct worship.In India, the agency of human trance mediums, as I have described it in the *boil* ritual of the Bora Sambar region, is a widespread mode of communication with a goddess (Assayag / Tarabout 1999). Ritual goddess embodiment is generally characterised by trance, ritual language, often ecstatic forms of expression like dance or other ritual performances and the existence of a specialised male or female priesthood.[57] Enactments of goddess-embodiment or goddess-spirit possession are regularly accompanied by music, performed exclusively by initiated male musicians on highly symbolic instruments which at the same time provokes and indicates spiritual transformation. Goddess-spirit possession is specific to non-Brahmin social groups and mostly found in rural regions of India (Roche 2000: 288-295).

## *Boil as a theory of the Sacred*

To conclude this chapter, I would like to argue that the *thea-phony* of *boil* can not only be described as a ritual performance but in the same right as an indigenous theory of the Sacred or Sublime. An oral / aural culture as that of the local population of the Bora Sambar region implies that local value and meaning systems are enshrined and transmitted in acoustic or visual media as speech, song, music, dance or acting. The *boil* tradition of the Bora Sambar region shows a local meaning and belief system which is based upon the central idea that the goddess *is* the system of sounds mediated through music and embodiment. A sonic, sensual and intersensorial approach to sacrality thus shapes cultural ideas and mediates them in a specific way. The musically conceptualised sacred is on the one hand intangible as manifested in the sounds of *ganda baja*, on the other hand embodied in the trance medium *boil*, sacralising thus the message and the medium itself.

[57]For an impressive example of a female priesthood in spirit goddess embodiment, see Carrin 1997.

# *Third Chapter: Dance and Ritual as Idioms of Affinity and Alliance*

During the goddess embodiment ritual *boil*, the possessed priest, representing the goddess through his dance, dances forms of the traditional *dalkhai* dance. In the Bora Sambar region the *dalkhai* performance is another crucial form and medium of cultural and religious expression as well as of local meaning and value transmission. In the *dalkhai* dance and the corresponding rituals, the values of marriage in terms of affinity and alliance are re-enacted within a multifaceted ritual dance play whose principal actors are prepubescent girls.

## *Two Examples from Fieldwork*[58]

### *Duduki Jaria village*

In the Duduki Jaria village[59] *dalkhai* is performed during the time of *dusshara puja* or Durga *puja*, the veneration of the goddess Durga, on *osthomi*, the 21st day of the month *dusshara* and on the days that follow.[60] *Osthomi* is also the day of *bhai juntya*, the ritual veneration of brothers by their sisters. Thus, in one sense, *dalkhai* is a dance of sisters who dance for their brothers. The dancers are mainly girls aged between 3 and 13 years, led by an elder female lead dancer (*dekha guru*). Sometimes the *dalkhai* it is also danced by young married women, as the custom prescribes that every married girl has to return to her mother's house on the occasion of the Durga *puja*.

On *osthomi,* the worship of Dalkhai is performed in front of the *dalkhai kutti* (altar of Dalkhai), which is simultaneously named *durga kutti* (altar of the goddess Durga) and *dhunkel kutti* (altar of the *dhunkel* instrument). The *dalkhai* girl dancers offer rice paddy *(chaulo)* and incense *(duppo)* to the goddess and pray for their brothers. During the day of the *dalkhai puja* all girls are fasting. After the girl dancers have performed the *puja* inside the *Durga kutti,* they become *boil* – trance mediums embodying the Goddess Durga or Dalkhai. This happens without the involvement of any local priest

---

[58]Data was acquired between 2003 to 2009 during several periods of fieldwork (see above p. 11-13).

[59] In the Nawapara area of the Bora Sambar region (see fn 1 chapter 1). The population of the area mostly consists of Binjhal, Gond, Soara, Gour, Keut, Brahmin, Harijan, Sunari, Mali, Chomar, Boiragi, Mohant (Khondayat) and some Muslim communities.

[60] *Dalkhai* is also performed on *asuya,* the 8$^{th}$ full moon night of the year.

(*pujari*). The girls are from now on addressed as *Ma* (mother [goddess]) and are consulted by suffering patients searching relief for their personal sorrows and pains. The girls are also asked to forecast rain. While dancing, they are supposed to represent and embody the purity and beauty of a *devi*, a goddess.

The second day of the *dalkhai* ritual is the day of *bhai juntya.* The dancers put the offerings, which they have given the day before to goddess Dalkhai / Durga, on theirs heads and wish their brothers well. Sisters bind a thread (*juntya*) around the right wrist of their brothers (*bhai juntya*).

On the third day of the ritual cycle, the brothers (*bhai*) give clothes to their sisters. Then the brothers provide for musical accompaniment of the *dalkhai* dance by hiring *ganda baja* musicians from their own or from a neighbouring village. From the following morning on, which is the fourth day of the ritual, the young girls start to dance outside the village. The *Ganda baja* musicians accompany them with special *dalkhai* rhythms. When performing the *dalkhai*, the girl-dancers dance in one or two lines of two to six dancers facing each other, their bodies stooped, with small moving steps. The movement of the dancers does not follow any prescribed choreography; it is spontaneous but never uncontrolled or wild. Their dance seems rather monotonous, rhythmically responding to the music of the *ganda baja* orchestra, which guides the dance. While dancing, the girl-dancers sing the *dalkhai geet* – the song of *dalkhai*, which often has an erotically provocative character. The song is intended to tease and ridicule those who encounter the group of dancing girls on their way. The whole day long, the girls fast and dance outside their village, accompanied by the *ganda baja* party. As there is no rigidly fixed time schedule for the ritual dance, the *dalkhai* dance might sometimes start on an earlier day, before the ritual of *bhai juntya*.

### *Ambahalli village*

Another village where *dalkhai* is practised is the Ambahalli village, situated among the Gandamardhan hills of the Bora Sambar region. The area is populated by communities of Dhol Khond, Goura, Harijan, Boria/Binjhal, and Patro (Paika). The village god (*gram devta)* of Ambahalli is the goddess *Mati Devta Ma,* the goddess of the Earth. At a crossroads, the Durga and Dalkhai altar (*dalkhai kutti)* are placed nearby the *Ma Mati Devta* altar, which is a triangular shaped natural stone under a tree. The altars of the goddesses Durga and Dalkhai are represented by similarly shaped stones. The priest (*pujari)* of the *dalkhai kutti* belongs to the Dhol Khond community. Only once a year, during *bhai juntya* – the celebration for brothers by their sisters - he performs the *dalkhai puja*, the worship of the goddess Dalkhai.

For this occasion, the priest himself paints images of goddess Durga on a wall of a house near by the central place of the village with colours which the girls (*tukelmane*) have collected from the other villagers. While he is painting, *boil* – the spirit of the goddess – comes upon him and under her inspirations he draws the divine images. The place of the images of the Goddess Durga and Dalkhai is also called the *Dalkhai/Durga kutti.*

From around 10 in the morning to 4 in the afternoon, all young girls of the village dance the *dalkhai* dance. The polyrhythmic *ganda baja* music leads the stooped dancing movements of the girls. While dancing, the girls carry a short casual saree and cover their arms with a small untailored cotton cloth. The girls approach all houses of the village in order to collect money for the musicians of the village orchestra, which accompanies their dance. Together with the musicians, the group of girls then starts to dance outside the village and to move around on the roads leading to the village. They demand money from passers-by who cross their way. Often they are led by an older woman, who dances in front of the young girls and invents rhymes mocking the passers-by. The dance is always accompanied by teasing, provocative lyrics full of sexual allusions. Only after a donation of 10 to 100 Rupees, the traveller, who encounters the group of girl dancers, is allowed to move on. The older woman leading the dance is called the "teaching teacher" (*sikha-guru*). The girls learn the dance by watching and imitating her movements and thus also call her *dekha-guru* "the teacher to look at". The girls dance *dalkhai* only outside their village. Only outside "*behere*", they do not feel ashamed while dancing, since their dance is considered to be of a sensual and erotic character. Before dancing and going outside, "*behere*", the girls offer to the goddess Dalkhai a *mohuli* donation of wine and small bowls made of banana leaves filled with uncooked rice. The burning of incense sticks and high screaming sounds called *hurli hurli,* created by a vibration of the small singer's tongues, accompany the *puja*. The goddess Dalkhai/Durga is considered to protect the girls who become her dancers and worshippers. The girls' dance is on the one hand conceived as a ritual to make the goddess happy; on the other hand the goddess herself is identified with the dance of the girl children.

## *Dalkhai Dance*

### *Dalkhai in transition*

Traditionally, *dalkhai* is supposed to be an Adivasi dance of the Soara, Binjhal and Gour communities. In the course of tribal migration and the corresponding cultural transformation processes, it has spread to the urban centres of western Odisha and is performed today also in the guise of the urban *Sambalpuri* folk dance. As the *Sambalpuri* dance, it has become the most characteristic and popular dance style of the region and the core of various folk dances of western Odisha. Through public performances, the *dalkhai* dance has become one of the most important identity markers of *Sambalpuri* identity, synonymous with the regional identity of western Odisha with its core centre Sambalpur town.[61]

In its ritual form, the *dalkhai* dance is today only preserved in some very remote villages of the Bora Sambar region. As a common village dance tradition of the region, *dalkhai* is about to vanish because most mothers do not want their girl children to dance in front of men and boys. Often, the villagers themselves have decided to abandon the *dalkhai* tradition due to its supposed sensual character. But what are the reasons for such sudden cultural prudery? The ambivalent perception and assessment of the *dalkhai* dance can be explained as a reaction to the pejorative values of urban mainstream Hinduism. In urban Hindu society, the *dalkhai* dance is associated with the culture and lifestyle of Adivasi societies – hence with people who are discredited as *jungly*, as having the stigma of being uncultivated, wild and sexually easily accessible. In minority and subaltern communities an interiorization of external prejudices is a sign of a violent alienation from one's own cultural heritage. In his essay on "*Adivasi Knowledge and Aphasia*" G.N. Devy has extended the medical term *aphasia*, designating the pathological loss of speech, to the loss of the cultural capacity to recognise one's own systems of knowledge and to the loss of the power of expression through one's own cultural knowledge techniques (Devy 2006b: 95-122). For the fragile community of the Soara, Piers Vitebsky describes this process as a dramatic cultural "inarticulacy" and "cultural forgetting" (Vitebsky 2008: 243-261). The abandonment of the traditional *dalkhai* dance and ritual can be interpreted as a self inflicted cultural *aphasia* and cultural forgetting, and thus as a sign of the accomplishment of a cultural hegemony of urban

---

[61] See chapter 8.

Hindu values, which persistently have been interacting with the indigenous traditions of the Bora Sambar region. Due to an urban process of re-traditionalization and re-invented remembering, which has its centre in the town of Sambalpur, the emergence of urban *Sambalpuri* folklore has, however, re-valuated and re-defined the *dalkhai* dance: as folklore it has become an important political and regional identity marker.[62]

## *Etymological and metaphorical levels of the term dalkhai*

The term *dalkhai* is considered to stem from *dalo*, the branch of the *dalo* tree. During the *dalkhai* dance, the people tell, the *dalo* branches are symbolically planted. The branch of the *dalo* tree in turn is the symbol of the goddess Durga, who is associated with *shakti*, the female power. *Dalo* branches also stand for brushwood, evoking the picture of young shy girls dancing in the brushes. The *dalkhai* dance is thus considered a shy (*surmili*) and sensual (*bhabo rossa*) dialogue between girls and boys. Moreover, "*Dal*" (rice) and "*khai*" (eating) also signifies eating rice, generally associating the goddess Dalkhai with rice. Some tell that the *dalkhai* dance is performed on *dusshara* days in order to prevent the paddy from insects. The vibration of the *dhol* drum of the *ganda baja* orchestra accompanying the *dalkhai* dance is believed to affect the air and disturb the flight of the insects, so they are fended off the paddy. The term *dalkhai* does not only designate the ritual dance and the local goddess Dalkhai, in whose honour it is performed, but it may simultaneously refer to other goddesses such as the pan-Indian goddess Durga, Shakti Devi, the local goddess of power, Bandurga, the local forest-goddess, or Samley the regional goddess of the Sambalpur district. Indian goddess worship often implies a polysemic inclusion of diversified goddess concepts. One goddess is regarded and venerated as an integral part of another. While displaying one personality she may simultaneously incorporate other manifestations of her divine identity.[63]

## *The legend of dalkhai*

Local narrations about the *dalkhai* dance relate the dance to stories of seven sisters and seven brothers venerated in the *dalkhai* or *sula kutti*, the altar of the goddess Dalkhai, also called "altar of the sixteen". In order to ex-

---

[62] See chapter 7.

[63] On the multifaceted features of goddess worship in South Asia see: Kinsley 1985; Bakker/Entwistle 1983; Jacobsen / Basu / Malinar / Narayanan 2009: 457- 828.

plain the origin of *dalkhai*, an old priest of one *dalkhai / sula kutti* in the Bora Sambar region recounts the following story:

> *"Once upon a time a rusi [holy man] told the seven sisters: in case you can not bath in the Ganga, you will die. One time, the seven sisters could not find any water to bath during seven days and thus decided to commit suicide on the seventh day. But before they could carry out the deed, the seven brothers came to the jungle and rescued the seven sisters from suicide by marrying them. The seven brothers, who all where sons of a king (raja putra), then took the seven sisters to their kingdom. It took the seven brothers sixteen days to reach their kingdom with the seven sisters. When the seven sisters entered the kingdom they performed the Kudrukuni puja ("ussa"). Then they danced the dalkhai dance. Kudrukuni Goddess told them not to take any water and any meals before they had accomplished the goddess worship. If they could not resist eating something, they only were allowed to take a cake (pita) from seven leaves. After fasting (upvas) and after performing puja for the Kudrukuni goddess, the seven sisters performed first Pankaldaki puja, then the Shiva puja and then the Durga puja. All in all, the sisters performed sixteen pujas. When fasting, the sisters danced in order to forget the hunger."*

Embedded in the complex configuration of the ritual sequence described, the legend highlights the value of marriage for individual and social continuity by depicting it literally as a life saving event. The legend also preserves a variety of names of local goddesses which over time have been suppressed in the general narrations about the *dalkhai* dance. Today, only the names of dominant trans-regional goddesses such as Durga are usually mentioned in connection with the *dalkhai* dance and ritual. The narration harbors the remembrance of certain local goddesses, who otherwise have completely vanished from the collective memory. The ritually based oral culture as well as the ritual itself acts as an indigenous archive of culturally specific meanings.

## *Dalkhai and sula kutti - the altar of the sixteen*

Traditionally, no temple exists for the goddess Dalkhai. She is worshipped through the dance inside or in front of her altar, the *dalkhai kutti*. The *dalkhai kutti* which is also called *Durga kutti,* the altar of Goddess Durga or *sula kutti,* the altar of the sixteen, or *dhunkel kutti*, the altar of the *dhunkel* instrument, is mostly a quadrangular room within a mud house considered as a sacred abode. On the upper part of one of the room's walls, 16 images of the goddess Dalkhai or Durga together with her seven sisters (*sato bhani*)[64], performing the *dusshara* ceremony [65], are painted.

Photograph 12: *Durga kutti /dhunkel kutti /dalkhai kutti/sula kutti*, village of Dhumabatta, 2004, L. G.

[64] 1) Subkeshi, 2) Oholya, 3) Tulsabati/Irani, 4) Dohona, 5) Kisteirani, 6) Sirya 7) Onjona.
[65] 21 jars (*kolos*) brought to the *kutti* during *dusshara* are supposed to represent 16 goddesses and additionally the 7 sisters of Durga (*sato bhani*).

Photograph 13: *Durga kutti /dhunkel kutti /dalkhai kutti/sula kutti*, village of Dhumabatta, 2004, L. G.

The images themselves represent “the altar of the sixteen” (*sula kutti*). The painting of the pictures is part of the ritual cycle performed during the Durga *puja*. The first 16 pictures representing single goddesses will be painted and worshipped by the local painter artists of the Maharana caste on *ostomi,* the ninth day of the *dusshara* month. After the artists of the Maharana cast have painted a new *dalkhai / sula kutti* it is ready for the appropriate worship of the goddess Durga (*Durga puja*). At *dosomi*, the tenth day of the *dusshara* month, the double pictures representing goddesses in company of their seven sisters and their husbands will be painted and worshipped by the villagers. It is believed that all the goddesses and gods, the seven sisters and their married seven god-brothers reside in the *dalkhai kutti*. As mentioned above, the *kutti* is also the sacred abode of the *dhunkel* instrument.[66] Every year, a new

[66] For a description of the instrument see chapter 2.

*dhunkel* instrument is brought into the *dalkhai kutti* while the old instrument is destroyed and thrown away. This is why the *dalkhai kutti* is simultaneously called the *dhunkel kutti*. Ideally, the *dalkhai / dhunkel / sula kutti* is supposed to be renewed every seven years, but factually the frequency of its renewal depends on the financial capacities of the particular village. This event is celebrated as *sasti*, the holy marriage of goddesses and gods.

The *dhunkel* instrument is used by the *dhunkel* singer and player (*dhunkelya*) to accompany his recounting of the *dhunkel bandana*, the story of the *dhunkel* instrument, and its relation to the worship of goddesses, the notion of sound and to the concept of *dalkhai*. The following song, performed during the *dalkhai* ritual, is an exemplary fragment of this sophisticated oral tradition:

### *Dhunkel bandana song*[67]

*Bandhu achhen mui re*
I do the invocations to [goddess] Dalkhai

*Bandhu ache mui Samalai*
I do the invocation to [goddess] Samlai

*Feda mor kasana*
To remove my difficulties.

*Baja baja jhumka badi re*
Please infuse sound in my musical stick

*Baju thibu re siba dhanu*
You will continue your sound in my Shiv's bow

*Chhaachuri kheli bure devi*
You will play pleasantly my goddess Mother.

*Aasi gala mor Subhakeshi re*
My [goddess] Subokeshi has come

*Biswa Mohini lo devi*
You are the snail of the world.

*Bandu acchen mui grama pati go*
I am invocating the village goddess Grampati [=village earth]

*Bandhu acche mui aadi Shakti go*
I am invocating the goddess Aadishakti [=first power]

---

[67] The song was recorded on October 15, 2004; the transcription is by Surendra Kumar Sahoo. For another version of the *dalkhai bandana*, see Appendix.

*Bandu acche mui Nilaaraani*
I am invocating the queen Nilaaraani-

*Bandhu ace mui Tulsa raani*
I am invocating the queen Tulsa.

*Danya Danya Rohelya baati re*
So many thanks to Rohela Bati.

*Rupe Guneta Maahasati go*
Her looks are beautiful, inside she is virtuous.

*Orissa buli gala*
She moved to Orissa.

*Jagata mohila re jemaa*
She overwhelmed the world.

*Bandu acche mui Mahaa Maai*
I invocate the goddess Mahamaai.

*Tor Paaden sarana je Maata*
I pray before you my Mother.

*Baaja baaja mor ratna handi*
Please make my pot sound.

*Runu jhunu ta rumu jhumu*
With a booming sound.

*Ulashe khelibu*
You will dance.

*Aasi gala mor Banabassi*
My [goddess] Banabasi has come here.

*Parvati Nandini*
Oh Parvati oh Nandini!

*Bandu acchen muin Saptasati*
I invocate the Goddess Saptasati.

*Prasanna huibe re maataa sudayaa karibe*
Please make me happy and take care of me.

*Bandhu acchen mui dahanaa raani*
I invocate the queen Dahanaa.

*Raja raghu rani re myi raja ra dulani*
All are the housewives of the king.

*Raaja kuanri Rupabati*
The beautiful princesses.

*Bayesa heal re jhia ulashe badhilaa*
They have grown with luxury and got maturity.

*Chaata Saali ke padhi gala*
They went to school.

*Sundara disilaa*
They looked beautiful.

In its first part, the song describes the invocation of a divine presence through the sound of the *dhunkel* instrument: The *dhunkel* is supposed to call different goddesses and gods to the *dhunkel kutti* [I *do the invocations to [goddess] Dalkhai - I do the invocation to [goddess] Samlai - I am invocating the village goddess Grampati [=village earth] - I am invocating the goddess Aadishakti [=first power] - I invocate the goddess Mahamaai*]. This is accomplished through the sounds produced by the *dhunkel* instrument [*Please infuse sound in my musical stick - You will continue your sound in my Shiv's bow]*. The sound of the *dhunkel* acts as a mediator or magnet for the divine sphere.

The song contains a metaphoric and fragmentary language, alluding to local ideas and values: The "snail" [*You are the snail of the world*] refers to local cosmological narrations about the birth of the universe, where the snail is a metaphor of fertility; the figures of the divine king and queen [*I am invocating the queen Nilaaraani - I am invocating the queen Tulsa - All are the housewives of the king*] and the ideas of "*beautiful princesses*" who "*have grown with luxury and got maturity*" allude allegorically to the inclusive cultural value of marriage – linked to reaching the age of maturity [ *They went to school - They looked beautiful*]. In the Bora Sambar region, a girl's maturity is the starting point for marriage arrangements, which are ideally made after the pattern of preferential bilateral cross-cousin marriage (see below). The *dhunkel bandana* is at once the enactment and the description of the worship of Dalkhai by means of her dance, the sound of the *dhunkel* instrument and the sung oral narrations. Moreover, it is another moment of the synaesthetic transmission of the core value of marriage within the ritual, symbolic and aesthetic meaning system of the Bora Sambar region.

### *Narrations about the dalkhai/sula kutti*

Oral narrations about the altar of the goddess Dalkhai and the 16 goddesses generally transport the idea of 16 gods and 16 goddesses, which means that all in all 32 gods and goddesses (*botis*) are held to be residing in the so called "altar of the sixteen" (*sula kutti*). A taxonomic mysticism can be retrieved from these narrations, stressing the numbers sixteen, thirty two, seven and eight. The numeric correspondences seemed to represent an abstract value in themselves, designated to enforce belief contents and stabilize the divine order by their numeric symbolism. What seemed important to all of my interlocutors was the existence of a numeric taxonomic logic as such, not an empirically coherent numeric system. The enlisted number of names of gods and goddesses accordingly may vary, depending on the narrators and the mnemo-techniques employed - with the *dhunkel* players being the mostly specialized and trained story tellers or singers. The following gods and goddesses are regularly named as belonging to the sixteen goddesses and gods:

| **16 goddesses (*devi*)** | **16 gods (*devta*) and goddesses (*devi*)** |
|---|---|
| 1) Durga | 17) Jakya Pati |
| 2) Samley | 18) Lakshmi |
| 3) Dula Samley | 19) Mandala |
| 4) Chara Bahati | 20) Sundala |
| 5) Maha Lakshma | 21) Boru |
| 6) Borul Ma | 22) Durbasa |
| 7) Adi Mata | 23) Vishwa karma |
| 8) Shiva Parvati | 24) Ongira |
| 9) Oholya Mata | 25) Polostya |
| 10) Rohelia | 26) Maricho |
| 11) Chanchala | 27) Sopta Rusi |
| 12) Kosala/Bimali | 28) Vishwa ritra |
| 13) Subrokeshi | 29) Hanuman |
| 14) Chandra Tara/Promila | 30) Dohana |
| 15) Subratara | 31) Kartika |
| 16) Bihma Goura | 32) Ganesh |

Figure I: Indigenous names of the sixteen gods and goddesses

But also other goddesses and gods are often named as residing in the sula kutti, for example:

| | |
|---|---|
| 1. Durga | 6. Rakta Mauli |
| 2. Shiva | 7. Sato Bhani |
| 3. Parvati | 8. Rayala |
| 4. Mauli | 9. Donmauli |
| 5. Kanda Mauli | 10. Karamsani |

Figure II: Diversification of indigenous goddess-names

or:

1. Maha Kali
2. Ma Tarini
3. Maha Mangala
4. Subokeshi
5. Oila devi
6. Sat Bohoni
7. Hanumat
8. Chamunda
9. Lakshmi
10. Saraswati
11. Sriya
12. Indrani
13. Shiva
14. Omrika
15. Kayeti

Figure III: Variation of goddess-names

Sometimes a priest-musician cannot remember all the names immediately or even at all. Often priests start to chant, in order to recall the names and their arrangement while singing. The order of names however, is always individual. What is important is the symbolism of the number sixteen.

A special significance is ascribed in local narrations to the mythical figure and taxonomy of the seven sisters *sato bhani*. The seven sisters Ohalya, Rohelia, Chanchala, Kosala/Bimali, Subrokeshi, Chandra Tara/Promila, Subratara (see fig. 1, no. 9 to15) are told to be married to the seven brothers *sato bhai*. The seven brothers in turn are supposed to be the ancient *rusi* (wise men) who accompanied Shiva and Parvati during their marriage (fig. 1, no 21-27). The names of the seven brothers may also vary in local narrations. An old priest of one *dhunkel kutti* recounts the couplings of the seven sisters and seven brothers as follows:

1) Oholya is married to Gauton Rusi
2) Rohelia is married to Puspa
3) Chanchala is married to Chandrahasia
4) Bimali is married to Sumonu
5) Promila is married to Okyaya
6) Subrokeshi is married to Oniradha
7) Subratara is married to Kirakarua

By establishing a link between the mythical marriage of the seven sisters with the seven brothers and the marriage of the holy couple Shiva and Parvati, local narrations relate this collective marriage alliance to the mystical number sixteen:

$$\begin{array}{l} 7\ \textit{bhani} + 7\ \textit{bhai} = 14 \\ \underline{+\ 2\ \text{(Shiva and Parvati)}} \\ 16 \end{array}$$

The *sula kutti*, the alter of the sixteen, represents thus the symbolic and abstract veneration of the local value of marriage, manifested by the taxonomic mysticism of the number 7 and personified by the mythical seven sisters and seven brothers. The addition of the divine couple Shiva and Parvati reinforces the value of alliance and marriage. The taxonomic symbolism is finally unified in the metaphoric power of the goddess Dalkhai and her dance *dalkhai*.

The aesthetic and religious expression of the *dalkhai / sula kutti* in the Bora Sambar region of western Odisha reveals an artistic mimesis of the marriage pattern between the mythological sisters and brothers. This mythological pattern corresponds to the factual social structures of the region: The mythological alliance between 7 sisters and 7 brothers represents the common preference in the Bora Sambar region to marry the bilateral cross-cousin, called *bhai* or *bhani,* the classificatory brother or sister. The children of opposite sex of two opposite sex siblings[68] are considered the preferred marriage partners, a pattern reflected in the mythological taxonomies.

## *Dalkhai music*

The *dalkhai* dance is accompanied by a specific music, performed by the village orchestra *ganda baja. Dalkhai* music is distinguished by particular rhythms and *matras* (drum strokes per beat). *Dalkhai* rhythms are characterized by 6, 10 or 14 *matras,* considered by the musicians as the rhythmic foundations of the worship of goddess Dalkhai (Dalkhai *puja).* They are vivid, joyyful and played within a pentatonic scale. In the context of *dusshara* ceremonies, *dalkhai* music (*dalkhai baja*) with 6, 10 and 14 *matra* is linked with the ritual dance entertainment of young girls outside the village. In order to stimulate the dance, the pentatonic melodies are repeated in rhythmic cycles. *Dalkhai* music necessarily has a vocal component: It is associated with the *dalkhai* songs (*dalkhai geet*) of the dancing girls. In contrast, the rhythms of the *durga puja* played by *ganda baja* inside the local king's palace are not designated for dancing. Through an ascending rhythmic tempo, a tensed and fearful sacred atmosphere is created, which culminates in the *sula bharni par*, the sixteen rhythms of goddess possession.

## *Dalkhai geet*

*Dalkhai* songs are extremely popular in the Bora Sambar region. In their modernised and popularised versions they are known as S*ambalpuri geeta/gana* and are well represented at the folklore festivals of the region. In their ritual context they are sung as rhymes (*stanza*s) by the older women acting as lead singers and repeated by the chorus of the singing and dancing girls. *Dalkhai geet* from village Kanda, sung by Mrs Beikhai, a song leader of about 65 years of age, who has for many years been a famous *sikha-* and *dekha guru* for young girls:

---

[68] MB=mamu =MBC = bhai bhoni marry children of FZ= nana=FZC = bhai bhoni.

### *Dalkhai geet* (song)[69]

**I. Song Leader**

*Dalkhaire, Dalkhaire, Dalkhaire*
*Suna gala - Bala gala- Manena Padila*
Gold lost- Round ring lost- did not remember

*Chhabis – bhari- mudi gala – bela ke*
Twenty six-bar of gold – ring lost- at a time

*Jhuri –Jhuri- malaa- kain*
Thinking- Thinking – was – at
[the meaning of the stanza could be rendered as follows: *When she lost much gold, she did not mind; But when she lost a good friend, she started to think and think* (gold may also stand metaphorically for a friend)]

**Girl Chorus**
[repeats the complete stanza]

**II. Song leader**

*Dalkhaire Dalkhaire Dalkhaire*
*Udi gala – Pen kuali*
Flew – Aquatic bird

*Hiti- Padla- Tiha*
Fall- down- Tiha

*Balut kalu- biha haiche- nani ke*
Young Age- marriage completed by the girls

*Deu kete-tia-kain*
Pay much - waiting at
[The meaning of the stanza could be interpreted as follows: The blue bird flew. The Tiha bird fell down. Auspicious bird and the auspicious time have passed. Early marriage is achieved by the girl. When her lover wants to meet her now, she always postpones his visit (she invents excuses not to meet him any more).]

**Girl Chorus**
[repeats the complete stanza]

---

[69] The song was recorded in October 2004, at village Kanda gao, sung by Mrs Beikhai, song leader.

**III. Song leader**

*Dalkhaire Dalkhaire Dalkhaire*

*Kati neli - Bauns- nala*
Cut down- bamboo- took

*Duipaka- phula*
Two sides- whole

*Gala – salein - dekhi thili*
Last- year- had seen

*Chikanchakan- thila*
Finishing - was

Asur –sale-dekhiachhen -nanike
This year- looking to - girl

*Diaan-chari-gala kain*
White ants-eaten up- it seems
[The bamboo was beautiful last year (the bamboo = the young unmarried girl). This year it cut and damaged by white ants (cutting bamboo= the marriage of the young girl). Last year you looked beautiful. This year you look damaged / ugly. (The opposition alludes to the radical change in the life of a girl after her marriage, when her beauty quickly fades away as a consequence of the hard life she now has)]

**Girl Chorus**
[repeats the complete stanza]

**IV Song leader**

*Dalkhaire Dalkhaire Dalkhaire*

*Mor- Bahela- Bachha Kire*
My -moulded- calf bullock- weather

*Magur Gurike –dekhi- kari- babugo*
Brown fish - has seen - the boy

*Hiti – Gala - Kachha Kai*
Come –out- part of clothes – such as
[I have already used the bullock to plough (the ploughing of the earth with the bullock who has a plough fixed on his neck is a symbol of sexual intercourse) When the boy saw the brown beautiful girl (brown fish = beautiful girl) His under clothes fell down showing his naked masculinity.]

**Girl Chorus**
[repeats the complete stanza]

In *dalkhai* songs, sensuality, romantic emotions and the passage of time from childhood to adulthood are handled in a highly metaphorical disguise. Emotional or sensual contents are never expressed directly. The rhetoric images are always wrapped in a symbolic language. Meaning is transmitted through aesthetic ornamentation, fragmentation and multiplication. Symbolic allusions are made via rhymes and a highly hermetic language, employing systematic syntactic fragmentations. The first stanza, for example, introduces the metaphor of a lost golden ring to allude to the loss of friendship. The image of an aquatic bird fallen down in the second stanza hints to the emotional states of unanswered love and disappointment. The third stanza drastically deplores the passage from childhood to marriage as the loss of beauty. Finally, the fourth stanza poetically expresses the corporal pleasures of love and beauty by allusion to common erotic symbolisms, such as the brown fish as a metaphor for an attractive woman and the bullock ploughing the earth as a common symbol for masculine sexuality. The metaphoric content of sensuality is thus synaesthetically expressed in the *dalkhai* dance and ritual through the interrelatedness and the intermediality of rhythmic language, body movement and the poly-rhythmic music of *ganda baja*.

## *The dalkhai dance as a multi-dimensional cultural medium*

*Dalkhai* unfolds its social effectiveness both through its ritual performance and through its metaphorical symbolism. Only after years of field work in the Bora Sambar region I started to understand the interrelatedness of the *dalkhai* dance with the values of the local culture and the implicit symbolic meanings and images. After many conversations with musicians, girl dancers and their parents; through repeated visits to distant villages where the *dalkhai* dance was performed; through recordings of music and various narrations, always transcribed by Surendra K. Sahu, and finally through my attempts to include as many views and perspectives as possible, I grasped the effectiveness of the metaphoric symbols used in *dalkhai*. *Dalkhai* unfolds its power through the combination of the performing arts of dance, music and oral poetry. Its social and cultural efficacy may be described as an effect of aesthetic distancing through its metaphoric disguise comparable to those which Roseman and Laderman (1996:7) have identified as central for the efficacy of healing performances. Even if *dalkhai* is not a healing performance in any strict sense, the *dalkhai* performance nevertheless is, like a healing performance, centred around a moment of crisis – the critical passage from infancy to adulthood, with the coming forth of the problems of adult life, family relations and work. In the jocular and playful presentation of the dance and the fragmentary and metaphoric language of the *dalkhai* songs, these elements are 'put in a distance': they can be dealt with in perspective and thus loose part of their terrifying aspect, something that may well be compared to a kind of 'healing'. *Dalkhai* turns out being a multi-dimensional representation of values and facts of local culture, operating on various levels of metaphorical representation:

1) The *dalkhai* dance is a form of local goddess worship expressed through the dance of young girls, which represent and incarnate local goddesses during the time of the ritual. The girl-child is associated in Bora Sambar region with the goddesses Dalkhai and Durga respectively with the regional goddess Samlay/Samleshwari. The *dalkhai* dance represents ideas of divine purity and beauty, symbolised by the unripe, joyful and child-like state of the dancing girls.[70]

2) The worship of brothers by their sisters represented in the *dalkhai* dance simultaneously celebrates the biological and classificatory sister-brother-relations and enshrines the idea of a crucial bond between sister and brother. Notably, the classificatory terms *bhai* (brother) *bhani* (sister) indicate both: the life long bondage between brothers and sisters, which continues after marriage[71] and the marriageable partners. *Dalkhai* is, on the one hand, a celebration of the sister-brother bond as an elementary kinship relation containing social and ritual obligations after marriage and the patri-local establishment of a new household: biological brothers and sisters have a lifelong duty to care for each other. On the other hand, the terminological *bhai-bhani* relationship celebrates the value of bilateral cross-cousin marriage in Bora Sambar region: the children of a brother preferentially marry the children of his sister[72] in order to settle patri-locally in the bride-groom's family. In a joyful way the *dalkhai* dance celebrates and enshrines the complex cultural value configurations of marriage. While dancing, the girls are symbolically prepared for their marriage life. In the same vein, the mythological dimension of the

---

[70] The *dalkhai* dance and *puja* resembles the worship of Kumari Puja ("girl worship") in West Bengal. There, Kumari Puja is the worship of pre-pubescent girls during the second day - *Maha Asthami* - of the four day worship of goddess Durga. It is believed that during Durga Puja the goddess descends on earth and incarnates in different shapes. The small girl is considered Durga's favoured incarnation representing the values of creation and the forthcoming life-giving powers of female fertility (See the photographic print by Rosalind Salomon, 1984).
[71] The sister-brother relationship after marriage is a common ritual constituency in South Asia (See Jamous 1992: 52-73).
[72] MB=mamu =MBC = *bhai bhoni* marry children of FZ= nana=FZC = *bhai bhani.*

*dalkhai* dance, as it is expressed in the story of the seven sisters (*sato bhani*) and their marriage to the seven brothers (*sato bhai*) can be understood as an attempt to narratively establish the social structure of a continuous relationship and responsibility between brothers and sisters before and after marriage as well as the prescription of preferential marriage between bilateral cross-cousins. The homonyms *bhai-bhani* thus indicate a crucial social category. The *dalkhai* dance can be seen as a sensual and bodily metaphor of a social system where the relationship between brothers and sisters is a fundamental bond shaping the whole life of a person.

3) The time of the *dalkhai* dance as well as its symbolism is connected with the basic aliment rice and with the cut paddy of the harvesting time. In this context, the *dalkhai* dance becomes a metaphor for production, creation, life and wealth. Vigorously danced and sung, *dalkhai*'s poses, songs and rhymes often have a flirting and provoking sensual connotation. The typically stooped movements of the dancing girls are associated with both, a pose of sensual attraction and with hard work, namely the stooped working position while harvesting rice. As well, dancing "outside the own village" seems metaphorically linked to both the awakening of sensuality and work in the fields. The dance outside the village also metaphorically hints to the social fact of exogamy, where marriageable partners are preferably found and chosen outside the own village. The marriageable partner is always supposed and imagined an "other" even if he is classified as brother or sister.

4) *Dalkhai* can finally be considered as a puberty initiation ritual for the girl-child, where the girl is socialised through playing, joking, singing and dancing to become a woman ready for marriage. *Dalkhai* thus represents a ritual of transition, a ritual of life-cycle and social movement which is itself a movement – a dance. It is a fluid – dancing - transfer from girlhood to the next steps in life as sisterhood, marriage, motherhood, and hard work. Early from childhood on, the young girls are prepared for their social role as women. This process of preparation and ripening takes place within a divine play performed in the dance of the girls and the goddess. The *dalkhai* dancing girl becomes a homologue of the goddess Durga and Dalkhai associated with the rice harvest. The *dalkhai* dance symbolises hence the social and biological ripening of the girl by correlating it with the ripening of rice. The socialisation of the girl child in the Bora Sambar region is implemented particularly by dance and music – with the *dalkhai* dance as a crucial medium of indigenous education transmitting the socially encompassing values of affinity and alliance.

## *Tin Sali Yatra - a Ritual of Divine Marriage*

In the Bora Sambar region, a further ritual symbolically re-enacting of the crucial value configuration of marriage is practised, the *tin sali yatra* of the Binjhal community, also called the *Brahmani Potari yatra.* According to the tradition of the *tin sali yatra*, every three years the Binjhal gods Bura Raja and Brahmani Patri[73], who are recounted to have reunited after marital quarrels and separation, visit the houses of the goddess' mother and the goddess' mother's sister (*mausi*) after their symbolic remarriage. These visits are ritually performed by the Binjhal community through processions to the seven Binjhal villages of the Bora Sambar region. At night, a fisherman's bamboo basket, containing an abstract anthropomorphic clay figure which represents the goddess Brahmani Patri, is carried from one village to another. The procession is accompanied by the village orchestra *ganda baja* which welcomes and evokes the goddess. While the *ganda baja* plays, *boil* comes upon the priest carrying the goddess: the goddess awakes and takes possession of him.

The tradition prescribes that the divine couple visits first the goddess' elder sister's (*boro mausi*=eZ) house at the village Bora Sambar, where they reside for one night. The next morning, the god and goddess move on to Bengrajpur to the house of Brahmani Patri's mother, the goddess Patkandha. Until midnight, the couple is supposed to stay at Bengrajpur. Then it is expected to move to Jhengnadihi village, the home of the younger mother's sister (*sano mausi*=yMZ) of Brahmini Patri. During the following days, the procession completes its route by visiting the Binjhal villages Temri, Shura and finally the village of Khoira. At each village, the gods are welcomed by the village orchestra and thus *boil*, the goddess spirit possession by Brahmini Patri will occur. At the end of each visit, a special farewell ritual is performed to conclude their visit: A hen and a cock, symbolising the divine couple, are sacrificed after the hen has been hypnotised by the sacrificial priest (*junkhar*) and has shown rolling tears in her eyes. After this symbolic farewell tears, the hen and the cock are beheaded and distributed as sacrificial food (*prasad*) among the villagers. The ritual round of visits ends with the return of the goddess to Posada, the village of her origin, where a final festival of re-welcoming is celebrated around her village altar (*kutti*).

During the *tin sali yatra* festival, no bullock cars are allowed to be used and no harvesting is to be done. In the Bora Sambar region the earth is considered a metonym for any local goddess, while, as already mentioned in the

---

73 See chapter 1.

context of the *dalkhai*, ploughing is a metaphor for the sexual act.[74] Thus, the goddess is believed to be hurt and approached in her intimacy by ploughing and by agricultural work. This ritual taboo is transmitted in the following myth:

> *Once, a cultivator was harvesting during the festival time of the tin sali yatra. At that time a tiger came and attacked his bullocks. Shortly after this attack the farmer dreamt of Goddess Brahmani Patra who spoke to him: "Why are you harvesting at the time of my festival? The festival endures 7 days and covers my sacred landscape of Bora Sambar. Immediately stop your work".*
>
> *After having dreamt and heard this divine message the cultivator instantly stopped harvesting and joined the festivities of the village. Since then he lived in peace and happiness.*

To sum up, the *tin sali yatra* in its divine play and ritual underlines and reinforces a symbolic matrilineality as a crucial identity marker of the Bora Sambar region. After marriage the tie to the maternal line remains a key identity factor for the married woman.[75] The *tin sali yatra* also deals with the essential concept of locality and territoriality, demarcated by goddess worship related to specific local myths. Notably, the separation and remarriage of the divine actors of the myth and ritual points to a distinctive characteristic of the indigenous social structure where divorce and re-marriage – which are taboos in Hindu mainstream society – are a common practice.

## *Binjhal Biha*

The value of marriage is not only expressed in the *tin sali yatra* of the Binjhal but also in the idea of *Binjhal Biha*, the ritually performed ideal Binjhal marriage, which in former times has been taking place during the worship of the goddess Karamsani (*karma puja*) in October. The Binjhal consist of 30-40 patrilineal exogamic clans (*gotra*), which, as we have seen, prefer the marriage rule of bilateral cross-cousin marriage, where the opposite-sex children of the children of the opposite sex-siblings may intermarry. The ideal marriage is an arranged marriage, fixed by the families of the young couple. Usually, the bride is selected by the father of the bridegroom. Nonetheless, narratives tell of a legendary time when the adolescent girls of the

---

[74] The same metaphoric equation has been observed by Georg Pfeffer in Koraput (1997b: 183-208).

[75] A similar symbolic matrineality has been observed by Marine Carrin (2006: 213-240.)

Binjhal were free to choose their mates during *karma puja* in Bhojpur Godh, the sacred jungle place in the Gandamardhan hills.

An old Binjhal man spontaneously sings the following song in order to express his ideas about the Binjhal marriage:

**_Binjhal Biha geet_**[76]

*Tuinta raja Mainaa gada jaabe*
Oh king, who you are the king of Maina Garh [the sacred fort]!

*Titar maari raniku bhujan debe*
You have to kill the wild bird to satisfy the Queen.

*Raani gudar Bichuan Rajaa mare gahanaa*
When the king sees the ringing of the Queen's feets [the ringing sounds of the round and massif foot anklets which acoustically and visually symbolise the married woman] he feels happy.

*Raani gudar payendri raja mare gahaan*
When the king sees the rings surrounding the queen's legs, he feels happy.

*Tuinta raja Mainaa gada jaabe*
Oh king, who you are the king of Maina Garh.

Marriage is described through the metaphors of massive food anklets and their sounds associated with marriage life, sensuality and femininity, so desirable for the king that he has to go out and hunt a wild animal to please his wife. The arrow – symbol of masculinity and the male partner of a marriage – which is used to shoot down the bird is metaphorically implicated, but not explicitly mentioned, indicating thus a satisfied marriage life.

## *The Binjhal biha as a four days ceremony:*

1) On *matipoka,* the first day, seven female relatives of the bride (*konya*) go to a crossroads. There, they put soil (*mati*), which they have brought along, on a temporary earthen altar, *bedi*, the altar of the bride. The soil put on the marital altar is supposed to be purifying.
2) On *punami*, the second day, the bridegroom's (*boro pila*) male friends and relatives go to the bride's house and give her ornaments and clothes. Until today, *sear*, the bridewealth or bride price[77] is given by the father of

[76] Recorded by the author at Khoira village, 3 November 2003; transcriptions and translation Surendra Kumar Sahu.
[77] Donations of goods or money, made by the groom or his kin to the kin of the bride, in order

the bridegroom for receiving the bride in his family. These gifts are offered to 1) the elder sister of the mother (*nona sear)*; 2) the mother of the bride (*ma sear*) and 3) the grandmother of the bride (*ai sear*).

3) On the third day, *gonsa mangala,* the bridegroom's female relatives visit the bride, stopping at the crossroads. They purify themselves by turmeric powder (*holodi*) and pay reverence to the marital altar (*bedi).* A *bedi* is then also created in the houses of both the bride and bridegroom.
4) On *boro borthya,* the fourth day, the bridegroom (*bor pila*) is escorted in a procession from his home to the bride's house. The way from the bridegroom's house to the bride's house is called *kanya aniba*, the "bringing of the bride/girl". On this day, the bridegroom has to keep an arrow (*sor*) in his right hand.

In the last sequence of the marriage ritual, bride and bridegroom are carried in a kind of dance-procession, the *nachinya*, by the male friends of the bridegroom in a *dhula*, a traditional wooden marriage palanquin. The *Binjhal Biha* has been often presented to me as the ideal exemplary traditional marriage performance of the Bora Sambar. It underlines the value of symbolic matrilineality, expressed in the donation of a bridewealth[78] directed to the different generations of the bride's mothers' kinship line. But we also encounter the dominant patrilinear exogamic rule of leading the newly married bride to leave her mother's house for her in-laws' home. More and more the Binhal Biha as "the ideal marriage" of the Bora Sambar region is transposed today to stages of big towns of western Odisha, such as Sambalpur, where it is performed by artistic groups as local folklore.[79]

## *The value of marriage*

Through narrations, dances and rituals the value configuration of marriage, affinity and alliance is celebrated and re-enacted in the Bora Sambar region. The interplay of media, such as ritual and narrative performance, music and dance, transmit the social value configurations in a performative manner. The Bora Sambar region reveals itself as harbouring a dynamic culture of orality and performativity: With the *dalkhai* dance the social continuity - in terms of the crucial cultural value of marriage - is exposed and as such so-

to ratify the marriage.

[78] The local tradition of bridewealth is diametrically opposed to the hegemonic Hindu value of dowry, the money and goods the bride and the bride's kin bring into her marriage.

[79] See Chapter 8.

cially, ritually and musically enshrined. *Dalkhai* as a synaesthetic concept operates through a highly effective web of symbols mediated by dance, narrations, music and the rhetoric of a semantically and syntactically complex metaphorical language.

The *tin sali yatra* ritual discloses how social memory and matrilineal kinship are reconstructed through rhythms, narratives and performances ritually staging Bura Raja's transformation from a broken marital union and virtual death to a revitalised, regenerated marriage. The ritual of *Binjhal Biha* finally displays the vital celebration of the social and relational values of bridewealth and arranged marriage within patri-lineal clans. Re-enacted by rituals, myths and body-movements the comprehensive cultural value of marriage emerges in all these different ritual settings as a powerful factor of social and symbolic coherence.

# *Fourth Chapter: Music, Movement, Death and Ailment*

The Bora Sambar region is an example of the local predominance of non-Brahmin religious specialists. They are generally associated with a particular local community and bear diverse names and functions depending on their specific religious tasks. A wide range of non-Brahmin priests is engaged in the ritual handling of the inauspiciousness of death or in the cure of psychological and physiological ailment, interpreted as caused by non-empirical malevolent external forces. For the encounter with this spiritual world, non-Brahmin priests utilise music and the sound of their diverse musical instruments. In this chapter I will introduce a variety of local non-Brahmin priest-musicians and their handling of death, memory and ailment through music.

## *The "Guilt and Expiation Priest-Musicians"*

One central ritual task of non-Brahmin priest-musicians in the Bora Sambar region is the handling of the period following the death of a person.[80] Performed on diverse instruments, music is applied to ritual transformation processes during post-mortem rites. Each of the various communities in the Bora Sambar region has a specifically named non-Brahmin priest-musician. In the Goura and Soara communities he is called the *ghugia*, the Harijan communities name this specific priest the *birthya*, the Gond communities refer to him as the *porgonia* and the Mali and Kulta call him the *dusi*. These priest-musicians use specific musical instruments to perform their duties: the *ghugia* of the Goura use the *balu boisi*, a long bamboo flute, called the "flute of the bear"; the *ghugia* of the Soara and of some other Goura groups use the *brahma veena*, a cither-like instrument; the *porgonia* of the Gond use a *banna*, which is also a sort of cither, while the *birthya* of the Harijan communities use the *damburu*, a small drum whose shape reminds of an hour glass. In the following ethnographic description I will give a detailed account of the *brahma veena*, *balu boisi* and *damburu*.

The various vernacular terms designating these priest-musicians I will tentatively translate as "the guilt and expiation priest".[81] During mourning and remembrance rituals, these religious specialists take upon themselves the guilt (*daan*) of the dead person and accept the expiation (*daan*) of its family,

[80] For an overview how death is conceptualised in South Asia, see Schoembucher/Zoller (1999).
[81] For this terminology see Hertz (1988).

symbolised by the acceptance of ritual donations (*daan*). In distinguishing between guilt and expiation, I try to spell out the different meanings of the polyvalent term *daan*, which indicates both, the guilt of the deceased and the ritual handling of his death by his family. During my field work, I observed how important it was for my interlocutors to differentiate between the individual consequences of wrongdoing and the collective feelings of remorse in regard to the deceased which are both covered by the notion of *daan*.

The complex matter of post-mortem pollution has been discussed in the literature on Hinduism, especially in the work on pollution through alms in Hindu funeral rituals by Jonathan Parry (1988: 88-111) and Jeffrey D. Snodgrass (2001: 687-703). But while this discussion mostly focused on aspects of pollution in funeral rituals, I would like to underline the idea of an individual and collective responsibility created through the death of a person. This idea, I suggest, is expressed in the Bora Sambar region in terms of *daan* as the local concept of individual guilt and collective expiation.

Photograph 14: *Gour and Soara Ghugia*, playing the *brahma veena*, Khageshwar Bagh, Sakti village, 2004, L.G.

Photograph 15: The *brahma veena* kept in a sacred abode Sakti village, 2004, L.G.

Photograph 16: *Bhalu bans* flute played by the *ghugia* of the Gour, Sudarsan Raut, village of Doheta, 2006, L.G.

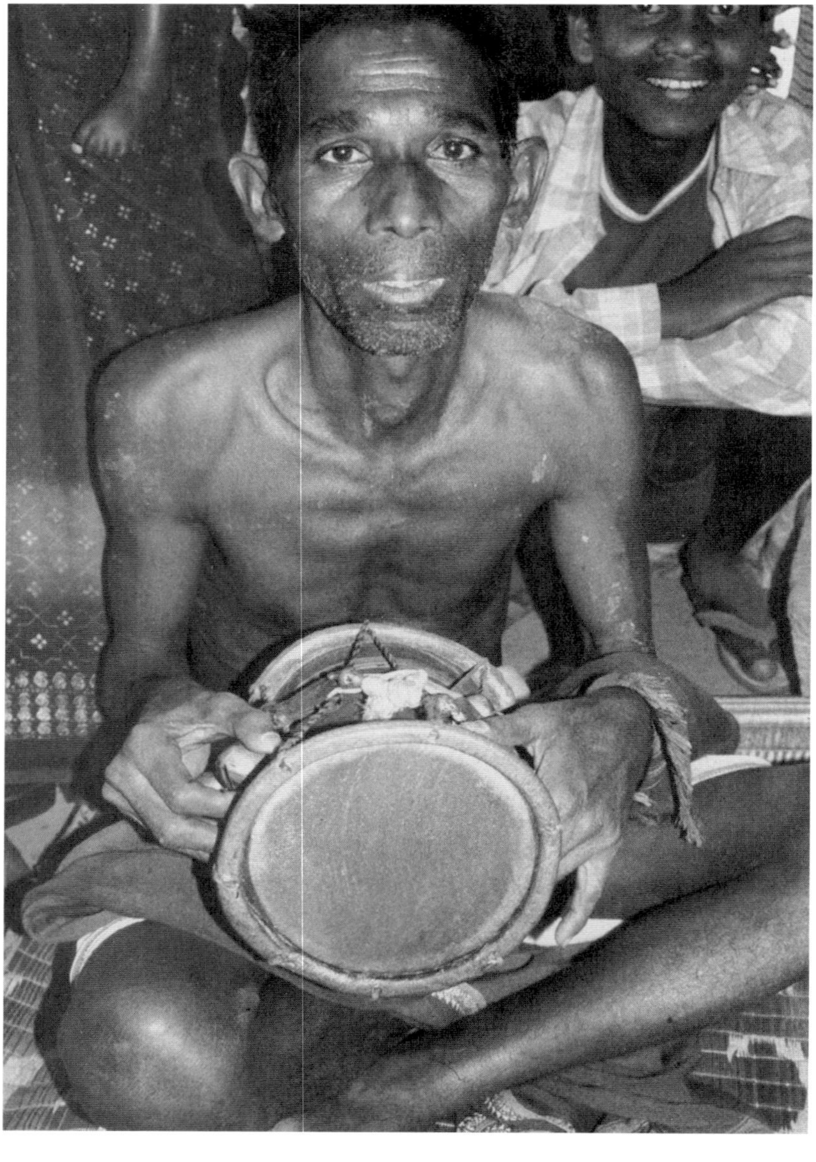

Photograph 17: *Birthya* of the Harijan Budu Mohanand with the *damburu* drum, village of Badgura, 2004, L.G.

## *Daan chheeka ritual*

The *daan chheeka* ritual is common to all of the different communities of the Bora Sambar region. On the night of the 11th day after the death of a person, the guilt and expiation priest sings songs and myths for the dead and for the ancestors. He sits at the threshold of the house of the deceased, playing a special instrument designed to communicate with the dead and the ancestors. The priest-musician advises the family to remain inside the house until the moment of giving *daan* – the ritual donations – to him. The whole night the priest-musician is supposed to sing *"purkha geet"*, the ancestor's songs to the deceased. In the morning, after having given the *daan* donations, the family of the deceased is allowed to leave the house in a symbolic act of re-socialisation and return to social life. This ritual and social transformation is called *daan chheeka. Daan chheeka* – "the breaking of guilt/rice"–symbolically signifies the "breaking" of the impurity and pollution, which death has brought upon the family. It is the central ceremonial act of remembrance as well as of purification. It is considered as both: the taking-over of the guilt of the deceased and the acceptance of the expiation of his family, both symbolised in donations made by the ritual clients to the priest. *Daan chheeka* indicates that the priest receives grains of rice, cooked food and new clothes from the family as well as bronze dishes used by the deceased before his or her death.[82] The acceptance of these ritual alms by the priest-musician is synonymous with the taking over of the guilt of the deceased. The receiving of the "gift" (*daan*) of guilt (*daan*) by the priest-musician is considered to transform the individual guilt into purity. The gift of guilt is never kept but always given away.[83] The priest-musician transfers the "guilt gift" either to another guilt and expiation priest or to a local goddess. Through the temporary acceptance of the "guilt gift", given from one ritual actor to the next, the inauspiciousness of death is mitigated and transformed. In the virtual circulation of the "guilt and death gift", the local goddess is the preferred final receiver. Only the goddess has the power and the potential of purity to put an end to the gift circle. The circulation of the guilt

---

[82] For comparison see Skoda (2005) who describes death rituals among the Aghria in western Odisha. There, two categories of Brahmin are employed to ritually handle the inauspiciousness of death. Up to the 11th day, a low Brahmin is responsible for the handling of the inauspicious *pret*, signifying the deceased who has not yet gained the status of ancestor. After the 12th day, a high Brahmin handles the ritual communication with the auspicious ancestor (Skoda 2005: 473-483).

[83] On the ambivalence and the "poisonous quality" of the gift and the "death gift", see the fundamental work by Marcel Mauss (1954); on the aspect of inauspiciousness of the gift see Raheja (1988).

gift is accompanied by popular hymns, sung by the priest-musician for the local goddesses. In the context of the *daan chheeka* ritual, the polyvalent notion of *daan* designates at the same time alms, guilt and expiation.

For the inhabitants of the Bora Sambar region, death is intrinsically connected to guilt. Guilt is either associated with the deceased's way of living and dying or with the part, the deceased's family had in his or her death. Death thus always indicates a social responsibility which has to be faced and handled ritually. Ritual processes of recreation and regeneration, of purity as well as of remembrance of the dead are operated by the specific sounds of the diverse musical instruments played by the guilt and expiation priest-musicians.

According to the priest-musicians I interviewed, it is the sound of singing and instrumental music during the *daan chheeka* ritual that mediates and transforms post-mortem inauspiciousness (*ashubbo*) to purity (*shubbo*). By means of the *dhaan cheeka geet* (song/music) individual and collective guilt is absorbed, transformed and purified: "...*When playing the daan chheka geet, I become heavy, very heavy – I take the burden of guilt* (daan) *from the deceased. I feel very exhausted, I feel very heavy after having played the whole night",* one of the priest-musicians explains. "*Daan chheeka music is purifying* (povitro); *sound is purifying* (dhaan chheeka git poche povitra heba; sur povitra koriba)", he continues. The whole burden of an ended life weighs on the guilt and expiation priest-musician. He carries this burden and transforms it by playing *daan chheeka.*

By playing *daan chheeka* music, the priest-musician also handles the ambivalence of death, which occurs through the dramatic experience of the radically and absolutely finished physical life and the belief that the soul of the deceased (*atma*) is leaving the corps and continues to live in another world. This transfer is considered dangerous, as the humans are still attached to the deceased. Their inability to give the soul leave to depart to the other world might have dramatically dangerous consequences.[84] Their attachment to the deceased might namely put an end to their own life by way of 'contagion'. In order to prevent such contagious contact between the deceased and his or her progeny, an emotionally neutral and specialised mediator is called. Instead of those who lost a family member, the socially marginalised and thus symbolically "untouchable" guilt and expiation priest-musician begins,

---

[84] Piers Vitebsky describes a similar phenomenon (2008: 245-248 and 1993).

through the medium of the sound of his instruments and his songs, a dialogue between the soul, the community and the ancestors.[85]

The ritual activities of the guilt and expiation priests of the Bora Sambar region reveal the local conviction that the medium of sound is fittest to catch the experience of death, its physical and empirical transformation processes and the intended transition of post-mortem pollution to purity. As Robert Hertz (1907) has shown in his fundamental study on the representation of death, its universal ambivalence and the affiliated concepts of inauspiciousness and impurity are closely related to the transformational phases of the decomposing human cadaver. The musical expressions of Bora Sambar's priest-musicians operate as ritual purifiers and absorbers during this precarious transformation.

## *The Concept of Sur – Sound and Liberation*

To all guilt and expiation priest-musicians of the Bora Sambar region I encountered, the notion of *sur* – sound – was crucial in their post mortem communication with the deceased and the ancestors (*purkho lok*) as well as for their ideas about the release of the souls of the deceased (*mukti*). The concept of *sur* points to the idea of sound vibrations (*sabad*) and their rhythmic-melodic movements, and to the power of sound to transgress empirical and unempirical spaces. The priest-musicians of Bora Sambar view the sound vibrations designated by the term *sur* as a mutual means of connection, communication and influence between the living and the souls of the deceased and the ancestors. "*When the soul is alive, then the beat of music is also audible* (sur au atma katha barta heba). *By listening to the sound, the soul will be released* (sur suniba bele atma mukti heba)*"*, one *birthya* explains.

*Sur* is perceived as a kind of moving vibrations, medium and expression of the fluidity between life and death, between the deceased, the ancestors and the living. According to the priest-musicians, the elusive sound created by their various musical instruments and by their vocal recitation and singing transports the memory of the deceased and accompanies the processes of transformation, purification and finally spiritual release. The concept of *sur* as sound vibration as it is formulated by the priest-musicians of Bora Sambar bears a certain resemblance to ideas formulated in the trans-regional South

[85] Piers Vitebsky (1993) describes these characteristic dialogs with the dead for the Adivasi Soara society.

Asian narrative *Natya Shatra*, a classical treaty on the performing arts including dance, drama and music of the 6$^{th}$ century B.C., where it is stated that the vibrations of sound are the origin of form and the universe (Vatsayanan 1996). However, although certain conceptual similarities are obvious, my local interlocutors never alluded to this source. I would thus suggest considering *sur* as an indigenous concept and theory of sound, incorporating local specific hypothesis on communication and transcendence as a musical dialogue but nevertheless reflecting the influence of trans-regional concepts.

## *Donations as cure - sound as spiritual liberation*

The texts sung by the priest-musicians during *daan chheeka* rituals establish multiform relations between death and donations, indicating processes of transformation and transfer mediated through the sound and voice of the priest-musician. The following fragment of a *daan chheeka* song enumerates and specifies some of these relations.

Photograph 18: Gour and Soara *ghugia* Khageshwar Bagh

Trancriptions of *daan chheeka geet* sung by

**_Gour and Soara ghugia Khageshwar Bagh_**[86]

*1. Sei Chandi Samalai Je Prabhat hoila.*
Down there, goddess Chandi is to be worshipped.

*2. Daana dele data punya pathe jibu.*
Oh donor, if you give me alms, you will go to a sacred place of virtues.

*3. Daana Jesane sarba byadhi khandanam.*
Oh donor! If you give me alms, you will go to the place of the sacred heavens.

*4. Daana Jesane sarba papa khandanam.*
By giving alms, we make good all types of sins.

*5. Epari lagichanti data sahe asta koti daana.*
Oh donor, there are one hundred millions of alms divided by god.

*6. Kansa daana dele data bansa badhutiba.*
If you donate bronze materials then it will help you to increase your next dynasty.

*7. Lauha daana dele data sani saanti heba.*
God Sani [the planet god] will be pleased by a donation of iron to him.

*8. Arna daana dela brahmananda santi heba.*
By donating rice as food, the whole world will be happy.

*9. Bastra daana dele pitru nabe sarga pure homa kundare basibe.*
By donating clothes, your forefathers will be seated in a sacred place in heaven

*10. Chhela daana dele data pitru loka je chandana banaku jiba.*
By donating a goat, your forefathers' souls will go to the sandalwood forest [a sacred place in heaven].

*11. Gairu daana deke daata Baitarani.*
Donating a cow's alms will help to cross the river Baitarani
[to reach the place where the souls will be released].

*12. Sapta prukha loka mane je mukti labhibe.*
Seven generations of forefathers will be released.

*13. Mahissi daana dele data akaala mrutyu.*
By donating a buffalo as alms you gain premature death
[i.e. an early liberation].

*14. Bhumi daana dele data preta astana suhie rahibu.*
After your death, your soul will obtain a good place to stay and to be happy.

---

86 Recorded by the author on 20th Februar 2006, in the village of Shakti; transcriptions and translation by Surendra Kumar Sahu.

*15. Ehipari Lagichanti sahe asta koti daana.*
Such like this, there are one hundred millions of alms we can take.

*16. Kakharu kati daana dele Chandi santi heba.*
By giving a white melon [during the ritual of goat sacrifice] you will make the goddess Chandi happy.

*17. Mendhaa daana dele Kali santi heba.*
Kali will be happy if you give her a sheep sacrifice.

*18. Hansa daana dele byaadhi Kati Jiba.*
If you give a duck as sacrifice, you will be released from all diseases.

*19. Kukura daana dele bakra roga kati jiba*
By donating a hen, you will be cured from paralysis.

*20. Sapta prukhara loka mane aasi ehi jaagare kara asirbada roga rasta kari dia dura.*
Oh! Seven forefathers' souls, you come to this spot, give us blessings and relief.

The text sung during the *daan chheeka* ritual indicates that the ritual donation incites a supra-empirical dynamism and exchange between the family of the deceased, the priest-musician and the non-empirical world of the ancestors and the gods. Post mortem "guilt" is evaporated by means of ritual donations directed toward the priest-musician. The ritual alms given to him symbolise trans-cosmic transactions and cause benevolent effects in the world of the dead and the ancestors. On the one hand, the text discloses that the ritual gifts set up a communication with the world of the ancestors. On the other hand, donations operate as means to attain a worldly as well as a soteriological rewards for the donors themselves – including the hope

1) to achieve a good afterlife (*Oh donor, if you give me alms, you will go to a sacred place of virtues*);
2) to obtain the cure of ailments in this world ( *If you give a duck as a sacrifice, you will be released from all diseases / By donating a hen, you will be cured from paralysis;*
3) to effect a release of their ancestors from the cycle of rebirths (*By donating a goat, your forefathers' souls will go to the sandalwood forest* and
4) to secure the appeasement of the divine non-empirical sphere in a general sense ( *God Sani will be pleased by a donation of iron to him. By donating rice as food the whole world will be happy).*

Underlying this otherworldly economy of donations, which reflects the crucial social and symbolical value of the gift,[87] is the local concept of *mukti* (spiritual liberation or release). The inhabitants of the Bora Sambar region hold that every human being is animated by a soul (*atma*). The *atma* is considered to be reborn during seven generations before being finally released ("*Seven generations of forefathers will be released").* This final liberation – the end of a circle of death and rebirth – of the soul, which may be conceived as a final absolute death excluding the possibility of further rebirth, is called *mukti*. The song of the priest-musician hints to the possibility of precipitating the soul's liberation by means of appropriate offerings: "*By donating a buffalo as alms you gain premature death"* – the absolute death is gained before the rebirth circle of seven generation has been run through.

The song of the priest preserves the idea of buffalo sacrifices in the context of ancestor worship which today are no longer practiced in the Bora Sambar region.[88] In *daan chheeka* on the one hand the cultural memory of the traditional ancestor worship as practiced through the buffalo sacrifice is reenacted through the poetic recitations. On the other hand *daan chheeka* establishes a continuum between the specific local ancestor worship tradition and the hegemonic trans-regional Hindu belief in divine animation of the world and the universe and the belief in the idea of the cycle of rebirths. According to the Upanishads of the classical Brahmanic tradition, the Absolute, the Immortal One is called Brahman; his human correlate functions as an *atman* (the "self") that, in human form, can attain redemption – *moksha* – from the cycle of rebirths (*samsara*) (Biardeau 1995: 32-34). Both in the local as in the Brahmanic tradition, the absolute death in terms of spiritual liberation (*mukti*) or redemption (*moksha*) is the highest aim of life.

The following poetic fragment sung during a *daan chheeka* ritual by Alekha Panigrahi, the *birthya* of the Harijan communities in the Bora Sambar region exemplarily expresses the complex interchange between donations, sound and ideas of transformation and spiritual liberation.[89]

---

[87] The idea of the "gift" as a most fundamental fact for the functioning of social communities has been underlined by Marcel Mauss. The social transactions operated by means of symbolic or factual "gifts" or donations incite a social dynamism crucial for the vitality of societies. The social principle of the "gift" is characterised by reciprocity, fluidity and transfer (see Mauss 1923/24; Godelier 1996).

[88] Buffalo sacrifices *gotr* as crucial expressions of ancestor worship are still a vibrant cultural trait among the indigenous Desya population of southern Odisha, such as the Gadaba of Koraput (Pfeffer 2001: 123-148; Berger 2007: 284-308).

[89] For further examples see Appendix.

The *birthya* accompanies his mythical recitations and poetic ballads by the playing of the *damburu* drum. The *damburu* is a small drum with two hemi-spherical bowls, in its shape resembling an hour glass. The two membranes made from cowhide are connected by fanlike lacing and stretched by a wrapping in the middle. The wrapping is held together by belts and small rattles. The *damburu* is played with both hands, while the sound of the small rattles backs the beats of the drum.

Photograph 19: The *damburu* drum, 2004, L.G.

Transcription of incantations recited by the birthya Alekha Panigrahi while playing the *damburu* drum[90]

*"This is the song of birthya for god* (Mahapuru), *for the ancestors* (pitru lok) *and for his community* (jati bandu)"

*"I am the ocean, the water and you will release me!"*
*"The mother cries for her son, oh son!*
*The sister cries for her brother, oh brother!*

[90] Recorded by the author on 1st April 2004, in the village of Siripalli.

*The woman cries for another son* [i.e. her husband]"

*"Why do you come here, my friend?*
*What do you bring from there?"*

*"You are the donor of my clothes and of my food.*
*If you give me food and clothes then your soul* (atma) *will reside in heaven* (boi-kunto)."

*"Brothers, friends, brothers!*
*Through my community* (jati bandu) *and through myself I venerate you, oh god! Relieve us!"*

*"Look at this woman. She cries for another son* [i.e. her deceased husband]
*Protect her! Take care of her!*
*Now your home is the damburu drum!"*

Through the sound of his drum, his voice and his ritual poetry, the *birthya* recalls the memory of the dead and reflects on the finality of life and the solitude of death (*I am the ocean, the water and you will release me!*). He gives consolation by hinting at the persistence of the social community, creating thus a social continuity after the loss of a family member (*Through my community and through myself I venerate you, oh god! Relieve us*!). The verse *"This is the song of birthya for god, for the ancestors and for his community"*, indicates that the *birthya* performs his songs both for the non-empirical world of the ancestors and the deities as well as for his social community. The dialogic form of the ritual incantations mirrors a structural pattern of exchange between the sounds of the *damburu* drum and the voice of the priest-musician. With the last line: "*Now your home is the damburu drum*!" the *birthya* expresses the identity between the drum and the non-empirical world of the deceased.

For the *birthya* and his Harijan community donations during *daan chheeka* guarantee a spiritual liberation of the souls of the deceased. (*You are the donor of my clothes and of my food. If you give me food and clothes, then your soul will reside in heaven*). This religious message is mediated through the sound of the *damburu* drum as well as the voice of the priest-musician (*Brothers, friends, brothers! Through my community* (jati bandu) *and through myself I venerate you, oh god! Relieve us!*). The *birthya* here ritually takes over both, the role of the ancestors (*pitru lok*) and the role of his community. The exchange between a god, the ancestors and the mourning community is thus mediated once more in a dialogic form, indicating a homology between the medium, its form and its content.

### *Music and liminality*

Besides being the medium of mediation, transformation and transfer, music in *daan chheeka* rituals is also an expression and a medium of liminality.[91] The threshold, on which the priest-musician sits during the ritual of *daan chheeka*, symbolises his factual, ritual and non-empirical location in-between the world of the humans and the world of the ancestors and deities. Music transfers the priest-musician into the in-between phase between post-mortem inauspiciousness (*ashubbo*) and purity (*shubbo*), death and life, gods, ancestors and humans. In former times, according to local narrations, the diverse guilt and expiation priests mutually exchanged their instruments during this liminal phase of communication with the deceased and ancestors. *Daan chheeka* ceremonies hence indicate a strong ritual interchange, transition and proximity between the local communities of the Bora Sambar region. It is told for example that in former time *daan chheeka* rituals were sometimes performed by two priest-musicians of two socially related communities. In this sense the priest-musician of the Goura, the Goura *ghugi,* was supposed to perform the *daan chheeka* ceremony both with his own community's instrument - the flute *balu boisi* - as with the ritual instrument of the Soara – the lute *brahma veena.* The *brahma veena* and *balu boisi*, so it is narrated, were first placed crosswise on the doorstep of the mourning-house and then played by the particular priest-musicians, either by the *ghugia* for his Soara community or by the *balu boisi* player for the Goura community. Today, the guilt and expiation priests generally use their own specific musical instruments. Some of the instruments of the priest musicians have been abandoned in the course of time. The *balu boisi,* for example, is no longer in use neither with the Goura nor with the Soara communities. Its playing has been replaced by the performance of *mantras*, religious recitations without any instrumental accompaniment. The *balu boisi* had become a forgotten instrument until it was unearthed in the course of the present research and has since gained a new regional popularity as an instrument for artistic musical performances during folk festivals.[92]

### *Ambivalence of social status and social change*

Most guilt and expiation priests have an ambivalent and contested social status. Generally, the priest-musicians regard themselves as having a higher

---

[91] For the symbolism of the threshold and the ritual in-between phase see Turner (1969) and Arnold v. Gennep's work on *rites des passages* (1986).
[92] See Chapter 8.

status than their ritual clients. Their self-esteem is backed by certain myths of origin of their instruments, as the following narration, told by the *birthya* about the origin of the *damburu* drum shows: "*The first damburu drum was created by Brahma for his elder son Shiva in order to venerate the dead and the ancestors. God Shiva himself killed the first cow from which the drum was skinned.*" In the context of the myth, the handling of the cow's skin, which in real life is a reason for the social marginalisation of the *Harijan* community, becomes an instrument and expression of positive identity. In the person of the mythical elder brother Shiva, social stigmatisation is inverted into religious specialisation. An equation of the guilt and expiation priest with the social category of the "elder brother" classifies him as socially and ritually senior to other members of his community. In the Bora Sambar region, fraternal seniority signifies a traditional hierarchical classification in a patrilinear social structure of status formation.

Yet contrariwise, the local lines of the guilt and expiation priests of the particular communities are generally considered by their ritual clients to be of an inferior, marginalised status. Thus, these religious specialists are always the social "other", regardless of the fact that they are sometimes perceived to be of a higher and sometimes of a lower status. Somehow, they belong to one's own community, somehow not.[93] Indeed, the *daan chheeka* work is generally regarded to be an *ashubba karjo,* an inauspicious religious duty. The handling of death and of the dangerous physical and spiritual transformations and transfer processes connected to it, involve an uncertain social status.

The ambivalent and precarious social status of the non-Brahmin guilt and expiation priests makes many of these priest-musicians extremely reticent to enter a public or official discourse about their handling of ritual pollution or contagion. Some families of non-Brahmin priests have completely abandoned or "cut" (*band korila*) their traditional ritual occupation and given up their role of spiritual "trash" absorber and cleaner. They refuse to continue their ritual tasks and have given up performing their music. They attempt to make forgotten or to change their ritual occupation in order to rid themselves of the stigma of ambivalence linked to their ritual proximity to the inauspiciousness (*ashubba*) and impurity (*ashudda*) of death. More and more the purifying process of *ashubba karjo* is reduced to the final step of donating

---

[93] For a parallel example of this ambivalence, see Fürer-Haimendorf's description of the role of the *pordhan* in [former] Madya Pradesh. The *pordhan*'s role is very much similar to the role of the *porgonia* in the Bora Sambar region (1979: 363-393).

the "guilt" of the deceased to the altar of a local or regional goddess or god – thus omitting the mediating work of the guilt and expiation priests, whose roles are taken over by the regional deities.

Photograph 20: A wandering *gosain* with his *sarangi* on the way from Paikmal to Padampur, 2006, L.G.

Some years ago for example, some *ghugia* guilt and expiation priests of the Binjhal, Goura and Soara communities, renounced to defining themselves as *ghugia* priests. Instead, they started to speak of themselves as *goswami* or *gosain* (=Hindu saint/ascetic). As an alternative to performing vocal and instrumental rituals for the ancestors, they began to carry out ritual worship for gods and goddesses such as Soni, Trinath, Durga, Ganesh, Shiva or Saraswati. The *gosain*s have changed their musical instrument, replacing the traditional *brahma veena* with a one-stringed violin, called *sarangi,* in which the goddess Saraswati is supposed to reside.

The former *ghugia* today recites the myths and songs from the Hindu Puranic narrative Bhagavadgita. He roams from village to village as a wandering singer and priest. No community calls him to perform his worship and he no longer chooses a specific community. He arrives by himself in order to recite and sing his various religious stories. In return for his performance, he receives lentils (*daal*) and uncooked rice (*dhan*) from the villagers. Besides the songs from the Bhagavadgita, certain melodic hymns for local goddesses, sung by these newly emerged itinerary priests, have gained a special regional fame.

The vanishing of the tradition of the guilt and expiation priests thus gives rise to a new popularity of certain local and regional deities of the Bora Sambar region. As a rising number of guilt and expiation priest abandon their ritual task of mediating communication with the hereafter, regional gods and their temples that fill this gap gain a new attractiveness. This is for example the case with the cult of the Goddess Tarini[94], who, being a former jungle goddess of the Kheonjhar region of southern Odisha, some years ago won pan-Odishan fame. Her popularity and vibrant worship is visible in the recently constructed Tarini temple by the road between Padampur and Paikmal. Her prominence is due to the fact that her worship is considered to finalise the circles of inauspiciousness and impurity passed through in the context of post mortem memorial rituals. Namely, by means of religious songs sung for her, the goddess Tarini can be incited to absorb ritual impurity. For the same reasons, the regional temples of Harishankar and Nursingnath have regained popularity in recent years.

Another example of social change is the recent discourse on *daan chheeka* led by senior representatives and authorities of the Gond community (Gond *sammaj*) from Chhattisgarh and Odisha.[95] The eldest of the Gond community have decided to completely abandon the tradition of *daan chheeka.* The ritual work of *daan chheeka* has been categorised by them as "*kin kamo*" - a bad or mean work, associated with begging (*magiba/vikya lok*) and thus a low social status. The senior authorities and representatives of the Gond collectively refused to be associated with the socially pejorative category of

---

[94] The Goddess Tarini is a former local goddess who gained an exceptional regional popularity around Odisha due to the spread of her worship through the Internet. See Mallebrein 2004: 155-165.

[95] The Gond of the Bora Sambar region are spread over the territory of both states.

beggars any longer. The *porgonia,* the ritual specialists of the Gond, thus had to abandon the tradition of musical recitations and invocations as well as the ritual begging for rice during the mortuary *daan chheeka* rites. Following the verdict of the elders of their community, they collectively destroyed their traditional instruments. The *porgonia* priest-musicians have today radically broken with the tradition of accepting the spiritually "poisoned" gift (*daan chheeka*). "*The community has decided – all is closed now*". The former non-Brahmin priests of the Gond are not inclined to make any further comment on their tradition. While silencing their tradition through a self-inflicted *memocide*[96], the former *porgonia* define themselves today simply as Gond. Their *daan chheeka* tradition has been totally abandoned and replaced either by 1) domestic ancestor worship where texts referring to dominant South Asian ideas of Brahman or to dominant trans-local narratives of the Vedas are recited; 2) by worship in the village temple of the god Bura Raja or Shiva where the dead are purified ("*suddo pai"* = in order to make them pure) or 3) by purification rites at the river Ganga where the dead are considered to receive an absolute and definitive redemption.

Through the shift from local dialogues to dominant South Asian narratives and through the destruction of their ritual instruments, a violent cultural amnesia seems to have spread in the subaltern Gond community of the Bora Sambar region. The local system of the non-Brahmin guilt and expiation priest-musicians and their music is generally highly vulnerable to processes of modernisation, memocide, cultural forgetting and the rejection and reduction of rituals. The social change which is traceable in a multitude of internal cultural dynamics becomes dramatically visible in the abandonment and in the highly symbolic collective destruction of the traditional instruments. In an act of auto-aggression, the community by force reinvents a new social identity, which adopts new religious and musical traditions, a process best noticeable in the rise and popularity of new religious centres with their devotional music characterised by ritual recitation (*mantra*s), devotional hymns and rhymes of praise dedicated to regional Hindu goddesses ( *devi sloka*s).

[96] The term *memocide* denotes the cultural dynamics of a collective and culturally destructive loss of the cultural memory of a minority society due to the influence of hegemonic value-ideas of a majority society. In the Indian context, the hegemony of Hindu values has produced a *memocide* in many small indigenous communities through the spread of hegemonic religious practices, ideas and hegemonic narratives (see Samaddar 1998).

### *Bhat – the praise-singers and genealogists*

Another category of non-Brahmin priest musicians are the *bhat*, the former praise-singers, story-tellers and genealogists of the kings and *zamindars* of the historical Raj Bora Sambar kingdom. The traditional tasks of the *bhat*s consisted in 1) singing the praise of the king's glory; 2) the daily announcement of the king's orders; 3) the daily wake-up calls for the king; 4) announcing the death of a king. In this context they also took over the function of "guilt-and-expiation-priests" by taking contagious alms (*daan*) from the king's mourning family in the course of death ceremonies and symbolically transforming and purifying them through the power of their mourning songs. A similar combination of tasks can be found with the *bhat* from Rajasthan who, as professional puppeteers and genealogists of the Rajput kings, act as the traditional praise-singers of the local kings, but also accept and transform funeral "contagion" and post-mortem "pollution" into "purity" through their recitations (Snodgrass 2006: 287- 691). As the Raj Bora Sambar kingdom has officially ceased to exist since the Indian independence, the category of *bhat* is today nothing more than a local cultural reminiscence of a vanished feudal social and ritual system. Today, most of the former *bhat* deny any kind of historical attachment to their past ritual duties of accepting the dead king's "impure" "death gift", and most former *bhat* priests no longer transmit their mnemo-techniques and songs to their descendants. The term *bhat* only remains as a social title or surname, no longer indicating any kind of ritual activity or obligation.

## ***Itinerary Non-Brahmin Priest-Musicians***

Besides those priest-musicians which I have subsumed under the category of guilt and expiation priests, a variety of wandering non-Brahmin priest-musicians and singers exists in the Bora Sambar region. They venerate local goddesses by playing specific instruments and often act as local healers. Specific healing capacities are ascribed to the music performed by these wandering non-Brahmin priests.

### *Sarmangalia*

The *sarmangalia* is an itinerant non-Brahmin priest of the goddess Mangala. He wanders from village to village, accompanied by his wife and children. The *sarmangalia* carries the goddess Mangala with him in a portable wooden altar, devoting the utmost care to her.[97] The *sarmangalia* and his family usually have no fixed abode but camp outside the villages by the roadside, sheltered by provisional plastic tents. The worshipping chant of the *sarmangalia* can be heard from far away[98]:

"*Dukho nee*
Take the pain.

*Sukho dee*
Give the happiness.

*Suke suke rohu*
Let the happiness remain.

*Apoti nahi*
I have no wish.

*Bipoti nahi*
I do not know any danger."

"*Ma Mangala likes the sound"*, the *sarmangalia* explains while playing the *sarmangalia dhol* drum. This is a small wooden drum made from lizard leather on the left and from goat's leather on the right side. The *sarmangalia* plays the drum with a stick in his left hand, while his right hand scratches the skin. The deep, monotone sounds he produces are conceived to evoke and represent the goddess Mangala. As he plays the *sarmangalia dhol* drum and sings the songs of the goddess, the *sarmangalia* begs for food for himself and his family as well as for food offerings for the goddess. In the morning and evening the *sarmangalia* conducts his ritual worship (*puja*) by food offerings to the goddess and by playing his drum. He mixes the sacrificial food (*bhog*) and distributes it among the villagers. The *sarmangalia* purifies the village he visits with some flattened rice mixed with cow dung. It is believed that the *sarmangalia*, who is also called *deheri* which means local healer, cures the physical or psychological ailments of those who give him donations. The sound of the *sarmangalia dhol* drum is assumed to appease and satisfy the goddess Mangala and to represent at the same time her voice and religious advice. It is believed that the drum's sound chases away bad dreams (*barna sapna*), protects against witchcraft (*tondei*) - especially when played at crossroads - and shields against bad spirits (*bhut pret*). Both the *sarmangalia's puja* and the sound of his drum are thought to prevent or heal illnesses such as small pox (*mata*), chickenpox (*bosonto*), fever (*jhoro*) and all

---

[97] Some *sarmangalia* priest-musicians also carry the goddess Thakurani with them.
[98] Documented by the author on a road to Padampur, 20 December 2006.

kinds of skin diseases (*khosa kujri*) or mental stress. Besides these healing procedures, the *sarmangalia* priest also sells self-made talismans (*dongria*) which are supposed to contain aryuvedic medicine.

Photograph 21 *Sarmangalia* priest with his *sarmangalia* drum, on the way to Padampur, 2006, L.G.

The activity of the *sarmagalia* represents the link between ritual migrant music and healing. His performance is a performance of cure, or a "performance of healing" as outlined by Laderman and Roseman (1996: 1-16). The deep resonating sound of the *sarmagalia* drum and the transportable altar of the goddess create an atmosphere of unfamiliarity, of temporality and thus of ritual effectiveness. The temporary character of his stay in a village, the ephemeral place of devotion which is established with the portable altar, the movement inherent in the *sarmagalia's* performance as well as the liminal, nomadic group he forms together with his wandering family all contribute to a continuum of strangeness around him which is operating on his ritual clients.

Photograph 22: Portable altar of goddess Sarmangala, on the way to Padampur, 2006, L.G.

### *Jawara geet*

Another example for the traditional connection between music and the task of healing illness is the *jawara* music (*geet*), played to chase away Mata, the goddess of the small pox and chicken pox (*guni sendri*), as well as to cure all

Photograph 23: *Sarmangalia* worshipping goddess Sarmangala through the sound of *sarmangala* drum, on the way to Padampur, 2006, L.G.

kind of *raga* (illnesses of the skin). *Jawara geet* musicians belong to the caste of the Ghansya, a Harijan category which is considered even lower than the Ganda. Their traditional occupation is the skinning of dead animals for the manufacturing of drum-skins. *Jawara geet* is performed by a singer or a group of singers, accompanying themselves by the playing of *mandal* drums. *Jawara geet* may be performed as a cure for acute illness or in the context of a preventive ritual.

In case a villager acutely suffers from one of the diseases named above, a singer of *jawara* music (*jawar gayak*) or a group of singers and players might be called, in order to sing nine nights and nine days in his village. As an invitation to perform in a village, the *jawar* singer is given a lemon (*lembu)*; he then has to donate the lemon as an offering to the goddess Mata and her manifestation Durga. The cutting of a lemon is considered auspicious. "*When goddess Mata sees the lemon, she will be happy* (devi shanti heba)", explains a villager. According to a local legend, the lemon symbolises the head of the demon Moisasur who, in the shape of a buffalo, was beheaded by the beautiful goddess Durga. As a general prevention against *mata* and *raga* diseases, *jawara* music is traditionally played on the ninth night (*noworatri*) of the month *choit* (April) and during *nowratri*, the ninth night of the month *dusshara* (October). During *dusshara* the goddess Durga is venerated synonymously as Mata. The *jawara* singers are acting as ritual assistants (*sevako*) to the local healer named *gunya* or *baiga* who, with the help of the *jawara* music, puts himself into a state of trance. He becomes *boil* – entranced by the goddesses- and in this state is supposed to be able to heal and protect from illness. The *baiga* acquires his healing and protective power while being venerated as the goddess Mata and at the same time venerating the goddess himself. Today, *jawara geet* is only rarely practised in Bora Sambar. Only some famous *jawara* singers and players still perform their music. As skin diseases could in recent years be significantly reduced by means of state or NGO sponsored health campaigns, *jawara* performances are no longer demanded by the village populations of the region. Another reason for its decline is that *jawara* players try to escape their low social status connected to their traditional profession and musical activity.

In many villages of Nuapara district however, local altars known as *mata gudi* are found. Dedicated to the goddess *Mata*, they indicate the memory of the tradition of *jawara geet.* And still, in front of almost every house in the region, dry lemons can be found hanging on the veranda. These apotrophaic symbols remain, even when the music has perished.

### *Bhairavi*

Another local category of wandering priest-musicians are the *bhairavi*, also called *Mali konti* or talisman makers. They fashion talismans from the *tulsi* tree and play the *kanjoni,* a tambourine made from lizard leather.[99] The *bhairavi* also teach theatre (*nato kirtan siksan*) and carry out ear invocations (*kana mantra*). They whisper secret spiritual advice into the ear of their barren or otherwise physically ill patients (*dukhi sukhi kosti*) who ascribe healing power to their whispering. They offer their services to everybody except the marginalised Gonsia and Ganda, considered as "untouchable" (*achut*). Even so the *bhairavi* are of a low and contested social status themselves, they still act within the socially constructed categories of "untouchability", maintaining what superiority they are able to secure in relation to other social groups.

Generally, *bhairavi* are regarded as healers for general purposes, such as skin diseases, stomach pains, mental frustration and the prevention against any kind of evil external influences. For healing and preventive purposes the *bhairavi* make talismanic threads which they sell while roaming from village to village. Similar to the *sarmangalia* families, the *bhairavi* priest-musicians move between the month *moxir* and *choit* (from December to April) with their wife and children. During the rainy season the *bharavi* families stop their wandering and stay at a temporary home. As in the case of the *sarmangalia*, their nomadic life style is imagined to be essential for the effectiveness of their healing powers. The migrant musician thus heals while passing by. While the male *bhairavi*'s specialisation is mainly to play *kanjoni* music in performing their ritual activities, the *bharavi* women are specialised in tattooing. They tattoo the women of the village communities they visit, but their trade is restricted to executing designs and patterns determined by these communities. For men, tattoos (*juti)* are not regarded as necessary: "*Education (bidha) is enough for men"*, people tell. For women however, tattoos are held to be effective after death, as a last covering of the carcass. In their tattoos, according to local beliefs, the forefathers (*pitru*) live on. As one legend tells, the god of death, *Jom*, will ask each woman: "*Do you have your tattoos*?" If she hasn't, *Jom* will chase her away from the world where the deceased and the ancestors live. He will shout: "*Go away! Your body is impure/not covered* (*pinda suddhha nahi*)!" If she is expelled from the kingdom of *Jom,* the dead women could become a homeless ghosts (*pret*), and

---

[99] The instrument of the *bhairavi* bears a remarkable similarity to that of the wandering Mahima Dharma ascetics of Odisha (Guzy 2002).

thus dangerous for the living. Tattoos are considered to convey an impression of injury and aesthetic mutilation, having an inverse effect in terms of spiritual security. Tattoos are seen as signs of a woman already wounded, marked by her blood. This symbolic and aesthetic "impurity" and imperfection gives her a spiritual guarantee not to die a bad death that could turn her into a *pret* and not into an ancestor (*pitru*), which is the aspired state of good death.[100] The male *bharavi*'s music and the female *bhairavi*'s tattooing seem to fulfil complementary roles: through the aesthetically distancing character of migrant ritual music and of tattooing the female bodies, male and female clients are protected from all kind of ailments in their lifetime as well as after death.

Photograph 24: *Bhairavi* with his *kanjoni*, on the way to Padampur 2005, L.G.

[100] For a further discussion of the categories of bad or good death see Alex/Heald 2008.

Photograph 25: *Kanjoni* instrument, with tatooing ingrediences, 2005, L.G.

## *Gopijantra*

Another category of itinerary priest-musicians are the *gopijantra*, literally the "musical machine" *jantra* played by the friend "*gopi*" of Rada. Rada is worshipped as the beloved girlfriend of the god Krishna who, in Hindu mythology, is the incarnation of the god Vishnu.[101] *Gopijantra* thus denotes both, the one-stringed instrument made out of a melon (*lou*) and a string as well as the itinerant priest-performer. Sometimes the *gopijantra* is also called *ekatara*, literally the one-stringed musical instrument. For the *gopijantra* performer the instrument itself is the altar of the goddess Saraswati, the Hindu goddess of wisdom and learning. By lighting an incense stick (*duppo*

[101] According to the mythology of the Hindu epic Mahabharata and to its local narrative counterparts, Vishu is believed to have been raised in a cowherd's family, vigorously playing the flute and often engaging in romantic episodes with cowgirls or other girlfriends (*gopi*).

*katti*) the *gopijantra* daily worships his instrument. Playing the instrument means an act of worship (*puja*) directed towards the goddess. A *gopijantra* features as the itinerary singer of the mythical local narrative (*katani*) of Gowind Chandra, a famous folk tale of Odisha, which meanwhile has been written down in the Gowind Chandra book (*bohi*). The *gopijantra* walks daily around 3 to 5 kilometres while begging, singing and playing. In the evening he returns to his home. Locals consider his activity as a religious devotion and an act of asceticism. Daily, the *gopijantra* sings the well-known rhythmic chant of Gowind Chandra:

**_Gowind Chandra katani_**[102]

*"The father of Gowind Chandra is Manik Chandra.*
*The mother of Gowind Chandra is the goddess Mukta.*

*Before Gowind Chandra was born,*
*Jom, the God of death decided that Gowind Chandra will live only 19 years.*

*In his 19th year he shall die, Jom said.*
*Only his mother knew this.*

*Anxious, she has forbidden her son to leave his home.*

*The only way for Gowind Chandra to be saved (mukti), was to leave the house - not as a son, but as a wandering ascetic (baba). Only as a baba he could mislead the god of death.*

*In order to meditate Gowind Chandra left mother and father.*

The meaning of the story- as the *gopijantra* explains - is that one crucial way to salvation (*mukti*) lies in the devotional practice of singing religious stories while begging. Here, the local concept of worldly renunciation and religious devotion amalgamates with the trans-regional Hindu value of as-ceticism[103] and the Indian Hindu mysticism of the *bhakti* tradition.[104]

---

[102] Documented by the author on November, 15, 2004, on the roads to Padampur.

[103] According to Louis Dumont's fundamental analysis, an Indian ascetic is an "individual outside the world" (individu hors le monde), who has left the world of castes, as opposed to the "individual in the world" – i.e., in the caste system. Ascetics, in the eyes of the faithful, have already reached in this earthly life the highest stage of religious release from the cycle of rebirths – moksha. (Dumont 1986: 324-350); on the diversity of modern ascetic traditions in South Asia, see Ishwaran (1999).

[104] The *bhakti* movement played a crucial role in the historical period of the Indian Middle

While begging and singing, the *gopijantra* accepts food or money donations (*vikhya*) from donors who in this way hope to attain good *karma* – performing good deeds to accumulate a "spiritual capital" for the next life. The Hindu worldview's central category of *karma* is, in short, a religious theory of action, which postulates that all the deeds of an individual have an effect on his or her next existences. Consequently, all situations and occurrences of the present life can be traced back to moral achievements or failures in a previous existence. Donations – "gifts" in terms of their socio-anthropological value – are meant to realize their value in an economy of soteriological reciprocity which aims at a final spiritual release. While the performance of the *gopijantra* is in its narrative and conceptual content embedded in the trans-regional Hindu mythology and its ideological context, the idea of goddess worship through the specific sound of a particular musical instrument and especially the identification of instrument and sound with the voice and utterances of a goddess seems to be an element specific to the Bora Sambar region.

Photograph 26: A *Gopijantra* singer playing his gopijantra lute, met on the roads to Padampur, 2004, L.G.

Ages (around the 12th century C.E.). The concept of *bhakti* emphasizes an intimate relationship to a personal god. In contrast to the "proper conduct" (*karma marga*) of Brahmanism and the "proper knowledge" (*jnana marga*) of Indian philosophy, the bhakti movement introduced the "devotional love of god" (*bhakti marga*) as the way to salvation. Its religious aim was to direct one's concentrated feeling towards a god while attaining indifference to worldly concerns; on the broad phenomenon of the *bhakti*-tradition in India, see Farquhar (1967) and Biardeau (1994).

## *Subaltern Musicians*

Apart from the itinerary priest-musicians, various other categories of subaltern musicians exist in the Bora Sambar region. With their music, these musicians enrich the musical and cultural landscape of Bora Sambar – even while as wandering and begging musical performers they have an extremely low social status.

Photograph 27: *Dopara* drum player, on the way to Raipur, 2008.

## *Cherchela*

The Cherchela is a begging musician who plays a big round and thin membranophone, the *dopara*, which reminds of an oversized tambourine. The *dopara* is made from the wood of the khorol tree (*khorol kat*) and is strung with goat's skin (*cheli chamara*). This big and thin instrument is played with a timsi, a small bamboo stick for the left hand and a stick (*kondha*) from the wood of the local sisu tree (*sisu kath*) for the right hand. Due to this handling of the instrument, which resembles that of the dhol and the nissan drums of the ganda baja orchestra, the dopara membranophone is considered - especially by Ganda musicians - as the ancient instrumental origin of the ganda baja orchestra. Musically the dopara drum might substitute the dhol. The cherchela musicians explain that dapara music is played especially for the worship of goddesses such as Saraswati, Samley, Lakshmi and for gods such as Ganesh and Vishwakarma. *"Cherchera par is the rhythm of begging (vikhya magiba)"*, the listeners of the *dopara* music tell. While playing the rhythm of begging, the *dopara* performer goes from door to door in order to collect voluntary donations. Giving donations (*vikhya deba*) to wandering and begging musicians in form of food or money is considered a religious merit (*karma*). The value of donations (*vikhya deba*) to the *cherchera* follows the same logic of an ascetic and devotional tradition already encountered in the case of the *gopijantra*.

## *Porushram*

With the *porushram* we come across the case of a specifically local tradition of the oral transmission of a pan-Indian epic. The subaltern *porushram*-musician is a local devotional musician and singer who has taken a special religious initiation in order to lead his life together with his wife as a *porush ram*– a wandering beggar-musician (*porushram dikhya*), devoted to the worship of the pan-Indian god Ram and to the recital of the narrations of theRamayana. Together with the Mahabharata,[105] the Ramayana belongs to the great lyrical epics of Indian cultural history. It tells the saga of the di vinehero Rama, his beautiful wife Sita and the dangerous king Ravanna. Its author is the saintly poet Valmiki[106], the origins of the text are considered how ever to trace back to the period between the 4th c. B.C.E. and the 2nd c. C.E. The Ramayana epic is very popular in lay Hinduism and its contentsare publicly declaimed or musically presented in sung narrations, the so called *kata*. *Porushram* is originally the name of a mythical figure, the creator of the god Ram, whose symbol is an axe. Retelling the stories of the Ramayana, the *porushram* roams the streets with an axe on his shoulder and utters the name of god the Ram. "*The porushram is always on the street (bate bate*

---

[105] The Mahabharata is a heroic poem that was collected between 400 B.C. and 400 A.D. and consists of more than 100,000 śloka (double verses). It contains myths, legends, parables and fables of an ethical, teaching character. The most famous section of the Mahabharata is the Bhagavad-Gita, "The song of the magnificent". The Mahabharata epic contributed greatly to the widespread popularity of the god Vishnu in South Asia (Glasenapp 1986: 66-93).

[106] For the retold Valmiki's version by Krishna Dharma see Valmiki, 1998.

*jiba)*", the people tell.Often the *porushram* is blind, making a living by wandering from door to door together with his wife, singing the story of Rama and begging for alms.

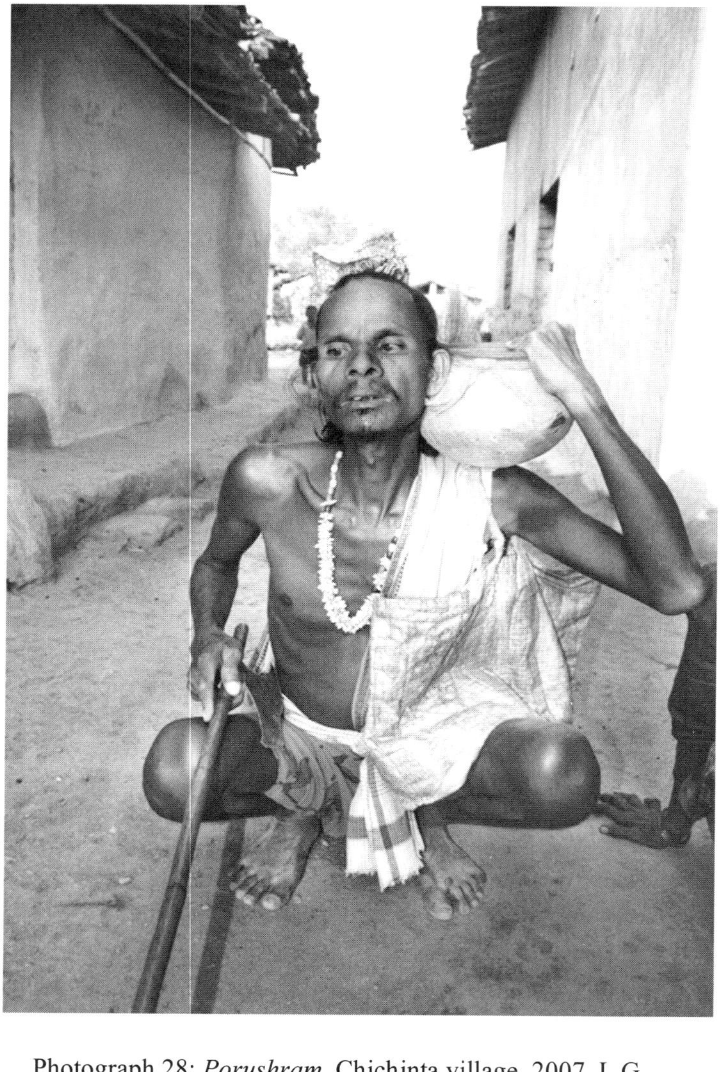

Photograph 28: *Porushram*, Chichinta village, 2007, L.G.

The *porushram* goes about his trade only in the morning hours. According to the prescriptions of his religious devotion, he is supposed to return after getting one meal a day. But besides this internal religious explanation, a practical reason might be that in the rural context with its poor infrastructure it is necessarily to reach home before sunset. As going by foot requires time to reach one's destiny, the return home requires the greater part of the day.

### *Devgunya: music and exorcism*

Another subaltern priest-musician is the *devgunya*, literally the exorcist of gods (*dev*= god, *gunya*=exorcist), who chases away malevolent forces. *Devgunya* designates at the same time 1) the Devgunya, a local subaltern community; b) a ritually specialised non-Brahmin priest and c) a lyre-like chordophone, also termed *veena*, played only by the Devgunya community. The non-Brahmin priest-musician called *devgunya* specialises in the worship of the goddess Lakshmi - the goddess of wealth and rice. One could understand *devgunya* as "the exorcist priest of the goddess Lakshmi" as it is believed that with the music of his lyre-like string instrument *devgunya* bad spirits (*bhuta*) are chased away. The chordophone *devgunya* is considered holy by the Devgunya community, representing the goddess Lakshmi as well as the goddess Mangala, the clan goddess (*ishta devi*) of the Devgunya community. The sound – *sur* - of the instrument is believed to invoke both goddesses.

The *devgunya* chordophone is a bar zither of about 1.20 meter in length, consisting of a bamboo bar, in the middle of which a resonance body fashioned from a melon gourd is fixed. It is strung with one string made out of cow's gut sinew and decorated with seven moulded knobs topped by seven mussel shells. On the left side of the bar a bronze casting and on the right side a wooden handle is attached. The musician presses the string with his left hand and plucks it with the right hand in order to create the sound.

The microcosmic morphology of the instrument corresponds to the divine macrocosm of the Devgunya community: The seven little knobs topped by mussel shells represent the seven notes and the seven sister-goddesses. The *bara bhai bentkar*, the twelve mythical brothers of the Binjhal community, are said to reside in the bronze casting. The cow's gut sinew used as string stands for "untouchability" but also for the strength of the instrument. No god can touch the instrument because of this untouchable string. This also explains why the very sound of the untouchable string is believed to drive away malevolent elements. The sounds of the *devgunya* zither and the recitation of the *devgunya* priest-musician expel bad dreams, bad spirits (*bhuta*) and bad thoughts. The local term for the exorcising power of the music of the *devgunya* is *baja dwara. Mantra dwara* denotes the power of the spoken word that, during the playing of the *devgunya* instrument, assumes the same exorcising power. When summoned, the *devgunya* goes to his mentally and physically suffering clients, where he plays and sings in order to chase away the malevolent elements haunting them. This musical exorcism is called *devta nacha*, the dance of the gods, which is also the name of a song sung on this occasion accompanied by the *devgunya* chordophone:

Photograph 29: *Devgunya*, at Bisipalli village, played by Anand Benya, 2009, L.G.

**Devta nacha geet**

Played with the devgunya chordophone[107]

*Chai chai chai olo*
Look my dear Chaichai [pet name of the goddess Lakshmi]

*Saas Pindiche banaa lugaa*
The mother in law wore decorated linen clothes.

*Toor kaahin kimaa*
Why you are wise?

*Hatara sukhuaa-Jhuri*
The sign is the salty dry fish [a metaphor connected to death]

*Uppar bandhar Chooli kilo*
The snail is at the surface of the pond [the snail may be seen as a metaphor for life, the pond as an image connected to the fertility of women and to goddess worship]

*Amar devi  naat karuche*
Our goddess is dancing.

*Chum Chhum Chhumre guri*
[an onomatopoetic phrase alluding to the tinkling sound of women's foot chains]

*Amar devi nat karuche*
Our goddess is dancing.

*Bohi Pindiche gailo*
The daughter in law wore a [simple] hand loomed saree

*Mor kahi ki mana?*
Why should I also wear it?

*Baari Baaina*
The aubergine of the garden [metaphorical allusion to wealth and prosperity]

*Tali Bandhar Gholi*
and the snail of the pond

*Sarge ude dhuli*
which also influenced the heaven's atmosphere

*Payejhal bajila*
[all] sounded in her feet.

*Mor mane bhabile*
This is what I thought.

---

[107] Recorded by the author on October 18, 2003, at Bisipalli village, played by Anand Benya, transcribtions and translation by Surendra Kumar Sahu.

Photograph 30: *Sarangi* player Jalandar Benya of the Devgunya community, at Bisipalli village, 2004, L. G.

The metaphoric language of the *devgunya* constructs a symbolic link between the microcosm of vegetables and animals and the macrocosm of the gods, which is expressed in the image of the divine dance and the sound of the dancing feet of the goddess Lakshmi. Lakshmi is symbolised and worshipped in India through the image of her feet, painted by women with rice paste on the threshold of their houses. The symbol of the goddess' feet alludes to wealth, prosperity and happiness, which are thus invited to come into the particular house. The sound of the goddess' feet relates on the one hand to a common acoustic metaphor of femininity and sensuality commonly expressed through the soft tinkling sounds of foot anklets accompanying the steps of women's feet. On the other hand, it is associated with the worship of the goddess through the sound of music which in this case again is conceived as both, the manifestation of the goddess herself and the medium of her worship.

The *devgunya* instrument is played particularly in the yearly ritual services for the goddess Lakshmi (*Lakshmi puja*). During her worship in the month of *maxir* (November/December) the exorcising power of the goddess is believed to be especially effective in protecting and preventing from all kind of misfortune and evil. In the course of this worship, the local epic Lakshmi *purana* is sung. The singing of the Lakshmi *purana* is intended to support the power of the music by the power of recitations and words (*mantra dwara*). The *devgunya* cither is considered by the Devgunya community as their sacred instrument which may never be sold. Their secular instrument, used for begging, is the *sarangi*.

Only males of the Devgunya community are entitled to play music. Devgunya women create small portable altars of the goddess Lakshmi – Lakshmi *murti* – made out of rice seeds, which are sold during the time of the ritual services of the goddess. The members of the Devgunya caste consider themselves to be the descendants of Narad, the mythical saint (*rusi*) and musician of the Vedas who, with his musical instrument, the chordophone *tampura*, is believed to have transmitted worship practices through his theory of sound. Narad's theory of sound is generally connected to the evolution of north Indian ("classical") *raga* music. It expounds that the universe and the cosmos were created by the sound (*nada*), the word (*shabda, vak*) and the rhythm of Shiva's drum (Daniélou 2004: 148).[108]

---

[108] The ancient Indian Vedic literature bears witness to the existence of very early indigenous theories on music and sound. Collections of religious hymns (*saman*) similar to the oldest Rig Veda hymns can be found in the Samaveda, the textbooks of the *udagatr* priests for Soma

In establishing a connection with the mythological context of the pan-Indian Hindu narratives and Vedic texts, the subaltern *devgunya* musicians thus ascribe a special cultural dignity to their ancestry, intended to counter their factual social marginalisation.

## *Music, movement and migration*

In the Bora Sambar region, music, movement and migration coincide. Music moves. It moves from village to village through *ganda baja* orchestras and along the routes of the itinerant non-Brahmin priests and musicians, and it moves by means of its sound vibrations. Its transgressing character is physical in the wandering movements of its performers and the rhythmic, sometimes dancing movements of their performance. But it is also metaphysical as it represents the sonic presence of the Divine. Regarding the wandering priest musicians or nomadic artists who offer their "musical services" to the villages of the Bora Sambar region, their mobility is held to be a crucial reason for their ritual efficacy.[109]

The diverse non-Brahmin priest-musicians and itinerant musicians of the Bora Sambar region keep a storehouse of cultural and musical wealth. Through their various musical traditions, they preserve a unique cultural consciousness and a local system of ideas and values about divinity, death and healing. In the *daan chheeka* ritual, human loss is made present in the experience and perception of the sound – *sur* – of particular instruments. The experience of sound seems to entail healing and re-structuring effects through its sensual and transformative powers. In this context, the people of

---

sacrifices (Nijenhuis 1974: 1). Fragments of Rig Veda (*Samaveda*) which are of unsure date (around 1750-500 B.C.E. according to Michaels (1998: 67) or much older – about 4000 B.C.E. according to Klostermaier (1994: 477-82)) expound through their hymns the spiritual und ritual characteristic of sound as *vak,* the sacred word, speech or language (Doniger O'Flaherty 1981: 61) which is equated with a goddess, especially with the goddess Sarasvati. Mystical texts of the Upanishads (secret teachings and Vedic tracts dealing with philosophical issues) of the late phase of the Vedic religion (1000-500 B.C.E.) show that the voice itself is considered holy. The most important holy verse (*mantra*) is the syllable "*Om*", considered as the expression of the creative process of the universe, originating from *shabda-brahma* (the ultimate in form of a sound). For later periods, "(t)*he most outstanding examples are the linguistic theories of the grammarian Bhartrhari (5$^{th}$ century C.E.) and of the Kashmir Shaiva philosopher, left-handed tantrist and poet Abhinagupta (11$^{th}$ centrury C.E.) or the Nada Brahman of the musicologists who claim the world is sound*" (Wilke 2008: 31).

[109] Christine Guillebaud (2008) describes analogous phenomena for the region of Kerala, where itinerant musicians offer their services to families of high status in order to treat malevolent influences and to protect from misfortune. In Kerala and in Odisha, the mobility of these musicians is seen as a crucial reason for their ritual efficacy.

the Bora Sambar region understand the symbolic and factual flow of donations during *daan chheeka* as a transfer of gifts from one world to another. The movement and flow of alms is metaphorically equated with the micro-movements of sound vibrations, expressing ideas of post-mortem transformation processes and the absence of the deceased. The concept of *sur* establishes music in the Bora Sambar region as a medium of spiritual purification, prevention and finally healing. *Sur,* the sound, which itself is transitional and temporary in nature, operates as a cultural metaphor of transfer, transition and memory.

Furthermore, ritual sound can establish an aesthetic distance, which becomes effective in the healing and exorcising powers ascribed to many of the discussed musical practices. The sound – *sur* - itself is associated with motion and linked to spiritual liberation (*mukti*). The effect of aesthetic distancing is metaphorically intensified by the migrant, wandering status of most of the musical performers. The attitude of begging, involved in particular traditions of migrant music, hints to connections between local concepts of religious musical performances and trans-regional religious traditions, such as the hegemonic Hindu value of asceticism.

All of the diverse musical traditions of non-Brahmin priest-musicians of the Bora Sambar region are connected by a proximity to ambivalent and dangerous rituals and situations of life – a social and ritual condition which classifies the non-Brahmin priest-musicians as "impure", as of a precarious and ambivalent social status. I would suggest that the symbolic identification of precarious and ambivalent ritual music with its performers, hints to a convergence between the medium music and its message: the transitional, migrant or passing character of music represents both: 1) the ritual transition and the ritual transformation of spiritual impurity and 2) the ritual passing and banishing of ailment. These transformations always imply a precarious being in-between the worlds. The liminality of the ritual music seems, in consequence, to stigmatise its performers socially.

Furthermore, the sounds of the specific instruments of priests-musicians of the Bora Sambar region are on the one hand acoustic metaphors and a sonic language expressing indigenous theories of sound and the sacred. On the other hand the importance of sound in the region demonstrates the interplay between trans-regional Hindu narratives and local concepts, indicating significant effects of hegemonic Hindu value-ideas in the region. Thus, the seemingly paradoxical situation emerges that moments of a *memocid*e of vulnerable traditional cultural and musical concepts go hand in hand with a flowering of musical creativity.

# *Fifth Chapter: Music and the Market*

## *Baja Bazaar – Sacred Music for Sale*

Since 2006, the phenomenon of *baja bazaar*, the "market of music", has emerged among *baja* groups of the Bora Sambar region. At a central intersection in Raipur, the capital of the newly created state of Chhattisgarh and in other urban settings near the capital, hundreds of *baja* groups from the neighbouring regions gather in order to offer their musical services to potential clients. These markets of music simply consist of groups of musicians presenting themselves with their instruments on the street sides – performing tunes for ritual events to attract customers. Clients approach them to select and hire groups for ritual occasions and marriages. The musicians then accompany their temporary patrons into their villages in order to provide the musical performances which are necessary components of rituals for village goddesses and gods or of ritual marriage preparations.

In the year 2000, the state of Chhattisgarh split from the former state of Madhya Pradesh. It was not least the awakening of an Adivasi consciousness and political resistance in the course of a pan-Indian Adivasi movement and indigeneity discourse (Karlsson 2003: 403-423; Devy/Davis/Chakravarty 2009), which led to the shaping of three new Indian states (Uttaranchal, Chhattisgarh, Jharkhand). The state of Chhattisgarh was formed around the core of the ancient cultural province of Dakshina Koshala, embracing its neighbouring provinces Jharkhand, Odisha, Maharashtra and Andhra Pradesh. In the year of its foundation, the government of the newly created state released a statement of cultural intent, announcing efforts to "*...identify, recognize, document, revitalize, present and disseminate the continuing cultural traditions of local communities...*".[110] The promotion of

---

[110] The complete statement of cultural intent by the state of Chhattisgarh runs as follows: "The State of Chhattisgarh will not announce or impose any cultural policy. It will identify, recognize, document, revitalize, present and disseminate the continuing cultural traditions of local communities.
The State will not set up artificial boundaries between classical, folk, tribal, visual and performing metropolitan and rural arts. It will recognize and respect the transitions and bridges among these.
The State will promote textual as well as non textual traditions, collection and documentation of tangible objects as well as recollection of intangible traditions, their ex situ display as well as in situ revitalization.
The State will try to work around existing cultural landscapes, festivals and institutions, rather than create new ones to replace them.
The State will be a catalytic agent, to support and advance the traditional connection among

local musical traditions has in fact since then been a recognizable objective of governmental policy in Chhattisgarh:

"Earlier we were called by our patrons (malik) to play our music for rituals", explains one musician from a village near Raipur, "but some years ago the new government (sarkar) started to stimulate musical competitions on the crossroads of Raipur with prizes to win and the baja bazaar started." Another musician from the Bora Sambar region adds: "I heard about the baja bazaar from my elder brother (boro bhai). I heard that we can earn there and so we started to come here each year". With the emergence of the baja bazaar in Raipur, the news about its new economic possibilities quickly spread among musicians of the whole neighbouring area. In this sense, the phenomenon of the baja bazaar has not been invented by the state but still relies on the traditional patron-client structure between musicians and their ritual customers. But governmental incentives nevertheless played a significant role in the formation of structures which revitalized local musical traditions, as the participants themselves acknowledge.

*Baja bazaars* are held in the Chenicheri market in Bilaspur (Chhattisgarh), in the Burhatalab market in Raipur and in the Champa market in Jharkhand. For the *baja bazaars, ganda baja* orchestras from the Bora Sambar region and from other neighbouring regions gather and present themselves in their full festive costumes: they cook, sleep and perform their music on the ba-

---

communities, between their life and their arts, and between forms and functions of these arts. It will respect and nourish culture as essential to eco-specific development strategies of communities, geared to resource management and subsistence. It will recognize culture as an essential ingredient in development. Effort will be made to recognize, embed and develop the cultural component in the programs of all Govt. departments, as culture is a component of all departments of life. Culture will not be reduced to a mere song and dance act, or to an exclusive concern of the Department of Culture.
Cultural impact assessment will be embedded as a component in the formulation and implementation of mega developmental projects.
The State will further cross disciplinary dialogues, inter institutional networking and decentralized field activity to replenish community identities.
The unique identity and polyvalence of the culture of Chhattisgarh will be promoted alongside its relationships and exchanges with cultural provinces and neighbourhoods of adjacent states of Chhattisgarh. The community cultural identity and landscape of Chhattisgarh will be presented in the national and global perspective.
(…)Tourism will be developed as a non-invasive instrument of biological, ecological and cultural conservation, and not as a bread and circus affair.
Chhattisgarh itself being treated as a living museum space, the in-situ and ex-situ exhibition and dissemination initiatives, will be designed as exercises in problem assessment and resolution, and not as passive displays. (…)(www.cgculture.in, retrieved, 20 February, 2010).

zaar. Especially during the months of *magho* (February), *falguna* (March), *choit* (April/Mai) and *boisaka* (June/July) and during the time of *kartika* (November), up to 1000 musicians (*baja mane*) gather at the diverse "music markets". "Baja bazaar", the people tell, "is welcoming the summer and winter season and it expresses a farewell to the rainy season. It is a market for the worship of the gods". Baja bazaars are also hold for the marriage season of the Raut/Gour (the caste of herdsmen), the dominant caste in Chhattisgarh, in the four months between magh (Februar) to boisaka (Mai). During this time, musical parties from the music market are engaged by patrons (malik) for the ritual of biha lagan – the approaching of a high status religious priest and astrologer, the Pandit or Brahmin, in order to ask him for a good marriage date. After hearing the baja music, the Brahmin priest augurs the right date (lagan) for the marriage, which should take place during the marriage season. During the marriage season two divine couples: Shiva-Parvati, the divine pan-Indian Hindu pair, and Goura-Gouri, the local mythical ancestors of the Gour caste are equally worshipped through the music of ganda baja. Also during various other times of the year, ganda baja music offered at the baja bazaar plays an important role for different ceremonial occasions:

### *Diwalli*

After *diwalli*, the "festival of lights", held on *amavasya* day, the day of the new moon after the ceremony of *dusshara* in the month *kartika* (around November), the *baja bazaar* begins to fill with different *baja* groups. In reference to the pan-Indian Ramayana epos, the festival of *diwalli* celebrates the return of god Rama to the holy city of Ayodhya after Rama's exile in the jungle, his victory against the demon-king Ravanna who has abducted his beloved wife Sita and after his happy reunion with his lost wife. In the course of a 7 to 8 days ceremony, many *ganda baja* orchestras compete with each other, in order to get engaged by *malik*s (patrons) of the Raut/Gour.

During this time, the *baja bazaar* is also called *Raut baja*. The biggest *raut bajas* are held in five main places: Raipur, Bilaspur, Champa, Raygada and Shakti, but there are also *raut bajas* in small towns and villages. A real musical competition takes place to attract a patron, who, in order to test the quality of the different *baja* groups, chants traditional Gour songs together with the orchestras and dances the *raut naach*, the traditional dance of the Raut, a stick dance symbolising the identity of the Raut as a cast of herdsmen. In case a Raut *malik* is satisfied with a *baja* performance, he engages

Photograph 31: *Ganda baja* at the *Baja Bazaar* in Raipur, 2008, L.G.

the group for a time of up to 8 days. The selected *baja* party then proceeds to the *malik's* village by foot, where it performs its musical services in the post-*diwalli* celebrations. After *diwalli,* on *ekadosi* which is the eleventh day of the rising moon in the lunar cycle and the $4^{th}$ day before the full moon, the Raut celebrate the god Krishna, who in Hindu mythology is depicted as a herdsman, as their ancestor. When listening to the performance of the *baja,* all women of the village become *boil*, possessed by the spirit of the goddess Gour Mata, the cow goddess. During the night, they are held to embody further deities, such as for example the pan-Indian gods Ishwar and Parvati. The possessed women and girls carry lights on their heads. Accompanied and guided by the *baja*, they submerge into the water of the village pond. On the next evening, the Gobordan *puja*, the worship of the god Gobordan, an incarnation of Krishna, takes place. After *diwalli, ganda baja* musicians are supposed to have collected enough money to subsist with their families for the following months.

In the context of the ceremony of *diwalli* the Ministry of Culture in Chhattisgarh has started to reward the best dance and music group with a considerable amount of money in order to keep the local dance and music tradition of *raut naach* and *raut baja* alive, respectively to re-vitalize them in cooperation with the local communities.

Photorgraph 32: *Raut baja* at the *Baja bazaar* in Raipur, 2008, L.G.

## *The Market of Gods*

The recent tradition of a *baja bazaar*, the market for ritual music, is intrinsically related to the old local tradition of "*dev-bajar*", the god's market. *Dev bajar* is a local ritual which traditionally takes place in the mixed "tribal-caste" villages of Chhattisgarh during the weekly bazaars (*haat*) of the local Adivasi communities. *Dev bajar* which is also named *dev khel* "the play of gods" is described by Nicolas Prévôt for the region Bastar in Chhattisgarh (Prévôt 2005, 2008: 75-88) as follows:

*"Music is an essential element of the ritual [the dev bajar L. G.] especially during the "play of gods" (dev khel). This marks the climax of the ritual. Musicians become central actors of the event as men, possessed by different gods, ask for their tune to be played so they can participate in the play of the gods.[. . .] The musicians please and entertain the deities – in the shape of men or in the shape of objects – by playing their respective tune(s) (called paR). The result is an unbroken line of melodies played on the shawm, using a circular breathing technique, and accompanied by specific rhythmic patterns on the kettledrums* [the *nagara*]" (Prévôt 2008: 77-78)

Photograph 33: *Baja Bazaar* and *Raut baja* in Raipur, 2008, L.G.

In the former local princely state of Bastar, the god's market *dev bajar,* respectively the "god's play" (*dev khel*), is linked to local spirit possession rituals where various kinds of spirits (*bhut, duma*), gods (*devta*), goddesses (*devi*) and other entities (*anga*-s) may be embodied either by a ritual specialist and trance medium (*sirha*) or by anybody susceptible and sensible to the ritual musical tunes played by the *ganda* musicians. Varying from the specific *ganda baja* ensembles of the Bora Sambar region[111], the *dev bajar* ensembles from Bastar consist of

> *"two or three GanDa musicians: the leader, often the elder, plays a shawm called mohri and is accompanied by a pair of kettledrums called nagoRa, and an optional smaller kettledrum called tuRbuli* " (Prévôt 2008: 79).

Even if the phenomenon of *dev bajar/dev khel* includes slightly different musical instruments than those of *ganda baja*, a similarity between the recently emerged *baja bazaars* and the traditional *dev bajar* can be ascertained. On the one hand, both the tunes of the music of the *dev bajar* and the musical 'services' offered on the *baja bazaar* mediate a communication with the divine sphere (Prévôt 2008: 86). On the other hand, in both cases the divine communication through music is intrinsically interrelated to a musical market, which takes place weekly in the case of *dev bajar* or on special times of the year in case of the *baja bazaars*. As Ganda musicians are always professional music makers, in both contexts their musical services have to be financially rewarded. The more recent phenomenon of *baja bazaar* thus seems to be embedded in a common local tradition of "god's markets" where sacred music is offered in exchange for remuneration. Generally, the weekly market (*haat*) plays a substantial socio-cultural and economical role in rural Adivasi regions. It is a meeting point of different local groups; a centre of exchange of commodities and information and a platform for personal networks. With the *dev bajar/dev khel*, where ritual and religious "services" are offered, presented and exchanged, the sphere of the sacred and the socio-economic sphere of the commodities market become intrinsically entangled if not congruent. The tradition of sacred music for sale during the social-ritual events of *dev bajar* has been revitalized today through the governmental encouragement of *baja bazaar* musical markets based on the traditional yearly cycle of socio-ritual activities and on the fact that ritual music has customarily been a good traded on the market. The cultural re-vitalisation policy of the Chhattisgarh State thus seems indeed to work as an "*in situ revitalization*" where the new State "*works around existing cultural landscapes, festivals and institutions, rather than create[*s*] new ones to replace them*".

---

[111] see chapter 2.

### *Economic empowerment and cultural politics*

"*Musicians always played for money and tried to get a prosperous call*", a musician explains. When receiving a "*call*" [the English term has entered the vernacular to designate a musical engagement] musicians might gain around 2000 Rupees. Even higher salaries of up to 5000 Rupees for one musician can be realized, as patrons are willing pay high sums for the best *baja* parties. For an engagement of about 8 days a *baja* party might gain a total of 22.000 Rupees.[112] Musicians explain that their economic situation has remarkably improved in the last years since the government of Chhattisgarh started to support the emergence of *baja bazaar*s through the initiation of musical contests and prizes for the best musical parties.

Since the cultural-political revitalisation of the *baja* music in *baja* bazaars, a new economic empowerment of the marginalised musicians has taken place. The cultural policy of the government's of Chhattisgarh Ministry of culture to treat Chhattisgarh "*as a living museum space*" with the attempt "*to provide a backdrop to the state's efforts to promote community well being and bounty*" seems to have successfully incited the continuation of a vulnerable musical tradition by utilizing the economic foundations of local traditions and through supporting them without an imposed intervention or reinvention of tradition. With *baja bazaar* a local tradition of sacred music for sale seems to have evolved into a self-dynamic socio-economic market of music.

### *Political discourse on indigeneity*

The Chhattisgarh's State politics of cultural revitalization, exemplified in this chapter through the case of *baja bazaar,* seem to be part of the self-fashioning of a "tribal" image for the newly constructed state. The "music markets" represent a part of the state's "tribal" identity in contrast to urban Hindu forms of ritual and secular music, such as for example north Indian *raga* music or the Indian wide popular marriage brass bands called *brass baja* (Booth 2005). Contrary to these pan-Indian classical and popular musical traditions, *Raut baja* or *baja bazaar* is embedded in the locally specific tradition of sacred music for sale, explicitly recognized as part of the Adivasi tradition of the state. Here, a political construction of identity through music becomes visible that may be compared with other global phenomena of eth-

---

[112] A daily wage is mostly around 100 to 200 Rupees; 2000 rupees can be considered an average monthly salary for a person without a higher education degree.

nicisation and re-traditionalisation of music[113] including the reconstruction and the revitalisation of marginalised, forgotten or vulnerable musical traditions. The construction of a cultural discourse of indigeneity is a recent socio-political phenomenon in India (Karlsson 2003: 403-423; Devy/Davis/Chakravarty 2009), representing a socio-cultural result of the rising consciousness of Adivasi identity articulated in an Adivasi literature (Gupta 2009: 191-202, Shah 2009: 130-137), its expressions of orality (Narjinari 2009: 84-101) and poetry (Patel 2009: 48-92; Tiwari 2009: 93-101), and addressing the problem of the cultural silencing and marginalization of subaltern indigenous groups (Devy 2006a; Devi 2003) on the subcontinent. The cultural politics exemplified by the "*in situ revitalisation*" of *baja bazaar* represent the state's interest in supporting and thus reconstructing its distinct indigenous "tribal" or Adivasi identity through its musical traditions, even though the rural and urban traditions of the new state are often characterised by a socio-cultural continuum between local Adivasi traditions and urban pan-Indian Hindu influences.

[113] see Stokes 1994; Hyder 2004, Yang 2008.

# *Sixth Chapter: Music as religious instruction and cultural transfer*

Besides their economical and socio-cultural functions, the musical traditions of the Bora Sambar region play an important role as media of religious, moral and socio-political instruction and of cultural transfer. This can be observed especially in the musical traditions which are discussed in this chapter: *sanchar, Krishna guru* music and *pala*. In contrast to the musicians described in the preceding chapters, performers of these musical traditions are neither professional musicians, like the members of *ganda baja* groups, nor "full-time" religious specialists, like the itinerant non-Brahmin priest musicians. They are musical laymen and receive no remuneration for their musical or theatrical performances.

## *Sanchar*

The local term *sanchar* is derived from the Sanskrit verb *sanchar*, which means "to spread", "preach" or "echo". Sometimes the term is said to be spelled *sam*-char, indicating four *(char)* artists playing together (*sam*): one singer, one dancer, one player and one narrator. The term *sanchar* is also linked with the notions of *somvar* (to explain) and *choroti* (to give). Local explanations reduce this field of meanings to the three main performing arts which are combined in *sanchar*: *geeta,* the song; *badya,* the play and *nurtya*, the dance. These three elements are performed simultaneously so that a *sanchar* performance is both musical and acrobatic in character. In their self-descriptions, contemporary *sanchar* musicians link their art to the historical personality of Chaitanya (1486–1533 AD), a charismatic religious personality, who propagated the belief in the god Vishnu through mystic-ecstatic singing and dancing.[114] Particularly in Odisha, Chaitanya's mystic poetry and sung performances led to an enthusiastic reverence for his person (Mukherjee 1986: 310-319). In the course of time, the popularity of Chaitanya, who himself came from Puri - the religious centre of eastern Odisha - was largely absorbed into the regional cult of Jagannath and in this form became a current of neo-Vishnuism (Behuria 1991: 28). Due to the influence of Chaitanya, religious *sanchar* songs about the Mahabharata and Ramayana epics were for the first time performed in the vernacular regional language

[114] Until today, Chaitanya's songs are performed in religious institutions such as the Shri Kalpataru Seva Ashrama in Bhubaneshwar (Malinar 2004: 175-202).

Orya. Vernacular interpretations of the pan-Indian religious texts thus began to be spread on a large scale. According to local legends, Guru Govinda, a legendary mystical singer and important religious and musical figure within the 16th century *bhakti* tradition in Odisha, was also a famous *sanchar* player, creating his own devotional compositions about his love for Krishna.

*"The playing of sanchar"*, one musician explains, *"was held to create a ritually pure atmosphere."* Sound, as a medium of transcendence, was supposed to have the power to purify its surroundings. Traditionally, musicians tell, *zamindar*s sponsored *sanchar* musicians in order to spread the belief.

Photograph 34: *Sanchar* players, Achut Behera with accompanying *kastal* players, Sohela village, 2008, L.G.

The principal instrument of the *sanchar* tradition is the *mrdanga* drum, which is accompanied by rattles (*kastal / jhang*), wooden sticks (*kati / gungur*) and sometimes by the *ghurka*, a traditional membranophone of the Soara community. The *mrdanga* is a big double-sided membranophone, tapered on both sides. The left side is called *dhaaya,* the right side *chaya*. Sanchar musicians relate that these *categories correspond to the classical tabla ensemble*: *dhugi* (a larger left-sided membranophone) and *tabla* (higher right-sided membranophone). *Kiran*, the black spot on the *chaya* and *dhaaya* sides of the membranophone, is made out of carbon black in order to modify the sound of the drumskin. The principal *sanchar* performer, who plays the *mrdanga* drum, is locally called *bahak*. *Bahak* signifies "he *who wears the* mrdanga *drum, who can sing, who can dance, and who can play simultaneously.*" The two to four accompanists who play *kastal* and *kati* are called *palia*. *Sanchar* music combines Indian classical (*sastria tala*) and folk rhythms (*loko tala*).

Photograph 35: *Sanchar* performance, village Gonthiapalli, 2007, L.G.

Photograph 36: *Sanchar* player, Sohela village, 2007, L.G.

According to local traditions, religious merits are attained by performing *sanchar*. It helps to gain the way to salvation (*mukti marga)* and inspires religious thoughts (*adhyatni cintan*). Thus, *sanchar* musicians emphasize, *sanchar* should always be performed in an ascetic, religious spirit. *Sanchar* music is traditionally only played by elderly men above 60 years. It is connected to the ideals of world renunciation and devotion through the wisdom of age. *Sanchar* performers such as Achut Behera[115] underline that asceticism, which is practised according to special rules of conduct (*nyam*), is indispensable for the *sanchar* artists and hence for a morally inspiring musical and religious performance. As *sanchar* is supposed to be played for the purpose of encouraging proper ethical behaviour, a "good artist" (*bhala kalakar*) must respect certain rules of conduct (*nyam*): He should abstain

[115] Achut Behera is a famous senior local *sanchar* artist who leads a local *sanchar* group and club/school in Sohela, a village about 30 kilometres from Padampur. The *sanchar* club's / school's building has been sponsored by the wealthiest landowner (*zamindar*) of the village.

from prostitutes (*dari*), thiefs (*chori*), murderers (*hoty*), liars (*mitya*), alcohol (*moda / moha*) and meat (*mastiarji*). A community of *sanchar* players (*sanchar sammaj*) belonging to the same musical school decides on the basis of compliance with *nyam* who is a good or bad *sanchar* artist and thus who, in a worst-case scenario, might be expelled from the musical community (*sommajru boiska koriba*).[116] A *sanchar* community - *sanchar sammaj* - defines itself as both: a particular musical school and a community with religious ethics that are binding for its members. Today, *sanchar* music is no longer very popular amid the younger generation in Odisha, who considers this ascetic musico-mystical tradition as "old fashioned" – as a music made by and for the old (*purana loko geeta*). *Sanchar* music with its elderly performers seems to express the particular religious devotion and morality of old age. But with its theatrical and acrobatic elements it, on the other hand, manifests a vital and active self-fashioning of old age in its rural context.

*Sanchar* music is a tradition which is not restrained to a special cast (*jati*) of musicians (as is the case with *ganda baja*). Basically, it is the choice of an individual artist to become a *sanchar* player, and to join the *sanchar* musical community means, besides adopting its particular musical and performative practice, foremost to subscribe to its ethical and religious ideas. However, even if it is theoretically possible to choose the playing of a *sanchar* instrument like the *mrdanga* drum as an individual musical preference, most *mrdanga* players state that they learned to play the instrument from their fathers or grandfathers – while they themselves start to perform regularly and publicly only in their own mature age –, so that several genealogical schools (*parampara*) of *sanchar* traditions can be traced locally. In this sense, *sanchar* is close to the ascetic, sectarian and mystical devotional traditions (*bhakti*) of Odisha. The texts sung in *sanchar* performances are derived from the pan-Indian epics Ramayana and Mahabharata as well as from the local epics Haribansa and Nrusingha *purana*. All these texts refer to the ancient scriptural and oral traditions of Veda, Vedanta, Upanishad and Shruti.

In order to understand the interweaving of narrations, music and religious oral texts, one must turn to the ancient pan-Indian Hindu tradition of the four Vedas (*veda*=knowledge), comprising - according to the Indologist's opinions - the oldest body of religious texts and the oldest literary creation of the Indo-European linguistic family. The term "Veda" generally refers to a cor-

---

[116] This structure of exclusion is similar to the practice of the ascetic orders in Odisha, such as Mahima Dharma, where ethical misbehaviour leads to exclusion from the religious community (see Guzy 2002).

pus of texts which did not necessarily have a written form. Before the texts were actually recorded in writing, they had for centuries already been transmitted orally. Veda in this sense, according to Wendy Doninger O'Flaherty, means *shruti*, "that which is heard" (O'Flaherty 1988: 1) and indicates a corpus of religiously "inspired" texts. Through meticulous, oral "syllable for syllable" transmission, they were communicated and preserved over generations. The Rig-Veda, that is said to have come from North India, is the most important part of the Vedic texts and the oldest source of this recorded oral tradition. It contains 10 song circles (*mandala*), consisting of 1028 hymns and riddle-songs for the carrying out of sacrificial rituals. The redaction of this text was probably completed around 1000 B.C. The Vedas, together with the corresponding ritual-exegetic literature (*Brahmana*) as well as the speculative, secret "Forest Books" (*Aranyaka*) and the Upanishads (secret teachings, Vedic tracts dealing with broad philosophical issues), the *sutra*s (collections of precepts, which provide the basic principles of the philosophical schools of thought), are considered to be revealed texts (*shruti*) and have exercised a great influence on later Indian religions. All other holy texts, in contrast, are considered as *smriti*, "the remembered", signifying a sacred tradition transmitted through human memory (Stietencron 1991: 13). These are texts that were written by human hand as commentaries to the *shruti*-texts. To this category belong, for example, the writings of the philosophical schools of Karma Mimamsa, Uttara Mimamsa, Sankhya and Yoga. The literature of the Dharma Shastra, including the law books of the Manu (Manava Dharma Shastra) and the great Sanskrit epics Mahabharata and Ramayana are also part of the *smriti* literature. The Dharma Shastra and the epics represent a narrative style with didactic objectives. O'Flaherty, in her thoroughgoing account, calls attention to what would seem on first sight an obvious paradox between the "heard" and "remembered" texts: because of the meticulous redaction of the ritual texts, the oral tradition of the *shruti* appears to be a "fixed" tradition, whereas the later written tradition of the philosophical schools and commentaries on the *smriti*-texts appears rather "fluid" (O'Flaherty 1988: 2-4).[117] The Vedas thus represent a kind of liturgical congealment, for their "heard" texts, containing strict liturgical prescriptions and instructions for formalistic ritual performances, have become rigidly fixed. Philosophical "memory" on the other hand, can unfold subjective and interpretative dynamics, thus leading to a diversification of contents. In

[117] "The *smriti* texts were written down at an early period, but constantly modified. Thus we are faced with what is to us a paradox: the Hindu oral tradition is fixed, the manuscript tradition fluid" (O'Flaherty 1988: 2).

the same vein, Harry Falk has outlined how since the beginnings of Indian literacy, it was always connected with oral traditions (Falk 1990: 103-119, 1993). Linguistic mediation of culture in "oral" civilizations works with virtuoso mnemonic techniques and a securing of the flow of words through bodily rhythms, song and dance (Schlaffer 1997: 7-23). A separation of the cultures of orality and literacy seems to be impossible in the Indian context. Moreover, it is the interface between the written and the oral which is at the core of Indian textual traditions (Goody 1968; 1986). In this context, the ancient Indian script culture of Sanskrit Hinduism can in general be classified according to Annette Wilke as an example of a "*culture of sound*" where "*eye and ear are not seen as contrast, but often appear synaesthetically related*" (Wilke 2008: 28).

During *sanchar* performances, local versions of *shruti* and *smriti* classical Hindu texts are presented. They are based on both written material and on mnemotechnically transmitted oral texts. A particular structure of semi-literacy can thus be traced in *sanchar*. The musicians perform the religious narratives, which they have heard or read, with rhythmic movements and through their songs. Prayers are sung in Oriya, some religious incantations (*prarthana, bhajana, manosikhya*) are recited rhythmically in Sanskrit and folk songs are performed in the regional language Sambalpuri.

An ensemble of *sanchar* performers consists basically of three musicians who are also singers: The leading *sanchar* musician is also the lead singer (*gayak*) who simultaneously plays the *mrdanga* and dances while singing. The second musician is a cymbal (*jhang*) player; the third musician's instruments are two wooden sticks (*katia*) which are hit rhythmically against each other in order to create a warm, energetic sound. While most sanchar groups are made up of three performers, a *sanchar* ensemble may comprise up to twelve members including up to three *mrdanga* players.

At the beginning of the *sanchar* performance, the lead singer and instrumentalist (*gayak*) starts to voice incantations in a smooth and melodious way. After he has accomplished his melodic, recitative introduction, he is answered by the chorus of the other performers who accompany themselves with the cymbals (*jhang*) and sticks (*katia*). While singing, the whole group starts to move in a slow circle. After some time, the rhythms of the songs escalate in tempo and the rhythmic foot dance movements become faster and more and more acrobatic. The sung and danced performance of religious narrations and incantations lasts between 15 minutes and up to 2 hours. After a rhythmic peak, the tempo of the performance de-escalates and the dance presentation slowly comes to a close.

The performance of sanchar is considered by the performing musicians as extremely emotional. Through *sanchar,* they explain, several categories of emotions are expressed: *rassa* (passion), *bhaya* (fear), *bibas* (pain), *roudra (*courage), *namra* (happiness), *basalya* (parental love) and *siddi* (peace). The *sanchar* players and singers are supposed to perform in a fully inspired manner, which they compare to the state of *boil* possession ("*ape ape ase*"). In this state, *sanchar* music is performed for the worship of 1) the god Jagannath (*Jagannath puja*) during the month of *isad* (June/July), 2) the god Ganesha (*Ganesh puja*) in the month of *bhudo mas* (August/September) 3) the goddess Saraswati (*Saraswati puja*) in the month of *magh mas* (January) 4) the goddess Durga (*Durga puja*) during *dusshara* (October) and 5) the god *Kartika* (*Kartika puja*) during the celebration and worship of the *oila* tree (or *panchko jatra*) every Thursday in the month of *maxir* (December). About the origin of the *mrdanga* drum various local myths (*kathani*) are told:

> *Earlier there was nothing, and then life arose. First insects, then small animals, birds, then manusya, human beings, and finally the trees appeared. The mrdanga arose from the bark (khonda) of an early tree. At that time, human beings ate the barks of trees. Once, suddenly, the whole of the tree was covered with leather and thus the sound (awaz/sur/sabda) of the mrdanga was created. First there was the sound (awaz/sur), the sound and the note; then, god's words (sabda) emerged. Shortly after the mrdanga came into existence, other drums, such as the dhol, nissan, tasa and tabla also came into existence. Then the potmaker (kumbhar) recreated the wooden structure of the mrdanga through a clay shape. The cover of the mud form was again the skin of the cow."*

Another myth traces the lines between the *mrdanga* and the worship of the god Jagannath.

> *The forefather of the local sanchar school (parampara) in the Bora Sambar region, Madhoba Behera, once set out on a journey to Puri in order to visit the Jagannath temple with his co-musicians [called samprada (Sanskr. group) = one mrdanga player together with 120 accompanying kastal players].*
>
> *All started the journey in a special way: whenever a rhythm ended, they all had to stop and change the rhythm by altering the movement of their steps. Sanchar implies: twenty two footsteps (bais pahacha); twenty two verses (bais sloka), twenty two beats (bais badhya). With these twenty two invocations the samprada group went to Puri to wor-*

*ship the god Jagannath. But as the group was about to enter the temple of god Jagannath in Puri, the priest barred them from entering because their mrdanga drum was not considered pure. The priest told them to go to the altar of Gouranga and to bring a paper certifying that the temple had requested and approved of their performance. The group did so while performing their musical acrobatics, step-dancing, singing and drum-beating. After the last step of the group, the Raja of Puri was so impressed that he raised Madhoba Behera from Behera to Das [titels of status]. The Raja then gave him a certificate, which implied new rules of behaviour (nyam) for performing sanchar.*

This myth shows how strict discipline and ascetic practices are combined with music-making. Adherence to a code of discipline is described as a means to enhance the social status of the performers of *sanchar* and to eliminate the stigma of impurity (*ashudha*) generally associated with village musicians.

It is this recurring element of individual choice which seems to distinguish sanchar from other local musical traditions. The *sanchar* performer – at least theoretically – opts for his vocation and his specific instrument on the basis of a personal decision. As well, there are no restrictions in the kind of instrument fit for a special performance: Each of the different *mrdanga* drums may be used in any kind of ritual worship. What is considered crucial for the success of a *sanchar* performance is the ethical purity (*povitra*) of the participants. *Sanchar* musicians hold that the quality of their musical expression is intrinsically connected with their respect for the ethical rules stated by the respective *sanchar* schools and communities. They underline that within these musical collectives, performers correct and improve each other both ethically and musically. In addition, the non-professional character of *sanchar* adds to its being regarded as ethically and devotionally superior. *Sanchar* music is performed free of cost and thus simultaneously free of any stigma of a commercial impurity.

## Krishna Guru Parties

Besides *sanchar* groups, so called Krishna Guru Parties – the English term is used in the local vernacular –, musical ensembles honouring the god Krishna, are popular as performers of devotional music in the Bora Sambar region. *A Krishna Guru Party* consists of the following instruments: *khanjani*, the traditional tambourine stretched with the skin of a lizard or contemporary tambourines, stretched with plastic skin; *gini* (small gongs), *kastal* (big gongs), *kubja* (middle sized gongs), *nal* (a kind of combined *tabla* and *dhugi* drum), *mardal* (a small-sized *mrdanga*-like drum made out of clay) and *daskatia* (small wooden sticks played with two hands).

The *mardal* drum is the leading instrument of the Krishna Guru Party. *Daaya*, the left side of the *mardal*, is made out of cowhide, *ekot talli.* The left side is beaten with the plain left hand, while the smaller right side is beaten with four fingers only. The *mardal* drum plays a counter rhythm to the beat of the wooden sticks *daskatia.* The players are usual villagers who exercise with each other out of individual enthusiasm for music and religious devotion. Krishna guru parties are essentially open to everyone – men and women - who likes to participate. However, they consist mostly of older men and occasionally of older women. The music does not require sophisticated instrumental skills or acrobatic movements. Nevertheless, a collectively and rhythmically consistent performance is regarded as a valuable expression of *bhakti* – the local notion of religious and musical devotion. Many times, however, I encountered highly talented singers and players in Krishna Guru Parties, who could easily compete with professional musicians.

In the villages of the Bora Sambar region, Krishna Guru Parties are regularly engaged by the local authorities for educational purposes or for the transmission of information: with their music and songs medical information or methods of family planning are communicated and socio-political measures announced. Thus, dance, song and music are not only used as techniques of religious but also of secular communication of social and cultural meaning.

## *Pala*

*Pala* is a vocal and dance performance popular in the villages of the Bora Sambar region, representing a musical and religious transfer between Hindu and Muslim cultures. Going back to Mughal India (1526-1858), Pala has assimilated the cult of Satya Narayana, an incarnation of Vishnu, with the Muslim *Pir*-worship, the adoration of a living or dead local religious leader, who is supposed to embody a spiritual charisma (Werbner / Basu 1998). Out of these traditions, the mixed character of Satya Pir ("the holy spiritual leader") emerged, who is worshipped simultaneously as both, Narayana Vishnu and a Muslim Pir. The rural *pala* dance performances are intended to worship Satya Pir and to obtain the well being of his followers by means of music, dance and sung narrations. *Pala* performances bear certain similarities to *sanchar*, but differ in costume and in the texts presented by the per formers. Four to six artists participate in the ritual performance: one chief singer, called *bayak*, is accompanied by two side singers who play cymbals (*kastal*) or / and *daskatia* (wooden sticks). The side singers (*palya*) explain the meaning of the sung verses to the audience in a kind of danced panto mime. A bunch of peacock's feathers is held by the main singer (*gayak*). It is called Satya Pir, representing the holy character during the musical performance. One of the side singers embodies the figure of Chamar, a low caste Hindu sweeper. The singers are accompanied by two or three rhythm players (*palya*), who play either a *mrdunga* drum or a slightly smaller drum in the same shape, called *khol*.[118]

Photograph 37: *Pala* performance, Mohurpalli, 2007, L.G.

[118] The difference between the *mrdanga* and the *khol* drum is that the *talli* side of the *khol* drum is only made for 2 fingers and not for the whole hand as on the *mrdanga*.

Photograph 38: *Pala* performance, village Mohurpalli, 2007, L.G

During *pala* performances, Hindus may appear as Muslims, dressing in a Muslim style, wearing for instance long colourful *kurta* shirts, a turban and bloomers. Songs presented in *pala* performances often highlight intersections and similarities between Hindu and Muslim beliefs and forms of worship. A popular narrative recited during *pala* performances, the story about the mythical origin of Satya Pir, may serve as an example:

### *Satya Pir pala*

The story of the birth of Satyapir[119]

*"King Maidan's virgin daughter Satyabati once took a dip in the river.*

*During her dip, she saw a flower floating. She took it, and while smelling the flower's fragrance she became pregnant. As her parents became aware of the fact, they understood it as the most serious offence and drove her away from home.*

*Under orders by Satya Pir, being in the womb of his mother Satyabati, the queen goddess Hanila built a palace for Satyabati where she could give birth to her child.*

*But she has born only a ball of bloody flesh! Satyabati threw it away into the river.*

*At the same moment, a female tortoise came by and swallowed the bloody piece of flesh. Shortly after, the tortoise gave birth to Satya Pir. She passed away after the birth but immediately went to heaven after her death.*

*The newborn was found by Kusaleswar, the Brahmin Purohit (priest) of the place called Maidanab. The Brahmin brought up the baby with great care. After years, when Satya Pir became a grown up and was one day taking a walk on the bank of the river Nur, Satya Pir found a manuscript of the holy book Koran. The Brahmin priest asked him to keep that book in the place where it was found. It should not be touched by anyone. The boy understood that there was no difference between a Purana and the Koran. "Hinduism and Islam are not hostile to each other", he concluded.*

According to oral traditions, the cult of Satya Pir has spread in rural Odisha in the 17th century under the Muslim Mughal reign of the Indian subcontinent. As *pala* performers are mostly Hindus, the *pala* tradition might be seen as the appropriation of socio-cultural influences through enacting. However, performances are directed towards a Moslem and Hindu public. In this sense, the believers in pan-Indian Hindu gods worship the Hindu god Satya Narayana during *pala* performances, whereas local Muslim believers venerate Sa-

[119] Collected by the author at village Mohurpalli, 10 December 2004.

tya Pir. Both are considered by the performers and by the public as interchangeable, as representing two profiles of one divine power.

The performance always begins with the invocation of the Hindu god Satya Narayana, the incarnation of Satya Pir, followed by recitations of Hindu epics and narratives, the *Purana*s, interwoven with poems of different Orya poets. The *pala* songs are often individual compositions of the *pala* artists.

*Pala* is usually performed on *Purnima* day, the day of the full moon, or on festive occasions related to the family and the family's home, as for example house building ceremonies or marriage preparations. *Pala* is also performed during the ritual of *ekusya*. *Ekusya* marks the 21st day after the birth of a child, celebrated in all households of the Bora Sambar region as an auspicious day and as the ritual birthday of the newborn. For the *ekusya* celebration, a *pala* performance is organised by the householder. A high status Brahmin priest conducts the religious performances.

In *pala* performances, the theme of cultural and religious transfer between Hindu, Moslem and local religious ideas is acted out in a lyrical and theatrical fashion; songs and ballads are presented by the singers in a melodious voice and performed in an alluring manner. Local narrations occupy a great part of the performance and the songs and stories are represented in a humoristic and entertaining way. The performers use local dialects and captivate the audience with their colourful dresses and through their skilled polyrhythmic play of the *mrdanga*.

The following transcription of a popular local ballad exemplifies some elements of the cultural and religious transfers and confluences between indigenous traditions and Hindu and Moslem influences:

***Mardagaji Biha Pala***

The marriage ceremony of Mardagaji[120]

*"There was a king named Gajendra. He had one hundred beautiful wives but only one son, called Mardagaji. The king ruled well and Mardagaji passed his time in luxury. He trained to shoot the arrow, played the lute veena and the flute.*

*One day, Mardagaji saw a beautiful woman in his dream. Her eyes resembled the eyes of a deer; her face was like a full moon. In his dream, Mardagaji was so attracted by this beautiful woman that, after*

[120] Collected by the author at Omlipalli village, 20 November 2010.

*waking up, he only urged to get this beautiful dream-woman back and to marry her. This was what he told to his parents. His parents became worried after listening. They proposed him that he might marry hundred beautiful women at once and then start ruling the kingdom. But Mardagaji refused everything. Mardagaji only wanted Sapnabati, the queen of his dream.*

*Queen and king were helpless. In search of help, they took a religious vow which should help to resolve their worries: they vowed to worship only God Satya Narayana in case their son might successfully find his dream girl.*

*Meanwhile, Mardagaji continued to be mentally confused and desperate in his unfulfilled love. He entered the tripatha - the sacred place where three roads cross - of the town Hastinapur. He could however not rest and find his way. In this moment god Satya Narayana in the shape of a beggar Brahmin priest approached Mardagaji. God asked him: "what are you searching?" Mardagaji started to tell him about his quest for Sapnabati, the queen of his dream. "Priest", he asked, "tell me, how can I get her?" Then god revealed his original identity. But Mardagaji could not believe. So, god showed the embodiment of his third incarnation (Avatar-Ramachandra). Then Mardagaji understood and prostrated beneath the feet of god. God said to him to go to the south of Lankapur in order to get his dream queen. Then god disappeared. Afterwards, Mardagaji entered the town kingdom of Maninagpur through the gates of birat nagar and kalinga nagar. Then, the forest Chandrabhaga came. That forest was very dense and dangerous, nobody lived there. However, Mardagaji heard that a bear lived in the forest. He was supposed to kill anyone who crossed his way. The bear was the king of that forest. Mardagaji however did not want to subdue to any threat. He got angry and planned to kill the bear.*

*After some days, Mardagaji found the bear sleeping under a Champa [Flower] tree. However, Mardagaji hesitated to kill the bear, as killing a sleeping animal appeared sinful to him. Thus, he woke up the animal and started fighting against it. It took some time, but finally Mardagaji killed the bear.*

*When the king of that region heard about the killing of the dangerous bear, he became very glad. He announced to marry his daughter Ratnabati with the brave man Mardagaji. Mardagaji thus married Ratnabati but he continued to search for his dream-queen. He left his kingdom to search her. He gathered all possible information about Sapnabati and finally he met her in another kingdom: she was the daughter of Soudagar, a merchant. The merchant however had a severe condition for giving his daughter away for marriage: there was a well in front of his house. Only the man who could fill up the well with rupees, gold or silver might be allowed to marry his daughter. Mardagaji was determined to meet this condition. He found a job for five rupees per month. Per month he put one rupee into the well. One day the daughter of the merchant saw this and thought: "If the young man puts only one rupee per month into the well, it will never be filled up. She prayed to God (Mapuro) to help her. She also went to the Shiva temple. God Mapuro embodied as a hungry Brahmin. He met her and begged for some food. She gave him food, and God showed her his original shape. Sapnabati requested God to fill up the well with golden Rupees in order to be able to marry Mardagaji. She was impressed by his strong will and desire, who experienced so many obstacles to marry her, but who however fervently continued his effort. God heard her wish. Sapnabati thus wrote a letter to Mardagaji that while he will watch the well at early night time [between 3.00 A.M to 6.00 A.M.] the well will be filled up. So it happed. The merchant however hesitated whether to allow a marriage between his daughter and Mardagaji. But finally God interfered and convinced the father to arrange the marriage of his daughter with Mardagaji. So it happened. After seven days passed, Mardagaji announced that he would go back to his own kingdom. On the return journey, Mardgaji with his two wives entered the kingdom of Karnat. A spy (Guptachara) of the king informed the king that - "a thief who has married the merchant's daughter and filled up the well of the merchant has come to our province."*

*After listening to the spy the king became very angry and ordered to arrest Mardagaji. The soldiers attacked Mardagaji. He fought against the king's soldiers and killed many of them. Finally, the king himself started personally to fight Mardagaji. God however sent eighty hundreds tigers to support Mardgaji. The tigers ate all the soldiers. The king was defeated and begged Mardagaji to leave his life. In return, he promised to give him two of his daughters, Chapala and Chanchala, for marriage.*

*Together with his four wives Sapnabati, Ratnabati, Chapal and Chanchala, Mardagaji left the Karnat kingdom. As they all came back to Mardgaji's native place, Mardagaji's mother became very happy to see Mardagaji not only with one but even with four wives! She quickly arranged the Puja ceremony of Satya Narayan to thank and to fulfill her vow."*

The story of Mardagaji and his four wives highlights the value of polygamous marriage, which in the Bora Sambar region is shared by Binjhal communities as well as by Moslem groups. The worship of pan Indian gods Shiva and Satya Narayan hints to the compatibility and convertibility of diverse religious ideas and values. On a local level, they converge in syncretistic religious practice and the shared tradition of *pala*. In its long-winded and detailed account of Mardagaji's errands and the trials and challenges he has to face, the legend is a good illustration of the ceremonious and slowly unfolding rhythm of *pala* narrations. In *pala*, as in many other kinds of local musico-theatrical performances, stories are celebrated rather than told in a straightforward way. For the audience, such performances combine evening and nightly entertainment with religious worship.

## *Pala and the interrelatedness of religions*

The *pala* tradition can be understood as a local attempt to trace and underline the connectedness of different religions. It particularly reflects the influence of devotional or mystical Islam, known as Sufism and connected to the Pir-worship.[121] The Islamic influence in India goes back to around 700 C.E., when the Muslims conquered Sindh – today a province of Pakistan – and first entered Indian soil. The rule of the Afghan sovereign Mahmud of Ghazni (997-1030) demarcates what might be called an Indian-Muslim imperial area. Around 1200 C.E., its administrative centre shifted from Ghazni to Delhi, which then became the focal point of an Eastern Muslim culture, marked by a blossoming of Urdu literature and poetry (Rothen-Dubs 1989: 499-509). The specific features of Sufism were in India influenced by the *bhakti* movement of devotional Hindu tradition. On the basis of his central mystic statement of divine love, Sufism was to some extent able to include the opposing principles of Hinduism and Islam, for instance the opposition between the Hindu caste hierarchy and the Islamic principle of equality. Particularly in the religious Urdu poetry of this age interconnections between Hindu and Muslim religious thought are explored. An example of this religious-literary syncretism are the works of the mystic poet Kabir (early 14$^{th}$ century - 1518), who treats Hindus and Muslims with equal respect, ac-

---

[121] On the history and poetry of Sufism see Annemarie Schimmel (1992).

knowledging that both the Veda and the Koran have an equal religious authority. Kabir is considered a key figure in the shaping of Indian Sufism (see Carpenter 1914: 244-250; 421-465).

Parallel to the traditions of *sanchar* and *Krishna Guru party* as local expressions of the devotional *bhakti* tradition, the theatrical musical *pala* performances of Bora Sambar seem to exemplify the influence of Indian Muslim devotion – Sufism and *Pir*-worship - on a local level. In *pala* sacred Hindu and Muslim traditions are enacted as entangled and of equal spiritual value. The *pala* play itself is a worship of the Muslim Satya *Pir*, without neglecting the Hindu worship to God Narayan. According to explanations of the performers, *pala* is considered a Hindu as well as a Moslem worship. *Pala* thus can be interpreted as a local expression of far-reaching influences of mediaeval Indian Sufism - in terms of a South Asian syncretism - on today's musical and theatrical village traditions. Besides, as an evening village entertainment *pala* is highly appreciated by all representatives of local religions as joyful and humorous.

With *pala,* the mutuality and the interchange between religious and social communities is expressed in a colourful and creative way. In the theatrical and ritual play cultural and religious differences seem rather to be integrated than to be excluded. *Pala* as a rural performing art manifests a play of social and religious harmony, highlighting mutual aesthetic joy and the comparability of local religious and cultural values. While laughing, all participants of the audience recognise their human and social interconnectedness and similarity.

### *Music as part of educational programmes*

In regard of the popularity and attraction of *pala* performances, local N.G.Os (Non-Governmental Organisations) today use the *pala* tradition for the promotion of social and environmental awareness campaigns, thereby putting to their use the traditional local technique of meaning transmission through music, dance and theatre. Thus, the Watershed Project, a N.G.O for irrigation and water problems in draught areas of Odisha, for instance, uses *pala* performances in order to transmit its message about water saving and establishment of irrigation in draught areas in a religiously neutral and integrative manner. Through *pala* performances the organisation's messages are supposed to reach all target groups independent of religious, ethnic or social differences. Currently, a trend seems to become visible in western Odisha that N.G.O.s use musical and stage performances as their preferred medium of socio-cultural awareness. Through the medium of music with its artistic performances, issues of culture preservation, health and environment education are communicated and re-enacted. M.A.S.S. (*Manap Adikar Seva Somiti*/Human Rights Service Organisation), for example, is an N.G.O. active in disaster management, malaria prophylaxis, the formation of self help groups and the organisation of micro-credits in western Odisha. Since 1995, it has systematically used folk song performances and competitions, financed by the Ministry of Human Resources Development, to spread its aims and ideas. Folk art performances have thus become a central medium of socio-political programmes. This trend reveals that with musical and theatrical performances such a *pala*, Krishna Guru party or *sanchar* socio-political as well as religious influences and an internal cultural transfer are mediated. Music and the performing arts furthermore seem to play a certain role in establishing and stabilizing a local socio-cultural harmony between different ethnic and religious groups.

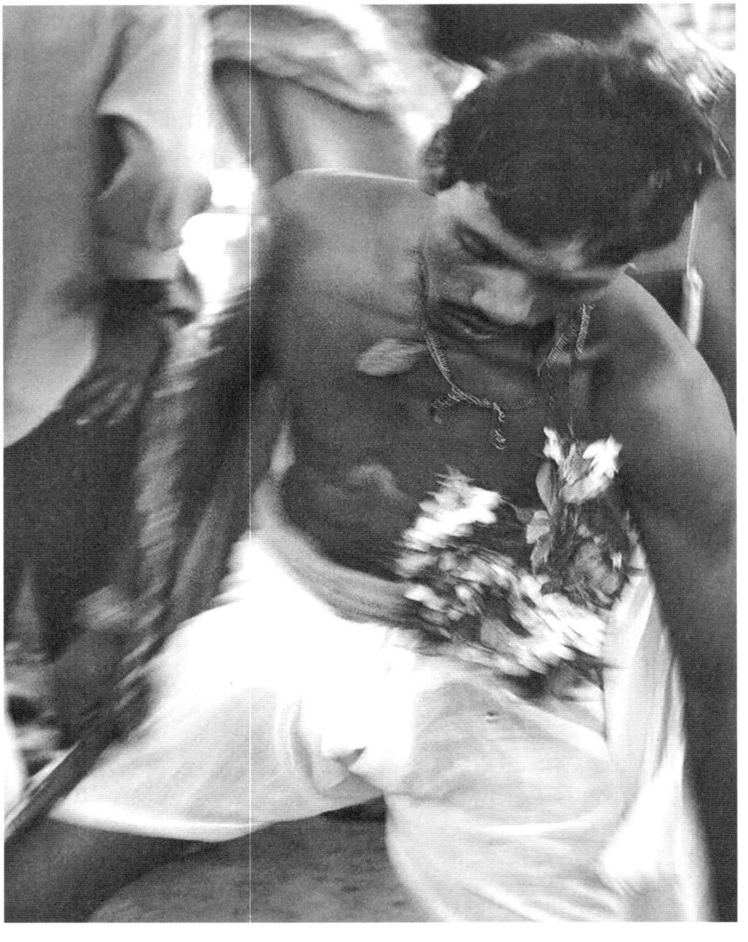

Photographs 39: Entranced *nag baccha*, village Munda palli 2006, L.G.

## Seventh Chapter: Possession and Performance in Western Odisha

Entranced, musically powerful possession rituals and ritual drama performances, loud and amazing in their creative and aesthetic expression, happen frequently in Bora Sambar. Ritual plays artistically connect local traditions with Pan-Indian religious and social concepts. During ritual drama plays, human fates and problems are transformed and enacted on a divine level.

### Nag Bacca - The Snake Children and Their Rituals

*Nag baccha* literally means the "sn

ake children". It is a local trance and possession cult combining the veneration of the snake god Nag - a local deity identified with the Pan-Indian Hindu god Shiva - with male peer group and initiation rituals, indigenous theatre, martial arts performance, music and healing traditions. It is mostly performed by young men from villages with mixed communities of Binjhal, Gond, Mali and Telli. A *nag baccha* group consists of around 25 to 30 young, mostly unmarried men, often of a comparatively fragile and feminine physical appearance. They have joined the group on their own decision and, after having undergone an initiation, are considered "snake children". The group is led by an older guru, an experienced master in the disciplines of *nag baccha*. The group members may belong to different communities from one village or from several neighboring villages.The *nag baccha* group is called by other villages in order to perform healing ceremonies or to bring the blessings of Shiva.

In the months of October (*dusshara*) and December (*maxir*), the *nag baccha puja* is performed on Mondays. Once started, it has to be continued for seven successive Mondays. On the seventh Monday the concluding and most important sequence of the *nag baccha* ritual takes place: the *binu jatra*, the veneration of the snake hole, a possession ritual that finds its climax before the earthen hole of a cobra in the jungle.

Before the start of the *binu jatra*, the members of the *nag baccha* group have to fast for one day. It is told that after fasting the *nag baccha* consume *godd*, an allegedly poisonous substance whose ingredients are kept secret. The taking in of *godd* has various functions. It is a crucial part of the initiation into the *nag baccha* group. Furthermore, it is said to be a counter-poison against snakebites, that when taken in, also bestows healing powers on its consumer. Having digested *godd*, the *nag baccha* are held to have the power to heal snake- and dog bites but also mute- and deafness, barrenness and sufferings induced by the so called bad eyes (*peten korab dusti*), the local term for the envious malevolence of others, and *dondei,* a term generally designating afflictions ascribed to external forces or influences, often translated by locals with the English term witchcraft. With the consumption of *godd*, which is distributed to them by their guru, the young men are also held to gain the knowledge of certain *mantra*s, secret verses or short sayings to which healing power is attributed. In fact, the *mantra*s are taught to the *nag baccha* by their guru. Through *godd*, the young men become initiated religious specialists, healers as well as members of a male peer group.

After *godd* has been consumed, a further preparation for the *binu jatra* takes place: To the sound of the *sulapar* – the sixteen holy rhythms of the trance ritual – performed by the *ganda baja* village orchestra, the *boil biha,* the "spiritual marriage" of the *nag baccha* comes about. In a state of trance, induced by the music of the *ganda baja* each *nag baccha* "marries" his favourite god or goddess, which means that from now on he is considered a medium of the spirit of this deity. In Adivasi Middle India, spiritual marriages are a common symbolic idiom of exchange and communication with the divine realm and of a ritual specialisation.[122] In contrast to the state of *boil* described in the context of goddess spirit possession rituals[123], *boil biha,* the spiritual marriage in *nag baccha,* is not conceived as the establishing of an identity between the medium and the deity that possesses him. It is supposed that the *nag baccha* does not entirely become the god or goddess he embodies but that he acts as a medium for the deity's spirit (*boil asibe nag baccha pila upore*) while retaining his status as therapeutic specialist, who maintains his separate personal identity.

When the *ganda baja* village orchestra begins to play the *sulapar*, the group of the *nag baccha*, surrounded by the villagers, sets out towards the jungle, where the hiding place of the cobra lies. The rhythms of *ganda baja* drive forward the entranced bodies of the *nag baccha* and direct the ritual crowd from the village towards the forest. The musicians guide the divine spirits by their music. On the musicians "*boil will never come - they are too*

---

[122] As described by Vitebsky (1993) for Soara shamanism and by Otten (2010: 33-51) for the ritual healing specialists of the Rona of southern Odisha. "Spiritual marriages" are also a common notion among the Alekh *gurumai*, the female ritual specialist of the new proselytising ascetic religion Mahima Dharma in Koraput (Guzy 2002).

[123] See Chapter 2.

*strong*", a villager explains. The spiritually "untouchable" musicians thus lead the procession.

During the procession, *boil*, the spirit of their respective spiritual spouse, possesses the *nag baccha* men. Villagers, searching cure and advice for their sufferings and ailments, now approach the snake children who, in their trance, are considered oracles and mediums of the divine spirits. But not only do sufferers that seek help approach the *nag baccha*. Also aggrieved and disappointed believers use the *nag baccha* as mediums to address their frustrations and aggressions to deities that did not fulfil their wishes, despite donations they made or severe ritual austerities they underwent. "*Why have you not heard my plead*?" shouts an angry man, "*How much do you want to take from me? I will not give you any more sacrifice! You are a cheater!*" In an alienated, rhythmically interrupted and spasmodically hiccup, a *nag baccha* answers his reproaches: "*Too much doubt in you, too much doubt. Don't look backwards; believe my mantra. I will help!*" The ritual disputation seems to relieve the accuser, and he calms down while the whole procession proceeds on its way deeper into the jungle. At times, the trance of the *nag baccha* men becomes wild and aggressive. They perform uncontrolled movements, often directed against themselves. In this situation, it is the task of the *nag baccha* guru, to take care that the possessed snake children do not hurt themselves during their ecstasy.

At some place on their way to the jungle, the *ganda baja* musicians, who lead the procession, stop. The marching crowd also comes to a halt. Now, a performance of the *nag baccha* unfolds which is part theatre, part display of acrobatics and martial arts and part healing séance. This performance is called *devta khel* - god's play. In the *devta khel* each of the *nag baccha* represents the god or goddess he is held to have embraced in spiritual marriage. In a wild mimicry and pantomime the snake children embody their divine parts. The way in which the entranced *nag baccha* move and behave indicates the personality of the specific spirit (*boil*) which possesses them. On the basis of his gestures and movements, the gods and goddesses represented are immediately recognised by the audience. The divine spirits (*boil*) coming upon the *nag baccha* are said to be those of the following gods:

1) The god Shiva, traditionally symbolised as the aniconic or phallic lingam or snake;

2) his wife Parvati;

3) the Bengali goddess Kali;

4) Ganesh, the elephant shaped god of luck and prosperity;

5) Saraswati, the goddess of education and wisdom;

6) the monkey god Hanuman, the popular and famous supporter of Ram, widely known from the Ramayana epos; as well as

7) Bhairu Dev, the forceful manifestation of Shiva, famous as Bhairava in Nepal and Kashmir – all these deities are widely venerated Pan-Indian divinities of the Hindu pantheon. In contrast

8) Samley, a regional goddess of the Sambalpur district and town;

9) the village goddess Gram Devi;

10) the bloodthirsty goddess Chandi Devi;

11) the snake mother goddess Naga Mata;

12) the fire goddess Agni Kumari and

13) the gods Thakur Dei,

14) Nepur Dei and

15) Bura Raja represent local deities of the Bora Sambar region.

The *guru* of the *nag baccha* group who, contrarily to the other performers, seems very much controlled in his way of acting, mostly represents the spirit of Shiva. Shiva plays the part of a presenter or narrator: he announces which god shall be represented next in the performance. Hanuman, the monkey god, is embodied by an athletic man, who starts acting in an idiosyncratic way: he climbs upon trees, where he greedily devours mango fruits, plays tricks at his fellow performers and scares the audience. The performer of Agni Kumari can be recognised by the spectators as he dances wildly and may jump through a fire which is lightened for the goddess. Parvati, Shiva's wife, can be identified because she always remains by Shiva's side. The performer embodying Kali's spirit symbolizes the goddess by sticking out his tongue. Bhairu is depicted in his persistent efforts to help and assist the other performers. The goddess Chandi introduces herself by uttering her own name. The performer of Ganesh can be identified by the audience, as he feasts on coconuts and advances in circular movements. The goddess Saraswati is characterized by her beautiful dance. The performers possessed by Gram Devi's and Bura Raja's spirit roam around the altar of the respective goddesses. Samley's and Thakur Dei's spirits announce their identities right away. The performer "married" to Nepar Dei's spirit tries to engage the other *nag baccha* in play and jest; and the performer embodying Naga Mata's spirit dances with snakelike movements. The *nag baccha* performance is interwoven with elements of acrobatics and martial arts. With their bodies, the participants spontaneously form human pyramid structures of up to four metres height. They also engage in mock duels, imitating fights while acrobatically avoiding any real bodily collision.[124]

During their performance the snake children are considered as divine oracles and healers. While the *nag baccha* performers are jumping, narrating, dancing or fighting in a state of trance, they are again and again approached by participants of the procession. The *nag baccha* feign to bite those approaching them, in order to suck out their inner poison (*onti*). The symbolical bite is held to be efficient against both mental and physical suffering.

The medical technique of sucking out the poison is in fact the common indigenous remedy for snake bites, which are a frequent accident in the region. The often life threatening snake bites are treated by immediately sucking the poison from the body of the victim, followed by the application of a local antidote made from plants and roots. The *nag baccha* also act as the local medical specialists for the cure of snake bites in everyday life.

*Godd*, the allegedly poisonous substance consumed by the *nag baccha,* is a cultural symbol of danger but also the symbol of a medical and social antidote. In medical terms, *godd* is the counter poison against snake bites; in social terms, it represents the values of courage and body control. After having consumed *godd*, the *nag baccha* are considered "poisonous" by those around them. It is believed that babies up to the age of six months may die when they come into touch with the sweat of the *nag baccha*. In case a suppliant is accidentally bitten by a "snake child" in the symbolic healing procedure of sucking the poison out during the *nag baccha* performance, it is believed, that he is condemned to die soon. The ritual healing during *nag baccha* is thus conceived to be of a highly dangerous character for the help-seekers. The atmosphere between the audience and participants of the procession is at once joy- and fearful. The audience laughs at the theatrical stunts performed by the embodied deities of *nag baccha*. However, the lookers-on are filled with respect and fear when faced with the assumed spiritual and manifest physical powers of the snake children.

---

[124] The mock duels of the *nag baccha* performance are a variety of the regional martial arts performance *bari khel*, where artificial duels avoiding bodily contact are fought with wooden sticks.

The male *nag baccha* group which uses the cultural idiom of trance mediumship symbolises on the one hand the transcendent power of a divine play surpassing human control. On the other hand, on a human and social level, *nag baccha* symbolizes the handling of danger through courage, specialised knowledge and body control, expressed by disciplined athletic and inventive body techniques, such as martial arts, drama performance and acrobatic movement. The initiated *nag baccha* performers also symbolise the ambivalence of power, which is potentially both: curative and deadly, as the healing ritual always contains a risk for the suppliant. The help-seekers are obliged to give themselves over to the ritually and socially constructed authority of the *nag baccha*; otherwise they put their life at risk. In this manner a dangerous sacredness of the healing process and of the healer himself is established, an unquestioned - divine - hierarchy between the healer and the patient.

The *binu jatra* ritual reaches its climax with an animal sacrifice in front of the earthen hole of the cobra. Situated under a big tree it reminds of an oversized mole hole. The rhythms of the *ganda baja* village orchestra speed up and escalate. The proximity to the perilous residence of the cobra raises the tension and fear of the crowd. "*Will the cobra come out*? I think to myself. A musician laughs: "*Our rhythms are strong*", he says, as if anticipating my doubts. He seems self-confident and at ease with the situation.

A male goat is sacrificed to the local goddess Chandi by the *junkar*, the ritual executor of the village in front of the cobra-hole. The temporary altar for the sacrificial act consists only of a stone placed in front of the opening in the ground where the cobra hides. The throat of the sacrificial animal is cut in order to let the blood slowly flow to the earth and into the cobra hole. With the flow of the blood a communication with the divine sphere is established: "*Goddess Chandi likes the blood*", says one villager. The sacrificial donation of a goat may be the fulfilment of a vow (*monosik*) made by the donator – a thank-offering for the granting of a supplication by the goddess. Or it may be a donation intended to enforce a plea made to the goddess. The sacrifice during *binu jatra* thus follows the universal sacrificial logic of *do ut des* (von der Leeuw 1920-1921: 241-253). After the sacrifice, the *nag baccha* and the spectators return to their village in order to prepare the meat of the goat for a common meal. The head of the animal is kept by the *nag baccha guru*, whereas the meat is cooked and distributed between the donator – who may be an individual or a family – and the other villagers.

## *A ritual for goddess Chandi*

The goddess Chandi, to whom the final offering and thus the climax of the ritual *nag baccha* performance is dedicated, according to explanations by villagers, incarnates the Pan-Indian goddess Parvati, the wife of Shiva. In this role she is also referred to as Shivani. In the identification between Chandi and Parvati, a shrewd distribution of roles between Pan-Indian and local deities and a carefully arranged interplay between the respective values they represent becomes visible. 'Officially', the bloody offering which crowns the *binu jatra* ritual is not donated to the Pan-Indian god Shiva, who is customarily honoured with vegetarian or floral donations, but to the local bloodthirsty female goddess Chandi. In this way, the responsibility for the powerful but bloody and thus, in regard to mainstream Hindu religiosity, problematic sacrifice is attributed to the local goddess. But by identifying Chandi with Parvati, Shiva's wife in the Pan-Indian pantheon, her spouse may indirectly profit from the potent bloody offering made according to local traditions. Locals underline that *"neither humans nor gods ever act in isolation but always in relation to each other"*. The divine couple Shiva and Parvati represents the pan-Indian and local ideal model of a relation between family lines, communities and individuals through the cultural institution of marriage (*biha*). In the ritual of *nag baccha* the divine couple also manifests symbolically the interrelatedness of different religious and social traditions: Shiva stands for the Pan-Indian Hindu tradition, where vegetarian sacrifices – coconuts and flowers – are preferred; the goddess Chandi represents the tradition of bloody animal sacrifice, regarded as especially efficient in Adivasi societies. By identifying the local goddess Parvati as the wife of the Hindu god Shiva, both traditions are shrewdly harmonized through the establishment of a matrimonial bond.

## *Becoming a nag baccha*

*"How does one become a nag baccha*?" I asked several *guru*s and members of *nag baccha* groups. All agreed that *"the idea and certainty to be elected to join a nag baccha group emerges through a dream"*. In a dream (*sapna*) the god Nag discloses his identity and calls the young man to serve him. The young man then starts to look for a *nag baccha guru* and group in the surrounding villages. It is only after examining his motives to become a *nag baccha* that the *guru* starts to teach him, to give him knowledge – *sikhya deba*. The term *sikhya deba* refers to the initiation, the teaching and the training of the art of *nag baccha*. Central elements are the knowledge of the secret *mantra*s, the technique of treating snake bites by sucking out the poison

as well as the preparation of herbal medicine, and a set of rules for an ascetic life conduct (*nyam*). The consumption of the allegedly poisonous *godd* – initiates the *nag baccha* as ritual specialists and healers. The *mantras* are secret verses or short sayings which are taught to the *nag baccha* adepts by their guru. Every *mantra* is supposed to heal a particular ailment. They are uttered in a low voice or whisper by the *nag baccha* toward the patients approaching them during the *binu jatra* or other healing performances.

Apart from the great *nag baccha* performances, healing procedures are enacted regularly during the ritual for god Nag. Every Monday (*somwaro*), the day dedicated to the worship of Nag/Shiva, *boil* comes upon the snake children at the altar of the *nag baccha* (*nag baccha gudi/kutti*). Framed by the ritual music of *ganda baja,* the ecstatically moving *nag baccha* then heal snake bites or mental sufferings, which are conceptualised as poisonous substances in the patient's body, by symbolically biting him and sucking the poison out. The art of sucking out the poison is said to rest upon long training and the spiritual advice of the *guru*. After the symbolical biting and sucking, the patient has to consume a medicine based on local roots and plants (*jori buti*). The ritual is then brought to a close with recitations of *mantras*.

Photographs 40: Entranced *nag baccha*, village Munda palli 2006, L.G.

## *Ascetic rules of nag baccha*

Each "snake child" is required to follow a set of strict rules of life conduct (*nyam*), which includes the following restrictions:

1) The *nag baccha* do not take any medicine from an urban doctor.
2) During the days of ritual performances the *nag baccha* have to abstain from meat.
3) *Nag baccha* have to restrain from fruits categorised as heating up (*kudru*), as for example the mango fruit.
4) Nag *baccha* have to abstain from long vegetables (*purdha*).
5) They are not allowed to take popcorn rice (*murhi*) from any other than their own household.
6) They are not allowed to accept cooked rice from others.
7) Before a *nag baccha* can perform a *binu puja*, he has to fast on the 7 preceding Mondays.
8) A *nag baccha* is not allowed to sleep in any kind of bed, but has to sleep on the ground.
9) A snake child has to consult his patient with an empty stomach; after the consultation and healing ritual the *nag baccha* must wash extensively.

These restrictions indicate important elements of the conceptions related to *nag baccha*. The interdiction to approach an urban doctor signifies a rejection of the urban medical systems and consequently a general rejection of the use of Western medicine. It can be understood as a challenge to medical authorities that indicates a strong self-consciousness and a firm belief in the effectiveness of the *nag baccha's* own practice of therapy. The temporary abstinence from meat in a society which values the meat of goats or fishes as delicacies, points to the common ritual idiom of temporary ascetic practice and vegetarianism connected to ritual specialisation, which is often found in Middle Indian Adivasi societies.[125] Abstinence from meat is considered instrumental to gain perceptive clarity and in consequence ritual effectiveness. The idea of pursuing psycho-physical self control through dietary restrictions is also expressed in the subsequent prescriptions. The idea of abstaining from fruits which are considered to "heat-up" the human body as well as from long and thus "phallic" vegetables is directed at a curbing of erotic sensuality. The prohibition of eating popcorn rice prepared by others hints to general notions of the capacity of food to transport "impurity". In the South

---

[125] Such as for example the Desya of Koraput (Berger 2001; Guzy 2002, Otten 2008)

Asian idiom of "purity and impurity" food transactions are generally conceived as dangerous. Food is not 'dead' or static. It has the capacity to take upon itself and thus to transport the dynamic substances of the "purity" or "impurity" of the food donor or cook, which in consequence affect the person digesting it. Particularly in cooked form, food is susceptible to the fluidum of "impurity". Uncooked food therefore can be more easily shared. *Murhi* – the popcorn rice is commonly considered in Odisha as resistant to the transfer of impurity. However, the *nag baccha* even resist from accepting *murhi* from any other than their own household. In this way, they underline their own extraordinary rigor in observing ritual cleanness and purity rules. The principle of commensalism within one's own household, community or caste is held to be basic to maintain protection from impurity and represents fundament of the Hindu caste hierarchy[126] as well as a basic social structure of the communal logic of Adivasi societies.[127] The idea of food purity is also underlined in the *nag bacca*'s rule of receiving patients with an empty stomach and to wash themselves after the therapy. In this way, a potential transfer of digested food substances from the *nag baccha* to the patient shall be avoided. The patient can thus be sure to address his ailments and sorrows to a truly pure – and thus effective - healer. The complete inner purity of the *nag baccha* is also held to heighten his capacity to absorb the psycho-social "dirt", the psychological suffering, of the patient. That he has taken this "dirt" upon him and inside himself is the reason, why the *nag baccha* has to wash himself extensively after his therapeutic procedure.

The asceticism of the *nag baccha* is on the one hand based on the creation of purity and ritual cleanness, on the other hand on the overcoming of fear, indicated by the rejection to use beds, which is highly dangerous due to the widespread peril of snakes that, moving on the ground, enter human dwellings especially in the night time. The *nag baccha* tradition is a practice of male peer groups to develop the values of purity, courage and psychophysical power in order to control "inner impurity", namely sexual and in a wider sense sensual impulses and fear as well as external danger. In overcoming their own frailty, fear and bodily inconveniences the *nag baccha* are supposed to transcend the problems of others.

---

[126] On the connection between food, eating, commensalism, connubialism and caste hierarchy, see Dumont (1986:168-195); on food substances, impurity and caste, see Marriott (1968: 133-172); on food as a potential bearer of pollutants, see also Douglas (1966: 33-35, 127).

[127] An impressive example of commensality of food as a central value for an Adivasi society, is given in Peter Berger's ethnography of the Gadaba of South Orissa (2007: 28-46).

Photographs 41: *Nag baccha* while treating a patient, Munda palli 2006, L.G.

Photograph 42: A *nag baccha* while enquiring the divine sphere, Munda palli 2006, L.G.

## *Conclusion*

The trance mediumship cult of *nag baccha* is an example of a possession cult, as they are vastly spread in cultures of orality. *Boil* in *nag baccha* seems on the one hand to represent a specific state of empowerment, giving the performers extraordinary forces to exert an influence on those surrounding them, an influence that rises to the capability to heal psychological or physical disorders and alleged or real poisoning. On the other hand, it is a highly exclusive category as *boil* is not supposed to come upon everyone, but only upon "*nyam loko*", the initiated, knowledgeable and devoted religious specialists. *Boil* in *nag baccha* seems thus to represent a distinctive state of social and religious power of its young male performers. But this state reveals itself as highly ambivalent: male and female, authoritative and healing, precarious and always potentially dangerous both for those attending the performance as for the performers themselves.

In *nag baccha* rituals the idea of evil and its handling is expressed in the cultural idiom of poison and antidote – *godd* and its handling during the creative trance state of *boil*. Evil, in the local context, seems to represent a dangerous sphere of the totally Other, imagined as the sacred and represented by the dangerous cobra snake. This kind of evil is not "evil" in a oral sense, but a perilous Otherness. In the local mythology the cobra is sacred as this reptile has an enormous digestive power (it can devour cows) and - like all snakes – it lives as well under the earth as above the surface.[128] The cobras' persistent transfer from a subterranean "underworld" where the dead are supposed to live and the sphere of the humans above makes this reptile both dangerous and holy. The dialogical encounters between the entranced *nag baccha* and the disappointed believers in the course of the *binu jatra* may be seen as a kind of practical theodicy, a performative justification of the embodied divine in the face of individual suffering and frustration. The *nag baccha* tradition is a local practice to deal with suffering, and thus an example of a local healing tradition, based on ritual music, trance-mediumship and the factual and symbolic removal of the individual psycho-social suffering as well as the real poison of snake bites. In this context it is significant to note that a certain vulnerability and receptiveness seems prerequisite for acting as a *nag baccha*. Compared to the musicians, at whom "*boil will not come*" for they are spiritually "*un-touchable*" and thus strong, the snake children are young, unmarried, often feminine and sensitive men who due to their socio-psychological fragility are held to be especially receptive towards the divine. This vulnerability and psychological receptiveness becomes the basis for the ritual effectiveness of the snake children: touched by their spiritual spouses (*boil biha*) they transform their vulnerability and frailty into power and the capacity to heal others. The performance of *nag baccha* turns out to be double-sided: On the one hand it celebrates the value of trance, in terms of a rejection of human control as a sign of divine presence. On the other hand the value of the control of the body is celebrated through ascetic rules and athletic exercises. Another notable feature of double-sidedness or ambivalence in the *nag baccha* performance is the simultaneity and intermingling of tension, fear, danger and a forceful presence of the divine with humoristic elements and outright comedy. The presence of joyful and humorous elements in the performance of the *nag bacca* constructs dynamics of tension and relaxation that are likely to contribute to the psychological and physical relief the patients experience during the ritual play.

[128] In the Bora Sambar region, as all over India, snakes are generally worshipped as divine manifestations.

Photographs 43: *Nag baccha* while treating a patient, Munda palli 2006, L.G.

## *Sobri Sobren Lila*

Another devotional performance with strong elements of comedy and hilarity is the musical and theatrical play - *lila* - of Sobri and Sobren. The play centres around a local version of an episode derived from the Pan-Indian Ramayana epos. It tells the story of Sobri and Sobren, an Adivasi couple of the Soara community, who meet the god Rama during his exile in the forest. The oral tradition of narrative and theatrical transmissions of the Ramayana epos has over time generated a diversity of variations on its motifs, with manifold local versions and plots all over India, which are enacted as *lila* – as dramatic and religious "plays of the gods" (Sax 1995, 2002). As far as I could enquire in the course of my research, the Sobri Sobren *lila* is today practised only in one single village of the Bora Sambar region – representing thus a unique local tradition.

In the village Bolongakot, inhabited by around 200 multi-community households of Mali, Telli, Lohar, Gour, Kulta and Saora communities, Sobri Sobren *lila* is performed on occasion of marriages (*biha*) and for the worship of diverse deities. Thus for the worship of goddess Oila (*Oila puja*) during the month of *kartika* (September); for the celebration of *Rama nowomi,* the birthday of god Rama on the ninth (*nowomi*) day of the month *chaitra* (August), and generally for any religious worship (*sabu puja pai*) such as for the local goddesses Bihari Path Devi, Boranga Path Devi, Kodel Path Devi, Bausen Path Devi, Thakur Devi Rakot Mauli Devi, Mauli Ma, Buri Samley or Dhan Mauli Devi. In recent years, the Sobri Sobren *lila* has been represented at some urban folklore festivals (*Loko Mohatsav*) in Sambalpur town by a group of performers from the village.[129]

The Sobri Sobren *lila* is enacted exclusively by male lay performers of all ages. The male performers and singers thus also embody female parts in the play: their faces are powdered and artistically rouged, and they wear their long hair open or as a pony tail. With their feminine attitude, Sobri Sobren *lila* artists follow the common traditional practice of rural artists (*kolakar*) to switch gender codes during their performances.

Apart from the gender of the actors, there are no obvious restrictions or necessary ritual preparations for the performers. The only pre-condition for a Sobri Sobren *lila* to take place on one of the occasions outlined above is that a sufficient number of male villagers come to gether which are inclined to masquerade, sing and perform in front of the community. Apart from the

---

[129] On the *Loko Mohatsav* festivals see chapter 8.

core roles of Sobri, Sobren and the god Ram, the characters depicted in a performance may vary. A performer may choose impromptu to embody a certain figure from the Ramayana Epic, for example Hanuman, the ape god, Lakshmana the younger Brother of god Rama or Ram's wife Sita. The performers representing the diverse goddesses and gods from the Ramayana dress up in fantasy costumes of their own invention and are sometimes equipped with props associated with the diverse deities, such as the thunderbolt for the god Brahma, the trident for the god Shiva and a wedge symbolising the god Hanuman. The players embodying Sobri and Sobren masquerade and make up themselves with furs, bows and arrows, in caricaturesque Adivasi-style costumes. The actor who represents the god Rama has his face coloured blue, as this colour is widely considered the symbol of Rama's divinity (Blank 1992).

Photographs 44: Sobri Sobren *lila* at Borongakot, 2007, L.G.

If a sufficient number of male villagers has assembled in the right mood, the Sobri Sobren *lila* may start. Sobri Sobren *lila* performances are supposed to be enacted purely out of joy without any pay – only then are they considered a religious worship. The *lila* has no fixed choreography or story line, but is an impromptu musical and vocal play with invented rhymes and songs, presenting variations on mythological themes. Songs are improvised while the story of Sobri and Sobren is narrated and sung by the performers. The story itself is rudimentary: Sobri and Sobren go into the jungle in order to hunt and to collect fruits and berries. There, they meet the gods Rama, Lakshma and Hanuman and support and advice them in their battle against the demon Ravanna. The Sobri Sobren *lila* thus consists of melodious songs and narrative ballads, accompanied by village instruments such as *kanjoni, dand dhol* and *kastal*.

Photographs 45: Sobri Sobren *lila* at Borongakot village, 2007, L.G.

Photographs 46: Sobri Sobren *lila* at Borongakot village, 2007, L.G.

The performers embodying the various personas and deities, play and sing their improvised songs and ballads while promenading through the village, frequently mocking women and children from the audience. The actors as well as their audience laugh about the narrated and sung jokes, which are a crucial part of the performance. The whole village enjoys the masquerade and village parade expressing in this way the ritual value of laughing.

A Sobri Sobren *lila* performance usually takes about two hours. It lasts until the variations of the story of Sobri and Sobren and the inventive energy of the performers are exhausted.

The strong presence of humour, laughter and jokes[130] reveals a facet of local religious devotion and a specific way of the veneration of the local as well as of the pan-Indian gods and goddesses in Bora Sambar. While in South Asia *lila*-narrations and plays based on parts of the Ramayana epic and plays are a common practice of oral tradition, the Sobri Sobren *lila* is quite unique in its focus on the roles of the mythical Adivasi couple.

---

[130] For an outline of the anthropology of laughter and humor see Apte 1985.

## *Dand Nacho*

*Dand nacho* designates a further local ritual theatre play, widely popular in the Bora Sambar region. *Dand nacho* (*nacho*= theatre / dance) is often referred to simply as *dand*, *dand lila* or *nila*. It is a compendium of narrations and ballads about the love between Radha and her divine lover Krishna. As the night time is considered the time of Krishna's amorous activities, the play usually starts around 11 pm and ends at about 5 am in the morning. The nightly play is a vibrant interplay between musical brilliancy, poetry and highly sophisticated artistic aesthetics, performed by professional stage artists who play the particular gods.

Originally however, *dand nacho* refers to a sequence of two ritual theatrical plays, the first of which today is only rarely performed due to its austere character. The first part of the original sequence is the *pen dand* (*pen*=gods; *dand* = expiation, penalty), a ritual dance theatre performed exclusively by male volunteers calling themselves *danduas*, and considered religious devotees (*bhakta*). It is traditionally performed in the Indian summer month *choit* and *boisako* (April/ Mai), during the hottest time of day, as an expression of particular devotion for the Pan-Indian goddesses Kali, Parvati and for the god Shiva. Today, *pen dand* performances can only occasionally be encountered in Bora Sambar as a ritual practice performed for obtaining religious merits and for the realisation of religious vows (*manosik*). During my research in the region from 2002 on, I was only able to witness three *pen dand* performances. "*Young men reduce today a lot of parts and the ritual character of dand*", older locals complain. Only some old men claim that they have frequently performed all parts of *dand*, including the *pen dand*. "*In earlier times a* dandua *only could eat small snacks* (tifin) *during the day; during* pen dand *he never was allowed to touch any water* (kahari pen ni chion)*"* they remember the traditional ritual rules (*nyam*) for *pen dand,* implying that today they are no longer followed with appropriate severity.

The second part of the *dand nacho* sequence is the nightly play *dand lila*, depicting the amorous entanglements of Krishna and Radha, which today enjoys great popularity as an independent performance. In former times, locals tell, the nightly entertainment of *dand lila* was also performed by the *danduas*, the lay performers of the ritualistic *pen dand* daytime part of the sequence. Today however, the *dand lila* is performed by highly professional *dand* troupes consisting of male and female actors. Many of my interlocutors underlined the kinship between the *dand nacho* of Bora Sambar and the *dand nato* performance tradition of southern and eastern Odisha. But even if similarities can be traced between the *dand nato* in southern Odisha, which has extensively been documented by Burkhard Schnepel (2000: 156-171; 2008), the *dand nacho* I encountered in the Bora Sambar region seems to have a particular and distinct character: Whereas the ethnography of *dand nato* in southern Odisha discloses a sophisticated and coherent ritual drama tradition, the *dand nacho* practice of Bora Sambar has a much more fragmentary appearance. Even if these fragments are grouped together by local oral tradition, they today have each developed a life of its own, which would make the reconstruction of a supposedly original *dand nacho* ritual drama sequence largely hypothetical.

## *Etymology and myths of origin*

Etymologically, *Dand nacho* refers to expiation and penalty. *Danda* is a Sanskrit word designating a stick that symbolizes castigation for committed misbehaviour or sins. As Burkhard Schnepel (2008: 21) has pointed out, *Dando* can be associated with the stick of a father or king who punishes his children. An old villager tells the following myth about the origin of *dand nacho*:

> *After goddess Parvati had killed two demons, she returned home. On her way home, she met her husband Shiva. He was in a very angry mood, lying on the road and shouting. When Parvati saw this, she became furious and stepped on Shiva's right leg. She immediately became Kali. Shiva felt humiliated being stepped on by Kali and he punished Parvati. He said to his wife: as a penalty you have to go to your brother's villages and you have to perform dand for punishment. Only after performing dand in 13 villages you will get mukhti, the release of your sins and thus salvation.*

Another myth elaborates another version of the penalty and expiation motive:

> *Taranga Rusi had 14 sons. He once came with all his 14 sons in order to destroy the holy fire jagia. At that moment, Brahma came and punished all 14 sons of Tarangi Rusi. All became infected with leprosy. They then went to lord Shiva to the hills of Kapilas in order to pray. During their meditation the demon Ohing Asur ate one of the sons and thus only 13 were left. Shiva wanted to kill all the sons, but his wife Parvati interfered: "you should not kill them, but you should punish them". While she was telling this, a wooden stick rose from Parvati's*

*left hand. With this stick, she gave a light blow to each of the remaining 13 sons. After her beating, they were cured from leprosy.*

*Rusi Turunga came happily to Shiva when hearing about this incident. He promised Shiva to remember this event during dand in the month of choit.*

## *Pen dand – the dance of penalty*

*Pen dand,* the first part of the *dand nacho* dance play sequence, is conceived as a performance in honour of the goddess Dokini Kali, a local manifestation of the goddess Kali. It is a dance drama of expiation and penalty, considered to be a very harsh kind of divine worship (*kasta puja*). The rare contemporary *pen dand* performances have the character of parts and fragments of an imaginary narrative and performative whole. *Pen dand* is performed after *purnima*, the full moon during the Indian summer month *choit* (April) and *boisako* (Mai) for 7 to 15 consecutive days. The performance has to take place at midday, in the hottest time of the day, when temperatures may rise to over 48 degrees Celsius. The exposure of the *danduas* to extreme temperatures and the burning sun is an essential element of the ascetic and self-chastising character of the *pen dand* performance which may last for up to three hours. *Pen dand* is performed mostly by childless men as part of a religious vow to practice austerity and severe spiritual and physical exercise in order to get progeny. By the vow of *dand* a man commits himself to perform *pen dand* for seven consecutive years. The completion of a seven years commitment is believed to lead to fertility and a large number of children. A *pen dand* group consists of 10 to 25 lay performers, who are considered as *bhakta*s, ascetic devotees enacting a ritual story of penalty and expiation. It is led by the *pen dand guru*, usually an older member of the group, who orchestrates the parts of the performance. For a *pen dand* performance to take place, it is prerequisite that a certain number of men – at least about ten – come together, who have taken a vow to perform *pen dand* during seven consecutive years. Besides the austerity of the performance it is the difficulty to meet this condition that has contributed to the vanishing of the *pen dand* tradition in recent years. A second precondition for the performance is the invitation through an "inviter" (*boron*). The inviter sponsors the props and materials for the performance as well as the food for the performers and thus "invites" the ritual drama play to his village. Usually, the ritual "inviter" of *pen dand* is a rich person with a "strong house" – which in the Bora Sambar region means a concrete and brick house with more than one floor, in contrast to the widespread one floor mud houses with partial brick structures.

Through the performance of *pen dand* which starts in front of his house the "inviter" gains religious merits and may fulfil a personal vow.

During the days of the pen dand, the *dandua*s have to fast (*upvas*) – only in the evening, after the performance they are allowed to take some food. As a preparation for the performance, they perform *puja* (worship) connected, as in other rituals of the Bora Sambar region, to sixteen "divine stories" (*sula kunja*) of different deities. Again, the taxonomic number sixteen is encountered in this *puja*. The worship for the goddess Kali and for Shiva, who are particularly venerated, is expressed in special songs for these deities (Shiva *bandana*; Kali *bandana*) sung by all the *dandua*s. The moment to start the performance is chosen by the *pen dand guru*. To initiate the performance, the inviter of the *pen dand* worships the *danduas* by sprinkling water over their feet. Besides the invitation by water, the ritual beginning of the play is marked by the lighting of four *danda*, clay sticks filled with straw, by the *pen dand guru*. This sequence is also referred as *homo,* the ritual fire. From this fire, the *pen dand* performers lighten a rice straw crown *(benthya*). The straw crown is believed to be ignited by Brahma Agni, the God of fire. The fire has to be kept alive for the duration of the *pen dand* performance. A *pen dand* performance has no fixed story-line or choreography, but emerges from a repertoire of elements. The parts actually performed are chosen according to the inspiration of the actors and the demands of the spectators. Key elements of this repertoire are stories of deities and stories of agrarian labour, which are presented in songs and an elaborate body theatre; acrobatic performances like body-pyramids (*deul bandana*); and the imposition of – often painful and humiliating – tasks on the *dandunas* by the audience. The roles in the ritual play are not fixed but adopted impromptu by the performers, according, as they report, to divine inspiration.

The *pen dand* performance begins in front of the "inviter's" house and later proceeds to the centre of the village. The stage of the ritual play is shaped by the bodies of the *dandunas,* demarcating the scene on the sand (*duli*) in the middle of the village. During the performance, the *dandua*s are almost naked, only wearing a kind of traditional underwear, the *dhoti*, consisting of a cotton fabric wound around the waist. The players carry umbrella- or banner-like structures with them, symbolizing various divine personalities. These props of up to two metres height are made of black or white fabric or paper, mounted on wooden frames. A black banner, named *porba,* is associated with the goddess Kali; other deities as the village goddes *gram devta* or the god Shiva are symbolized by a white banner, the *chotor*. Further props carried by the *dandunas* include a trident, the *trishul*, which is associated with the role of the god Bairava, the gatekeeper of Shiva; a burning straw (*betua*), an earthen pot (*astro sombo*) and a wooden stick of an arm's length (*danda*). A central element of *pen dand* is the body performance *bina basi*. By waving the *danda* stick and striking up introductory songs, called *bina-kar*, one of the performers initiates this sequence of the ritual play. The other players then, by means of pantomime and physical mimicry accompanied by songs, begin to enact or rather literally to embody certain stories such as the popular agrarian narration of the ancient farmer (*holia*) and his wife (*holen*). The story begins with the farmer couple demarcating a field in the middle of the village, which is represented by a quadrangular body structure formed by the *dandunas*. The performers then plead to the god Kuver, the local god of farming, for the tools and seeds needed for cultivation. They finally plough the field three times, until a wild pig breaks in and eats all their seeds. The performers designate the corporeal structures they enact as sentences (*kata*) made up of the single bodies of the *dandunas*, which are understood as scriptual signs (*kia*). The narrations presented in *pen dand* are thus "body-stories" in the full sense of the word. Another crucial element of *pen dand*, which stresses the expiatory character of the ritual play, is the imposition of tantalising and painful tasks on the *danduas* by the village audience. Such tasks imposed on the *danduas* may include:

1) to collect stones from the road;
2) to clean the village road;
3) to fill the road with heavy iron pieces needed for road construction;
4) to roll oneself around in the hot sand of the midday (*dholiba*);
5) to construct a temple (*mandir*) by forming a pyramidal structure with their bodies (*deul bandana*);
6) to purify the body temple with their bodies;
7) to make Shiva bath in the body-temple;
8) to represent Hanuman eating fruits. The *bhakta* are supposed to eat symbolically the leaves of a tree;
9) to wash the grains in the fields;
10) to compose a lotus flower with their bodies symbolizing meditation.

After the *pen dand* has lasted for about three hours in the heat of the summer's midday, two hens are sacrificed by a village priest (*dehuria*) for the goddess Kali. One of the *danduas* carries a black *chotor* banner around to indicate the end of the day's performance. In the evening, the *dandua*s are allowed to rest at the pond and to take some food, sponsored by the "inviter" (*boron)* of *pen dand.*

In a similar fashion the daily performances are continued for a period of 7 to 15 days. The overall length of *pen dand* is dependent on the decision of the *pen dand guru* as well as on the sponsoring capacities of the *boron*.

When the *pend dand* reaches its last day, all *chotor* used in *pen dand* are thrown away. This is a ritual necessity as the *chotor* have been representing the sacred images of goddess Kali or Durga, which outside the ritual transform back to useless wooden structures. As these wooden structures have however already "touched" the sacred sphere, they are still ambivalent and might be dangerous for the living if used in every day life. The destruction of the former ritual requisites prevents the misuse and misdirection of these vessels of the divine energy against humans.

Agrarian stories centring on the hardships of cultivation and the cultivation process where favourite topics in the *pen dand* performances I witnessed. They represent basic experiences, ideas and values of an agrarian community such as the cycle of the seasons, hard bodily work and discipline and the sometimes benevolent sometimes hostile forces of nature. These stories are "body-stories" both in their representation of physical labour as well as in their representation of a sophisticated body-culture and language. The central role of the body in the ritual theatrical composition of expiation and penalty in *pen dand* has also been underlined by Burkhard Schnepel in his work on *dand nato* in southern Odisha. He particularly accentuates the role of the body as a human paper on which cultural ideas are inscribed (Schnepel 2008: 120-123). Schnepel identifies "*patiency*" as the central quality of the *dandua*s' bodies - a capacity of empathy, to embody the divine powers which are corporally absorbed and re-enacted (Schnepel 2008: 123-125). In this way the passive bodies demarcating the stage, the field and diverse structures in *pen dand* serve as a platform on which "social dramas"[131] unfold.

Childlessness, one has to keep in mind, is considered an extremely serious misfortune in the rural society of the Bora Sambar region: It is seen both as an individual failure and as a divine penalty or curse. Most of the *danduas* whose biggest wish is to get children, thus suffer under grave social pressure and presumably a feeling of personal inferiority, when they engage in per-

---

[131] In terms of the model of Victor Turner, a social drama implies the phases of 1) breach; 2) crisis 3) redressive actions and 4) reintegration (Turner 1957; 1974; 1982)

forming *pen dand*. This personal situation seems to reflect itself in the virulence of the performance and in the severity sometimes amounting to violence of the ritual dramatic exercises the *danduas* undergo. According to the analysis of "social drama" outlined by Victor Turner, one might observe that by becoming a *dandua*, the performers enter a state of liminality, a ritually vulnerable state of being "betwixt and between" (Turner 1964: 4-20), or, to be more precise, that their liminal and precarious state as childless men is expressed in a ritual idiom. The half naked appearance of the *danduas* physically underlines this vulnerability. The demanding tasks imposed on the performers by the audience, which are carried out under extreme outward conditions, inflict real corporeal suffering on the *danduas*. In this collective choreography of individual pain and expiation, the dramatic elements of crisis and redressive action become manifest. The ordeal they undergo, on the other hand, gains the performers the esteem and admiration of their audience. They are no longer considered as men with a personal shortcoming but are respected as religious devotees (*bhakta*). A social reintegration takes place which not least is a restoration of the performer's self-respect.

## *Dand lila at night*

In contrast to the vanishing tradition of the austere ritualistic *pen dand* performed by lay devotees, the professional nightly *dand nacho / dand lila* performances seem to enjoy an ever increasing popularity in the Bora Sambar region. In the darkness, vibrant sounds of *dand* music can be heard. Melodious ballads, colourful costumes and beautifully made-up female and male performers fill the quadrangular stage (*mandoli*) erected for the nightly performance or simply the central place of the village where the artists start to perform. Around them, the village population assembles. In the crowd, the men significantly outnumber the women. The nightly scene with its colours, sounds, melodious voices and sensual movements of the dancing actors merges into a frivolous sometimes obscene performance full of musical virtuosity. The delightfully dressed and made-up actress embodying Krishna's lover Radha evokes the night-time fantasies of her male audience. The spectators seem exhilarated about Krishna's divine urge for Radha's love and the cunning tricks he plays to win her favour. The audience is joyfully entertained by the sensual allusions, gestures and movements of the performers, especially by the wild *dalkhai* dance movements of Radha. The energetic and escalating music of *dand* fuels the nocturnal excitement.

*Dand* music consists of a *ganda baja* orchestra with the *dholya*, the musician playing the *dhol* drum, taking a central part in the performance. The *dhol* drum used for *dand* is a specific instrument: Contrary to the common *dhol* of the *ganda baja* orchestra, the *dand dhol* drum is not made of wood, but of clay, and is slightly bigger than the usual *dhol*. The sound of the *dand dhol* has thus a bright and insistent resonance. Besides the common *ganda baja* instruments such as *nissan, timkiri/tasa, jumka* and *mohuri* modern instruments as clarinets, trumpets, keyboards and harmoniums may be used. The central musical performer is, however, the *dand dholya* who, during the whole nightly performance, is exposed as the musical hero of the play. With his rhythms, by which he introduces and accompanies the different artists entering the stage, he leads and drives forward the performance. The sound and rhythms of the *dand dhol* are held to transform the human personalities of the artists into embodiments of the deities whose roles they perform. During the play, the *dholya* is addressed as *mamu*, the mother's brother, by the other artists, who thus ascribe the influential but also intimate position of a maternal uncle to him.

"*Through the dand dhol beats the artists become gods*", explains a spectator, "*after greeting (namaskar) the gods through the music, all artists become boil*!" During their performance, the bodies of the artists become the body divine. The demarcated stage extends and moves with the movements of the artists, being transformed into a dynamic stage and a temporary moving altar of divine bodies. *Dand lila* performances are traditionally intended to be played on 16 consecutive nights, depicting 16 love stories of Radha. Today however, as the plays are usually performed by professional *dand* troups, the story cycle is mostly reduced to seven nights. *Dand nacho* troups consists of around 10 to 15 professional performers. A *dand nacho* performance is mostly organized and paid for by a village headman or a rich man, as an expression of his or the village's devotion for the Pan-Indian goddesses Kali, Parvati and for the god Shiva.

## *The characters*

The main characters of the dance drama are Radha and Krishna. One of the *dand* artists explains:

> *Radha means 'the great devotee'. When Radha was a baby she was very ugly, so she was thrown away by her parents into a pond. Radha's father was Supoko, Rathas mother was Supowa. After being thrown into the pond, Radha was however saved by a lotus flower where she remained 16 days. In the lotus flower she transformed into a beautiful woman.*

*Krishna then designed the fate of Radha: He arranged a marriage between her and Chandrasana, a hermaphrodite, in order to have a legitimate reason to start a love affair with her. Duti is a female mediator between Radha and Krishna. She will be punished in the play - as in fact she is not a real mediator between Radha and Krishna. Duti is intriguing a lot, not knowing how to act with Krishna and Radha in a proper manner.*

*Tetel is Chandrasana's sister. It is a humorous role. Tetel always makes jokes. Tetel is not married. Tetel and the dholya communicate easily with each other [=they flirt].*

*Chandrasana, however, is Radha's husband. As both Radha and Chandrasana have an unhappy marriage life, both are tragic characters.*

An old *dand dholya* tells another version of Radha's mythical story:

*Radha's father was the king Nilson Raja. Radha was his adopted daughter.*

*Radha's real mother and father were Sopokpa and Suprabha.*

*When Radha was a child she was extremely ugly with a rough figure. This is why her parents wanted to get rid of her, to throw her away. They thus put the small child into a small pot (monjusa). This small pot was thrown into the river, where it was stopped through a lotus flower. 16 days long the small girl stayed in the lotus flower. After the 16 days the pot broke suddenly.*

*At that time Nislon Raja was hunting and saw the small baby girl inside the lotus flower and took her with him. Radha became his daughter. Radha grew up to a most beautiful woman. Brahma then gave her white clothes (omblana bastra) [a symbol of inner purity and external chastity].*

According to the myths and narrations, Radha is supposed to represent the ideal woman: beautiful, seductive - chosen as the object of Krishna's erotic desires, but pure and chaste in her deepest inside. Krishna seems intoxicated by his corporal desire for Radha, playing out his divine powers as well as his boyish charm to obtain what he wishes for. With his cunning devices to win Radha for himself, he incorporates the powers of a trickster. Tetel as Krishna's sister depicts a scheming character. She quarrels a lot, and often adopts a vulgar tone in her communication with the *dand dholya* and Chadrasena. Chandrasena is an ambivalent personality. He is neither man nor woman, with no desire for Radha but often offensive, provoking and obscene in his responses to the other characters. The *dand lila* is always acted in the vein of comedy, focussing on the sensual side of divine and human life.

Photograph 47: *Dand dholya* master Biranchi Luha, Moturpalli village, 2007, L.G.

## *The artists*

*Dand* artists (*kolakar*) are professional male musicians, mostly from subaltern communities such as the Ganda or Gansya as well as professional male and female actors coming from local communities such as Binjal, Soara and Ganda. A common characteristic of *dand* artists is that they already wear the stigma of "outsiders" when joining a *dand* ensemble. Nearly all professional *dand* artists have critical biographies: women have often left their husbands and live with an actor partner; men have married out of love a partner of their own choice, a decision which in rural Bora Sambar as well as in the whole of Hindu India is almost inevitably followed by stigmatisation and social exclusion. Breaking religiously and socially sanctioned family rules - such as the rule of arranged marriage within one's own caste or local community – is seen as a severe disregard for the good of one's own family. The consequence of such individual (mis)behaviour is that the rule-breakers are expelled from their families. They are categorised as "socially dead"- with symbolic funeral rites performed for them by their family. Banned from their family homes, these persons often make a precarious living as day-labourers, roaming around the villages in search for a job. Some, who are artistically talented, affiliate with *dand* troupes. Such artistic groups offer a possibility to survive economically and to regain social admiration and respect at least for some nights - when during their performance the artists transform into admired and venerated deities on stage.

As a *dand* group, the artists form a separate community of their own. The group has a *dand manager* (the English term "*manager*" has been taken over into the vernacular) who organises performances and who receives the financial remuneration for his troupe. The *manager* is supposed to bear all costs of living for his artists. Usually, all performers live together in the *manager's* house. Generally, the actors negotiate a one-year contract with the *manager*. In addition to their daily expenses, which are taken over by the manager, the performers are supposed to get a salary for their performance on stage. However, the *manager* has the liberty to pay the actors according to his satisfaction and estimation, exerting thus a quasi absolute financial power over his troupe of performers. The manager's powerful and ambivalent role as head of a *dand* group is often expressed in rumours "*that the manager can abuse all female actors, whenever he wants*". Here, ideas of the role of the *dand* manager merge with fantasies and prejudices about female artists, who are held to be sexually easily accessible and who are generally discredited as prostitutes.

The ambivalent role of the artists becomes explicit in their ritual preparation for the *dand* play: the *dand* performers are not allowed to accept any water or food from other villagers. They are supposed to take water and to cook their food by their own. Vice versa, no villager would accept any water or cooked food from a *dand* artist. The artists are considered by villagers as *achua,* as "untouchable". It is once more their social "untouchability" that empowers the *dand* artists to embody deities on stage. Comparable to the case of the equally subaltern *ganda baja* musicians[132], social marginalisation creates a sacralisation through ritual inversion – the ritual theatre play generating a momentary social inclusion and integration and a surmounting rise in status for the socially excluded.

Photograph 48: Male artist playing Radha, Moturpalli village, 2007, L.G

## *Conclusion*

*Dand* in Bora Sambar is a religious and humoristic play, a divine comedy that mirrors the fates, emotions and desires of humans. It shows once again the crucial ritual role of the socially marginalised for the handling of the divine and the enactment of the sacred. In the tradition of *dand nacho* of western Odisha an amalgamation of different religious and social influences becomes manifest: the veneration of the Pan-Indian goddesses Kali and Parvati

132 see second chapter.

and of the god Shiva is interwoven with the popular vaishnaite topic of the love story of Radha and Krishna. Today, the austere devotional aspect of the dual sequence of *dand* plays, which is represented in the *pen dand* performance, seems to vanish, presumably because less and less lay performers are prepared to undergo the severe ordeal it implicates, whereas the nightly entertainment of *dand nacho / dand lila* flourishes, spread throughout the region by professional *dand* troups.

# *Eighth Chapter: From Ritual to Political Music*

Besides the symbolic dimensions of music as culture and religion in the villages of Bora Sambar, my study on musical traditions has led me to urban centres of musical and cultural activity. Over the last ten years, folk music festivals have become increasingly popular in urban contexts. Sambalpur, the municipality of the Sambalpur district of Odisha and the biggest town of western Odisha is an important regional urban centre. It has set an example of mega folklore events, replicated in many other towns of western Odisha such as Bargarh, Bolangir or Titlagarh. In 1997, *Lok Mahotsav* (The People's Festival), the annual Folklore Festival in Sambalpur town, was staged for the first time, playing a pioneer role for the region.[133] *Lok Mahotsav* deals with folk art traditions, regional cultural identity and socio-economic and environmental change. Organised by the Government of Odisha[134] and supported by local cultural activists, it represents an annual artistic multi media folklore event.

To understand the socio-political dimensions and the far-reaching claims of the *Lok Mohatsav* festival, it is worth citing from the festival's manifesto:[135]

> *A cultural manifestation of the hidden age-old traditional performing art of a vast geographical area is possible through this annual celebration of the festival in the name of "Lok Mahotsav". This festival is by the people, for the people, of the people & a reflection of the socio-anthropological evolution of the people of an area. Here "Lok" means "People" only.*
>
> *This festival is not only a source of entertainment & festivity; it is capable of exhibiting the amazing conglomeration of traditions, beliefs, sorrows & philosophies of the people which vitalize the rituals & festivals. One can feel by seeing the unimpaired preservation of these to the present day. These aspects of the people give meaning & depth to their lives & solidarity to their social structure.*

---

[133] Since 1997, Lok Mohatsav has been celebrated in Sambalpur each year from 4th to 6th January. Only in the year 2000, due to the super cyclone which hit Odisha, it was celebrated from 15th to 17th March (see http://sambalpur.nic.in/lokmahotsav/backandobj.html; retrieved 30. 03.2010.

[134] By the District Council of Culture, Sambalpur; by the Department of Tourism and Culture, Government of Odisha; by the Odisha and Eastern Zonal Cultural Centre, Kolkata

[135] http://sambalpur.nic.in/lokmahotsav/backandobj.html; retrieved 30.03.2010.

*Going back to a decade past, a constellation of sensible connoisseurs of culture & artists of this land, in the name of Artist Forum conceived a State level folk festival at Sambalpur to present the folk performing art on a single platform with a sincere motive of research, documentation, presentation & promotion.*

One of the aims of the festival is to encourage local artists to continue performing their specific art traditions. Local musicians from remote areas of western Odisha – considered to be the rural reservoirs of an almost lost cultural memory - are invited to Sambalpur. Among them, artists from villages of the Bora Sambar region play a vital role, as Bora Sambar is regarded as a culturally intact area which has been left almost untouched by industrial development. During festivals such as *Lok Mohatsav,* socially neglected and destitute rural musicians are supposed to receive recognition and money for their traditional performances.

But what are the reasons for the recent wave of urban interest in village art and culture? Sambalpur town is an example of the rapid urban modernization in western Odisha. In the post-Independence phase, Sambalpur underwent a brisk industrialisation, euphemistically called "development". The symbol of this development and modernization is Hirakud dam, the first Indian mega dam project and until today the biggest dam in the world.[136] The Hirakud dam across the river Mahanadi was inaugurated in 1957 by the then Prime Minister Pt. Jawaharlal Nehru who's saying that "*dams are temples for India*" is often quoted.

Officially intended for the improvement of living conditions, irrigation and power supply, the building of the Hirakud dam radically changed the socio-cultural life-situation of the area's peasant population. Village life was deeply transformed or had to be re-located to new urban contexts – a process which is universal for Indian "development" projects. Indian mega dam development projects, from Hirakud dam to the several mega dam projects which are under way in the Narmada valley today, are almost inevitably accompanied by huge environmental damage and the forced displacement of thousands of - mostly Adivasi – peasants.[137]

---

[136] http://sambalpur.nic.in/hirakud%20dam.htm; retrieved 31.03.2010

[137] Angana Chatterji, a member of the Independent People's Commission on Mega Dams, stated in an interview in September 2004"Adivasi and peasant movements reject the assumption that development justifies cultural annihilation. Since 1947, 4,300 large dams alone in India have displaced over 42 million people. Adivasis are about 8 percent of India's population but more than 40 percent of the country's displaced."

Systematic displacement of the rural population entails a forced urban migration. The construction of the Hirakud dam has effected the migration of a displaced rural Adivasi population to Sambalpur town, where the former farmers became low-paid urban day laborers.

When European tourists today visit Sambalpur, which is advertised in their travel guides as a "tribal region", they desperately ask themselves where to find any "tribals". With its hectic urban traffic, electronic and Internet shops, the incessant ringing of mobile phones everywhere, its steep concrete buildings and humble clay brick huts with aluminium roofs, Sambalpur town is far from an idyllic "tribal" abode with bare-footed, half-naked happy "tribals", as they are still advertised in tourist magazines.[138]

It is striking that in today's Sambalpur two generations are in search of their "lost cultural identity". The second and third generations of urban migrants begin to inquire what they were forced to give up in the course of the industrialization and modernization of their world. Out of this context, in recent years many cultural institutions and centers have emerged and grown in order to re-vitalize a "forgotten" local culture. Urban cultural activists such as college lecturers, Folklore professors at Sambalpur University or lecturers at private cultural academies (*kala kshetra*)[139] conduct research on traditional local dance and music in order recreate a "lost tribal identity" in a manner which is considered to be authentic and traditional.

In urban western Odisha, an extreme creativity in the performing arts can be noted, strikingly expressed in the famous annual *All Orissa Sambalpuri Drama Competition*, organised by the cultural organisation *Yuba Udayan*, inviting many local drama artists, drama and screen play writers and musical directors to present their compositions and creations on stage. Local playwrights are mostly college lecturers, as the famous Panjha Keshor Ranjan Pradhan or Ashok Baidar from Padampur, who have already won highest awards as Drama Directors. Local groups are invited by the organisers in order to perform traditional music and dance, transformed on stage into contemporary artistic expression.

---

[138]Such orientalizing "tribal" pictures are still to be found in various advertisements for "Orissa Tribal Tours" run by diverse "Tribal Tour" operators throughout India.
[139] The *kala kshetra*s are cultural centres where children up to an age of about 14 are taught the performing arts of the region, such as local dance, drama and song.

When I started my research in Orissa / Odisha in 2002, one of my initial endeavours was to visit the *All Orissa Sambalpuri Drama Competition*. There, I first saw Surendra Kumar Sahu with his group *sanskrutikaa* (=culture) performing on stage. I was deeply impressed by the creativity and virtuosity of the music and the artistry of the dance performances of this group with its ecstatic and devoted drummers, its brilliant *mohuri* player and its playful girl dancers. After their outstanding performance I approached the group in order to express my admiration for their artistic skills. I asked: "*Where do you come from*?" Surendra Kumar Sahu told me: "*From Padampur, please visit us and stay with us. You will understand our music*." This was the beginning of my long and decisive encounter and relationship with the region of Bora Sambar and its musicians and artists.

## *Sambalpuri Folklore*

In urban centres like Sambalpur town, in recent years an urban folklore called *Sambalpuri* has been created, referring to the rural musical and performative traditions in order to present a re-vitalised "traditional" regional identity. *Sambalpuri* folklore designates traditional musical and performative elements of *gada baja* and of the *dalkhai* dance which have migrated in the last 30 years to an urban context and there have been transformed into a new stage art. In this sense *ganda baja* has mutated into *dulduli* and the rural *dalkhai* dance has turned into *Sambalpuri nacho* (dance).

*Dulduli* as a recent urban musical creation resembles *ganda baja* music in its orchestral character: The instruments *dhol, nissan, tasa, mohuri* and *jumka* are played in the same configuration as in *ganda baja*. In *dulduli* however, the use of animal skin as drum-skins is more and more replaced by the use of industrially produced plastic membranes, avoiding thus the traditional stigma of "impurity" and "pollution" for the musicians. *Dulduli* players are in consequence no longer necessarily members of marginalised social groups like the *ganda baja* musicians. Today, they are mostly urban middle class stage artists, who belong to a second or third generation of former rural migrants from the villages around Sambalpur. They rehearse in private cultural centres (*kala kshetra*) in order to be hired to perform on stage in a range of folklore events, mostly sponsored by the East Zone Cultural Center (EZCC), Delhi, in the context of governmental "Revival Projects"[140]. Para-

[140] The EZCC's mission statement reads: "EZCC and the Ministry of Rural Development through the Special Project under Swarnajayanti Gram SwarojgarJogana (SGSY) scheme is creating self employment opportunities for rural artisans and helping them to grow as entre-

doxically, under a governmental scheme *"for rural artisans (...) helping them to grow as entrepreneurs by mobilizing them into Self Help Groups"*, it is mostly urban *dulduli* groups, performing on urban folklore stages, which are sponsored as the supposed "rural artisans". As the urban *dulduli* groups are actually in a better position to exploit the benefits of social and institutional networks than village artists, they tend in recent years to monopolize the cultural folklore industry. Musically, *dulduli* groups mix imagined traditional "village" rhythms with commercial trends of a growing *Sambalburi music* market, influenced strongly by international musical developments manifest in the extensive adaptation of "techno"-rhythms. The result is an extremely loud, rhythmically reduced musical repertoire, intended to evoke associations of rural "wilderness" and employing simplified folk melodies such as the *dalkhai* song. The deafening simplified rhythms and the forceful technical sound of dulduli songs are associated by locals with the power and noise of a thunderstorm. The *dulduli* performance is usually fuelled by a standardized *Sambalpuri* dance routine, danced by girls or young women representing an urban imagination of rustic "feminine wildness".

Parallel to the emergence of *dulduli* music, *sambalpuri* dance is the transformation of the rural *dalkhai* dance to an urban folklore dance drama stage performance. *Sambalpuri* dance is performed by young women or girls who have mostly learned the *sambalpuri* dance in one of the city's "cultural academies". On stage their performance is accompanied by a *dulduli* party. The *Sambalpuri* dance includes a uniform choreography presented in standardized costumes: the dancers wear a short *ikat* (tie-dye) saree printed with traditional quadratic red and white patterns on a black or red underground. The dancers are attractively made up, spreading a vibrant charm and attraction.

---

preneurs by mobilizing them into Self Help Groups. This project will revive and revitalize a few chosen dying art forms of eastern India and provide a sustainable livelihood to 4000 beneficiaries. The project period is 3 years ending on 31.03.2008.The selected backward districts and the dying art forms include [...]. Sambalpur with Sambhalpuri Dance." (http://ezccindia.org/revival-projects.html, retrieved 20.04.2010.

## *Media and folk music*

Songs from the *Loko Mohatsav* festivals lead the charts of the highly commercialized Odishan folk music market. The loud sounds of *sambalpuri* music reproduced on cassettes, CDs and DVDs appeal to the mass of former urban migrants and their children in Sambalpur and the other towns of western Odisha. Maybe the simple rhythms and technically alienated sounds of *dulduli* music are an adequate expression for their feelings, torn between a memory of rural tradition and their everyday life in a strenuous, technicized, extremely noisy urban environment. As the rhythms of *Sambalpuri* music and the high pitch voices of its mostly female performers blaze from every bus and cab as well as from every corner-store in Sambalpur and western Odisha, the *Sambalpuri* music industry and its market are booming. The starting point of *Sambalpuri* folklore was perhaps the famous "all-time-hit" *Rangabatti re Rangabatti* (Oh, colour light from colour light [a synonym for "colourful lady"]), a folkloristic love duet from the end of the 1970ies performed by the legendary folk singers Jitendar Haripal and Krishna Patel, which until today enchants local listeners, who download audio and video remakes from *You tube.*[141] Today, *Sambalpuri* hits have a stronger popularity in western Odisha than popular Bollywood songs. "Ollywood", the TV and video production centre of Odisha, uses *dulduli* music elements to incite the sale of its audio-visual products. With its appeal to cultural nostalgia and its new won "tangibility", urban *sambalpuri* folklore seems prepared for further multi media exploitation and commercialisation as a simplified and secular entertainment. The popular media culture brings to light the new face of an industrialised urban music culture, drawing on folkloristic elements, which re-invents itself permanently through medially transformed shards of a re-enacted rural cultural memory.

## *Re-traditonalisation*

Many urban cultural activists engage in the organization of folk festivals such as *Lok Mohatsav*. Such festivals are intended to offer a forum for the re-vitalisation of a rural cultural identity, "lost" through industrialization and the adaptation to an urban way of life. The re-enactment of a "rural" or "traditional" music and dance on stage is seen as a way of discovering one's

---

[141] http://www.youtube.com/watch?v=-BVBlQlZcoE; retrieved 20.03. 2010.

own "lost" cultural roots. For urban cultural activists *Sambalpuri* folklore thus becomes a crucial form of cultural expression.

Photograph 49: Sambalpuri *ikat* design, L.G., 2009.

Because of the vital work of these urban activists, art traditions are indeed re-vitalised and thus preserved through a re-enactement on stage. In this sense, rare local forms of oral tradition of the Ramayana such as the Sobri Sobren *lila* or specific instruments such as the *balu boisi* have been re-discovered through the *Loko Mahotsav* stage. However, re-enacted on the urban stage the local traditions transform dramatically: isolated from their rural context and alienated through an industrial musical aesthetic and through uniform stage costumes and decorations, they are becoming fragmented ingredients of a new and different socio-cultural totality. Nonetheless, in Sambalpur town *Sambalpuri* music and dance seem to bundle up and express the invisible roots of a local identity. The wilder the rhythms play and the wilder the *dalkhai* girl dancers whirl around on stage, the more the urban inhabitants of Sambalpur experience the music as an expression of their deepest feelings of identity. "*Dulduli is the beat of my heart*" says one visitor of a *Lok Mahotsav*. *Loko Mahotsav* of Sambalpur is an example of the on-going process of creation and re-creation of an urban folklore on stage interconnecting the local and the globalized world. In *Loko Mahotsav* local life is re-enacted and projected into the global community. Modern media and technology are used to promote the real and imagined local rural cultural varieties of music and dance and to transfer them as an expression of a unifying *Sambalpuri* identity of western Odisha to the World Wide Web.[142]

---

[142] http://sambalpur.nic.in/lokmahotsav/index.html; http://sambalpur.nic.in/lokmahotsav/2007/index.html; retrieved 30.03.2010.

On stage, the multi media events of *Loko Mahotsav* project an idyllic and romanticised imagination of a "former", "authentic" culture (*poscim sanskruti*), expressed in wild *sambalpuri* rhythms and moves. A lost tribal identity seems to express itself in re-invented "tribal" music and dance performances. In the urban centres of western Odisha folk festivals contribute to a strong medial re-traditionalisation of local culture as well as to a persistent re-invention of one's own tradition, considered as "lost" or "forgotten" during the ongoing process of urbanisation and modernisation of life. The *Loko Mahotsav* festivals may thus be interpreted as attempts at an "invention of tradition" in the sense outlined by Hobsbawn and Ranger, as "*a process of formalization and ritualization, characterised by reference to the past*" (1983: 4). In the case of *Sambalpuri* folklore the persistent cultural creation of a supposed "tradition" celebrates itself in the context of the new secular ritual of the folklore festival *Loko Mohatsav*.

## *Music, Politics and Ethnicity*

> "*Music has always been implicated in the social and political world. Its power to affect, disturb, rouse and subdue has been used to great effect by monarchies, armies and governments throughout history.*" (Leyshon et al 1995: 426)

In *Sambalpuri* folklore, the search for cultural identity meets a politically organised search for a unified regional identity. Corresponding to the cultural revival of traditional musical and other art forms on stage, a growing regional ethnic awareness can be witnessed. The cultural and political discourse becomes impregnated with strong references to an "authentic" rural *Sambalpuri* folk culture as basis for a regional identity. In western Odisha music today presumably represents the most vital expression of regional belonging. Village music, as it is re-enacted on stage in festivals like *Loko Mahotsav* and trasformed to S*ambalpuri* folklore music, has become *the* crucial symbol of regional identity and ethnicity of western Odisha. In the region, music and language are central to the construction of ethnicity, understood as a group identity based on the assumption of a common history, origin and culture.[143] Cultural and political activists use language, music and dance in order to construct a distinct regional identity of *Western Orissa*. Music and language have to provide evidence of the uniqueness of S*ambalpuri* culture.

---

[143] For definitions and discussion, see Guibernau / Rex 1997; Waltzer/ Kantowicz/ Higham / Harrington 1982; Ben-Ami / Peled / Spektorowski 2000.

In the urban centres of the region, the newly created S*ambalpuri* folklore is thus becoming one of the focal points of cultural and political aspirations.

The mass medial advantages of *Sambalpuri* music are exploited by local politicians who gladly distribute audio-visual messages accompanied by *Sambalpuri* music. In former times, rural *ganda baja* was patronised by landholders (*zamindar*) or by the local Bora Sambar king (*raja*). Today, urban folk festivals are patronized and financed by local politicians. The sacredness of the traditional *baja* is being used to sacralize or at least to provide a sacralizing legitimation to political statements and political personalities.

One of the political faces of *Sambalpuri* music is its instrumentalisation by the regionalist and separatist *Koshala* movement, which demands the political reconstruction of the ancient – mythological – regional kingdom of *Koshala* on the territory of western Odisha, respectively the creation of a new Indian union state under this name.[144] Often folklore festivals such as *Loko Mohatsav* - even if sponsored by the Central Government in the context of cultural programmes and intended to attract tourists to the region - operate as hot spots of an ethnic discourse and movement that is critical for the Indian central state. The *Sambalpuri* folklore festivals are frequently organized by Koshala activists. Loud, rhythmically catching *dulduli* sounds are supposed to evoke a feeling of regional identity. *Sambalpuri* music thus gains political virulence: *Sambalpuri* folklore is used to create a continuum between 1) locality – sensed in standardized local rhythms and sounds; 2) ethnicity – constructed through the imagination of a homogenous ethnic group belonging to the specific region and 3) a territorial idea of the area of an ancient kingdom.

The formerly sacred and ritualistic *ganda baja* seems to play a crucial part in this regionalist endeavour: transformed into secular *Sambalpuri* music, it becomes an emblem of political, cultural and regional distinctiveness and regional pride. The creation of *Sambalpuri* folklore and folk music in the construction of a regional ethnicity (see Stokes 1994) may be interpreted as a cultural metamorphosis – a process of secularization which at the same time

---

[144] The Koshal activist's webside as well as the Koshal Discussion and Development Forum have recently published a "Quit Koshal convention from April 1 2010" (http://www.koshal.in/index.php?option=com_content&view=article&id=89:quit-koshal-convention-from-april-1-&catid=1:latest-news&Itemid=50; retrieved 29.03.2010 ); (http://www.koshal.in/index.php?option=com_content&view=article&id=89:quit-koshal-convention-from-april-1-&catid=1:latest-news&Itemid=50; retrieved 29.03.2010).

can be read as a sacralization of local politics, which uses folk festivals as the new rituals of power.

Politically constructed musical identity is a universal phenomenon: it is observable in national anthems, musical folklore and popular music world wide. Music seems a crucial cultural metaphor to meet the need of global perception of a national or local belonging.[145] Music creates a space and a geographical imagination through the perception of sound. In the nation-state, cultural and personal identity and difference is homogenized and symbolically marked through its national anthem.[146] An "*ethnographic nationalism*" as "*the study, codification and idealization of peasant cultures in the interest of forging a new national culture*" (Gellner 1992: 290) seems crucial especially in the construction of national identities in post-colonial Africa and Asia. Musical and regional particularities such as local folksongs and folkdances are transformed into stage art and utilised in evoking and establishing an imagined national consciousness, and feeling of ethnic belonging, which can for example be traced in the rise of the "nationalised" Carnatic music in the beginning of Indian nationalism (Subramanian 1999: 131-163). The same analysis seems applicable for *Sambalpuri* folklore and its institutionalised presentation in *Loko Mohatsav* festivals. They can be read as examples of an ethnographic regionalism, pushed forward by regionalist Koshal and cultural activists, creating a romanticized picture of a lost homogenous rural and tribal identity of the region of *Western Orissa*. The recent successful history of administrative reorganizations and the creation of two new neighbouring states Jharkhand and Chhattisghar in 2002, which used their "tribal" character as a crucial argument for their regional claims, are concrete political models for their aspirations.

## *Music, Modernisation and Dalit Power*

Today, *sambalpuri* musicians mostly have an urban middle class background, often originating from families who have migrated from villages to the cities over the past two or three generations. In urban contexts, the musical tradition and the ritual power of the village orchestra *ganda baja* have been transformed by urban musicians for mega folklore events or by *brass bands* for the entertainment of urban marriage parties. Festive urban folklore

---

[145] For comparative studies on music and nationality see Biddle/Knights 2007; Wade 2000; Radano 2003; Sellers 2004.

[146] For an analysis of the function of national anthems see Anderson 1991; Gellner 1983; 1997.

and marriage music is no longer carrying the stigma of "untouchability" or "pollution" as 1) urban musicians originate from "general castes"[147] or the middle classes and 2) in the making of instruments plastic has replaced animal skin.

In recent years, the adoption of the Ganda community's intangible cultural heritage by more dominant social communities has brought about discussions about intellectual property rights, incited by a growing *dalit*[148] consciousness among rural and urban Ganda musicians. Traditionally oriented Ganda musicians denounce the entertainment-centred character of *brass bands* and *dulduli* parties as simplistic and profane. *Harijan* activists[149] accuse urban *brass bands* and *dulduli* bands of usurping the lucrative performances at marriage-ceremonies, and on a more general plane of "*stealing their culture and their intellectual property rights*". *Harijan* musicians calling themselves *bajinya* (musicians) actively reclaim their intellectual property from the middle classes by public allegations and criticism. By using the term *bajinya,* musicians indicate their attachment to the idea of the traditional *ganda baja* village orchestra, but, by using a new term, aim to avert habitual pejorative associations. *Bajinya Dalit* activists religiously identify with their music and insist that being a musician and performing *baja* should never be simply a musical performance, but should always be considered a *puja,* an act of worship of the goddess. One of the *bajinya* activists explains the relationship between music and religion as follows:

---

[147] The term "general castes" designates the middle class population of India which, according to administrative classification, comprises the "general categories" of the caste system and thus socially rather privileged groups. (On the social problem of administrative categorisation, see Assayag 1996: 493-499).

[148] The concept of dalit consciousness refers to the mass conversions of members of the so called "untouchable" Mahar caste from Maharashtra to Buddhism in the 1970s. Mahars reacted against social oppression by converting to Buddhism and in this context began to use the term dalit ("depressed", "broken," "torn into pieces") to designate themselves. In contrast to indigenous terminologies, the term dalit was chosen to avoid euphemism or pejorative connotations. The dalit Movement was the brainchild of Dr. Ambedkar – himself a Mahar, politician and activist. In contrast to Gandhi, who intended to reform Hinduism, Ambedkar completely rejected it. In a more recent work on Ambedkar and conversion as a socio-political tool of the Dalit Movement, Beltz (2005) analyses Ambedkar's options for conversion and his final choice of Buddhism in the face of alternative possibilities (Sikhism, Islam and Christianity). A few days before his death in 1956, Ambedkar converted, thereby placing himself in continuity with Aśoka's conversion to Buddhism and with Buddhist mythology. His conversion caused a wave of conversions to neo-Buddhism among the Mahar. The new religion became a potent factor in the socio-political struggle of this underprivileged group

[149] Gandhi's terminology harijan (=god's children) for marginalised "untouchable"communities has been adopted by many social and political activists.

> *"Gods live in four of our bajinya instruments: In the dhol Kalka resides; in the Nissan Buri Ma is manifested; in the tasa Mauli Ma lives and the black beauty Kali Sundari shows herself in the mohuri.*
>
> *In earlier times bajinya was never a performing art, but always a puja. Playing baja revealed a specific religious knowledge to perform the music and puja. The musicians as religious specialists arose from four brothers. Gradually that specific team became a bajinya orchestra."*

In this sense, the *bajinya dalit* activists of villages of the Bora Sambar region claim to be religious specialists *and* musicians at the same time. This recent evaluation of their traditional occupation is a sign of a new social and ritual self-confidence and self-consciousness. Local narratives trace the traditionally marginalised and powerless social position of the *bajinya* musicians to their inherently strong devotion to god which entailed a social naivety. This naivety is considered by the activists as the real reason for the social vulnerability and poverty of village musicians, as the following statement of another *bajinya* activist indicates:

> *"Only our economic disadvantages made us ashud lok ["untouchable people"]. But because of our artistic brilliance we were hired for musical services by the wealthy. This was the starting point when bajinya were forced to perform for money and where their social position declined".*

Today, the paradoxical combination of social marginalisation and ritual power which manifests itself in *ganda baja* is turning into a program of social empowerment. The consciousness of the ritual power of *ganda baja* music strengthens the self-awareness of the marginalised musicians and their communities. A new self-respect evolves hand in hand with a growing consciousness of their musical knowledge and skills, of the socio-symbolic power of their music and of their intellectual property rights. In the Bora Sambar region early stages of a *bajinya dalit* consciousness seem to become visible, which is grounded in the idea that the power of music is the power of the goddesses. The musicians as traditional mediators and transmitters of the conceptualised divine powers begin to question their former stigma of social marginality and to transform it into social power. They start to equate their ritual power with social value and dynamics. This semantic shift finds parallels in recent observations by C. Joe Arun on processes of self-assertion taking place between the socially stigmatised Paraiyar musicians in Tamil Nadu. Through the re-evaluation of the symbol of the *parai* drum, the marginalised Parayars have in recent times gained a new self-consciousness as well as real political power (Arun 2007: 81-104).

In today's India, as it becomes visible in the rural contexts of the Bora Sambar region as well as in the urban centres such as Sambalpur town, the power of village sound and rhythm seems to be no longer limited to traditional ritual contexts, but adopts new social and political roles: In an urban environment it plays a crucial role in the process of constructing political identities. In its rural context, the self-assertion of musicians is a sign to overcome the social stigmatisation and devaluation of the communities their music originally belonged to.

# *Post-Research Reflections*

In this panoramic ethnography of music it has been my aim to trace the sounds of a local culture amid its diversity, its oral history and its social change. I have attempted to document the multifarious facets of musical traditions in their socio-religious settings, in their socio-cultural processes and finally within the dynamics of musical industrialisation and globalisation. The complexity of music as a sonic, multi sensory, emotional and cultural medium of religious as well as socio-cultural dynamics and as a crucial medium of cultures of orality is difficult to grasp. In this study however, I tried to trace the sounds of Bora Sambar as resonances of socio-cultural processes and sensorially transmitted local meaning systems in terms of local theories. The sonic theory of the goddess manifests itself in a local *thea-phony,* a belief system expressed in sounds and rhythms and perceived through body movements and trance. Trance mediumship – visible in the concept of *boil* – revealed itself as a central local media theory and medium of cultural ambivalence. Music as both intangible and physically produced proved of ritual centrality. On the one hand, ritual music and the accompanying trance were crucial as cultural expressions of the locally conceived sacred. On the other hand sound and trance were found vital for performances of healing.

The intermediality of music in the Bora Sambar region appeared manifest in the interrelatedness of local performing arts like dance, theatre or poetry, so essential for value transmission.

In the Bora Sambar region I encountered a strong relationship between music and social structure revealing local hierarchies - visible in the key structure of marginalisation of village music and musicians. On the political level, the music of Bora Sambar is exposed to shifting identities and shifting contexts given today's processes of urban re-traditionalization and folklorization of culture.

I am aware that my presence in the villages of Bora Sambar, my endeavour to document the local rituals and musical traditions as well as the establishing of sound archives of the region, have in turn influenced the development and perception of the musical traditions and practices I studied. An international research funded by international research foundations exerts itself a great influence on the contents of research. Research topics construct realities. Research on subalterns possibly empowers these subaltern groups. During the years of my ethnographic visits, I recognised a changing self-awareness of the groups of Ganda musicians I encountered and re-encountered. I recognized a stronger resistance against commercial influences of urban *Sambalpuri* music among rural musicians. I witnessed that many village musicians denounced a popularisation of urban *Sambalpuri* music as not supportive for their village music, but only enhancing the profit of multinational multimedia companies.

My method of *sustainable documentation* was an attempt to establish a long lasting cooperation between researcher and local musicians who started to view themselves as research partners, responsible for a sustainable continuation and preservation of their musical culture. This modified the self-awareness of subaltern groups in regard to their cultural heritage: subaltern musicians started to consider themselves as valuable creators of culture. This, hopefully, has opened perspectives for a local resistance against cultural amnesia and aphasia due to socio-cultural marginalisation. Research on subalterns is changing its subject of research as well its research's subjects.

With my panoramic description of musical traditions of the Bora Sambar region, I have tried to grasp culture and religion without essentialisms. However, I learned that intangible culture (music) is a material of political agitation and plays a key role in the re-invention of an "authentic" subtantialised and ethnicised urban culture used for political programs of the urban regionalist Koshal movement.

Local rural music of Bora Sambar, it turned out, was not isolated but strongly interconnected with urban and global processes, creating thus local answers to global dynamics. The rural music of Bora Sambar however prevails - despite all kinds of external influences. As music moves, the musical cultures of Bora Sambar transform within their locally transmitted structures and meaning systems. The medium music nonetheless remains central for ritual and political messages.

# *Literature*


Alex, Gabriele / Suzette Heald (ed.) 2008. Good Deaths, Bad Deaths. Cultural Perspectives on Death and Dying, Special issue of *Curare* Vol. 31, 1.

Alldritt, Lesley D. 2000. The Burakumin: The complicity of Japanese Buddhism in Oppression and an Opportunity for Liberation. In *Journal of Buddhist Ethics*, no pages; online conference, retrieved online 20.02.2010. http://www.buddhistethics.org/7/alldritt001.html#barakumin

Anderson, Benedict 1991 (1983). Imagined Communities: Reflections on the Origin and Spread of Nationalism. New York / London: Verso.

Apte, Mahadev L. 1985. *On Humor and Laughter: An Anthropological Approach.* New York: Cornell University Press.

Arnold, Alison (ed.) 2000. *The Garland Encyclopedia of World Music. Volume 5. South Asia.* The Indian Subcontinent. London: Routledge.

Arun, Joe C. 2007. From Stigma to Self-assertion: Paraiyars and the Symbolism of the Parai Drum. In *Contributions to Indian Sociology* 41, 1: 81-104.

Assayag, Jackie / Gilles Tarabout (éd) 1999. La possession en Asie du Sud. Parole. Corps, Territoire. Collection *Purusartha* 21, Paris: Édition de l'École des Hautes Études en Sciences Sociales.

Assayag, Jackie 1996. De la Caste au »castéisme«. In Jafferlot, Christophe (ed.), *L'Inde Contemporaine. De 1950 À Nos Jours.* Paris: Fayard, 493-499.

Babb, Lawrence A. 1982. Amnesia and Remembrance among the Brahma Kumaris. In *Asian Folklore Studies*, Vol. 41, No. 1 (1982), 49-66.

Bakhtin, Mikhail 1981. *The Dialogic Imagination: Four Essays* (Caryl Emerson, Michael Holquist, Trans.). Austin: University of Texas Press.

Bakhtin, Mikhail 1973. *Rabelais and His World.* (Translated by Hélène Iswolsky). 1st ed. Cambridge: MIT Press.

Bakker, Hans / Alan Entwistle (ed.) 1983. *Devi: the Worship of the Goddess and its Contribution to Indian Pilgrimage: a Report on a Seminar and Excursion.* Groningen: Institute of Indian Studies, State University of Groningen.

Basu, Helene 2001. *Die Göttin und die Charan – Das Gedächtnis des Königtums, Verwandtschaft und Askese in Kacch (westl. Indien).* Berlin: Habilitationsschrift, Dept. of Social and Political Sciences, Freie Universität Berlin.

Basu, Helene 1994. Habshi Sklaven, Sidi-Fakire. Muslimische Heiligenverehrung im Westlichen Indien. (Indus 1). Berlin: Das Arabische Buch.

Behuria, S.N.C. (ed.) 1991. *Orissa State Gazetteers. Orissa State*, Vol. II. Cuttack: Gazetteers Unit Department of Revenue Government of Orissa.

Beltz, Johannes 2005. Mahar, Buddhist and Dalit. Religious Conversion and Socio-Political Emancipation. New Delhi: Manohar.

Ben-Ami, Shlomo / Yoav Peled / Alberto Spektorowski (eds.) 2000. *Ethnic Challenges to the Modern Nation State*. Houndsmills and New York: Macmillan Press and St. Martin's Press.

Berger, Peter 2001.The Gadaba and the 'Non-ST' Desia of Koraput, Orissa. Some Observations on their Interrelations. In Georg Pfeffer and Deepak K. Behera (eds.), *Contemporary Society: Tribal Studies*. Vol. 5. New Delhi: Concept Publishing Company, 57-90.

Berger, Peter 2007. *Füttern, Speisen und Verschlingen. Ritual und Gesellschaft im Hochland von Orissa, India*. Indus Ethnologische Südasien-Studien, Band 11. Berlin: Lit Verlag.

Biardeau, Madleine 1995. *L'Hindouisme. Anthropologie d'une Civilisation*. Paris: Champs Flammarion.

Biardeau, Madleine 1994. *Études de Mythologie Hindou II. Bhakti et Avatara*. Pondichéry: Publication de l'École Française d'Extrême-Orient.

Biddle, Ian / Vanessa Knights (eds.) 2007. Music. *Nationality and the Politics of location: Between the Global and the Local*. Hamshire: Ashgate Publishing Limited.

Bijoi, C. R. 2007. Adivasis of India. A History of Discrimination, Conflict and Resistance. In Aditi Chanchani / Mamata Dash / Rosemary Viswanath / Sinduja Ananthkrishnan / Vidhya Ragan (eds.), *This is our Homeland. A Collection of Essays on the Betrayal of Adivasi Rights in India*. Bangalore: Equations, 15–27.

Blacking, John / Kealiinohomoku, Joann W. (eds.) 1979. *The Performing Arts: Music and Dance*. Paris and New York: Mouton Publishers.

Blacking, John 1973. *How Musical is Man?* Seattle and London: University of Washington Press.

Blank, Jonah 1992. Arrow of the Blue-skinned God: Retracing the Ramayana through India. Boston: Houghton Mifflin.

Boal, Barbara M. 1997. *Human Sacrifice and Religious Change, the Kondhs*. New Delhi: Inter-India Publications.

Bourguignon, Erika (ed.) 1973. *Religion. Altered State of Consciousness and Social Change.* Columbus (Ohio): Research Foundation.

Boddy, Janice 1994. Spirit Possession Revisited: Beyond Instrumentality. In *Annual Review of Anthropology*, 23: 407-434.

Booth, Gregory D. 2005. Brass Baja. Stories from the World of Indian Weddings Bands. Oxford University Press: Delhi.

Bor, Joep / Philippe Bruguière 2003. *Gloire des Princes. Louange des Dieux*. Paris: Cité de la Musique.

Botanical Survey of India 1960. *Bulletin of the Botanical Survey of India*, 2, 1/2, 180-273. Calcutta, Botanical Survey of India.

Bräunlein, Peter J. (Hg.). Religion und Museum. Zur visuellen Repräsentation von Religion/en im öffentlichen Raum. Bielefeld: Transcript Verlag.

Bull, Michael / Les Back 2003. *The Auditory Culture Reader*. New York: Berg.

Cancik, Hubert / Hubert Mohr 1988. Religionsästhetik. In Hubert Cancik / Burkhard Gladigow / Matthias Laubscher (Hg.), *Handbuch Religionswissenschaftlicher Grundbegriffe 1*. Stuttgart: Kohlhammer, 121-156.

Carpenter, Joseph E. 1919. *Theism in Medieval India*. London: Garland Publishers.

Carrin, Marine 1997. Enfants de la Déesse. Dévotion et Prêtrise Féminine au Bengale. Paris: CNRS Éditions.

Carrin, Marine 2006. Le Meurtre Symbolique des Jumelles en pays Tulu: la Dramatisation Ritualisée de la Matrilinéarité. In Nicole-Claude Mathieu (éd.), *Une Maison sans fille est une maison vide. Genre, Matrilinéarité, Uxorilocalité*. Paris : Editions de la Maison des Sciences de l'Homme, 213-240.

Champion, Catherine (ed) 1996. *Traditions Orales dans le Monde Indien*. Collection *Purusartha*. Paris.

Chatterji, Angana P. / Harsh Mander 2004. *Without Land or Livelihood. The Indira Sagar Dam: State Accountability and Rehabilitation Issues*. (Report of the Independent People's Commission). New Delhi: Centre for Equity Studies.

Choudhury, Roy B. C. 1980. The Moon and Net: A Study of Transient Community of Marine Fishermen of Jambudwip. Kolkata: Anthropological Survey of India.

Chakraborty, S. B. 1986. Around the Plough. Socio-cultural Context of Agricultural Farming in an Indian Village. Kolkata: Anthropological Survey of India.

Classen, Constance 2005. McLuhan in the Rainforest. In David Howes (ed.), *Empire of the Senses, The Sensual Culture Reader*. Berg: New York, 147-163.

Clémentin-Ohja, C. 1981. Feminine Asceticism in Hinduism: Its Tradition and Present Condition. In *Man in India,* Vol. 61, No 3, 254-288

Clémentin-Ohja, C. 1990. *La Divinité Conquise. Carrière d'une Sainte.* Nanterre: Société d'Éthnologie.

Coplan, Ian 2002. Princes of India in the Endgame of Empire, 1917- 1947. New York: Cambridge University Press.

Coppet, Daniel de / Zemp, Hugo (1979). *Aré Aré. Un Peuple Mélanésien et sa Musique*. Paris: Seuil.

Crystal, David 1995 (1987). Die Cambridge Enzyklopädie der Sprache. (The Cambridge Encyclopedia of Language). Frankfurt/Main, New York: Campus Verlag.

Csordas, Thomas J. / Elizabeth Lewton 1998. Practice, Performace and Experience in Ritual Healing. In *Transcultural Psychiatry* 35: 435-512.

Csordas, Thomas J. 1990. Embodiment as a Paradigm for Anthropology. In *Ethos* 18: 5-47.

Daniélou, Alain 1979. *Introduction to the Study of Musical Scales*. New Delhi: Oriental Books Reprint Corp. distributed by Munshiram Manoharlal.

Daniélou, Alain 2004 (1975). *Einführung in die Indische Musik*. Taschenbücher zur Musikwissenschaft [Hrsg. Richard Schaal], Vol. 36. Wilhelmshaven: Heinrichhofen's Verlag Wilhelmshaven.

David, Saul 2003. *The Indian Mutiny: 1857*. London: Pinguin Books.

Demmer, Ulrich / Martin Gaenszle (eds.). The Power of Discourse in Ritual Performance. Rhetoric, Poetics, Transformations. Berlin: LIT Verlag.

Deva, Bigamundre Chaitanya 1977. *Musical Instruments. Their History and Development.* New Delhi. Munshiram Manoharlal Publishers.

Devi, Mahasweta 2003. *Chotti Munda and His Arrow* (translated and introduced by Gayatri Chakravorty Spivak. Malden, MA: Blackwell Pub.

Devy, Ganesh N. / Geoffrey V. Davis, / Kalyan K. Chakravarty, (eds.) 2009. *Indigeneity. Culture and Representation.* New Delhi: Orient Black Swan.

Devy, Ganesh N. 2006a. A Nomad Called Thief. Reflections on Adivasi Silence. Delhi: Orient Longman.

Devy, Ganesh. N. 2006b. Adivasi Knowledge and Aphasia. In ibid, *A Nomad Called Thief. Reflections on Adivasi Silence*. Delhi: Orient Longman, 95-122.

Doniger O'Flaherty, Wendy 1981. *The Rig Veda: an Anthology: one Hundred and Eight Hymns.* Selected, translated and annotated by Wendy Doniger O'Flaherty. Harmondsworth, Middlesex, England; New York, N.Y.: Penguin Books.

Douglas, Mary 1966. Collected Works. Purity and Danger. An Analysis of Pollution and Taboo. London: Routledge.

Dumont, Louis 1983. Essais sur l'Individualisme. Une Perspective Anthropologique sur l'Idéologie Moderne. Pars : Éditions du Seuil.

Dumont, Louis 1986 (1966). Homo Hierarchicus. Le Système des Castes et ses Implications. Paris: Tel Gallimard.

Dumont, Louis 1986 (1966). Appendice B. Le Renoncement dans les religions de l'Inde'. In ibid, *Homo Hierarchicus. Le Système des Castes et ses Implications.* Paris: Gallimard, 324-350.

Ellen, Roy / Holly Harris 2000. Introduction. In Roy Ellen / Peter Parkes / Alan Bicker (eds.), *Indigenous Environmental Knowledge and its Transformations. Critical Anthropological Perspectives*. Amsterdam: Harwood Academic Publishers, 1-33.

Eschmann, Anncharlotte 1986 (1978). Hinduization of Tribal Deities in Orissa. The Sakta and Saiva Typology. In Anncharlott Eschmann / Hermann Kulke / Gaya Charan Tripathi (eds.), *The Cult of Jagannath and the regional Tradition of Orissa*. Delhi: Manohar, 79-98.

Falk, Harry 1990. Goodies for India. Literacy, Orality and Vedic Culture. In Wolfgang Raible (ed.), *Erscheinungsformen Kultureller Prozesse*. Tübingen: Gunter Narr Verlag, 103-119.

Falk, Harry 1993. *Schrift im Alten Indien. Ein Forschungsbericht mit Anmerkungen*. ScriptOralia 56, Tübingen: Gunter Narr Verlag.

Farquhar, John N. 1967. An Outline of the Religious Literature of India, Delhi: Oxford University Press.

Feld, Steven 1990 (1982). *Sound and Sentiment. Birds, Weepings, Poetics and Song in Kaluli Expressions*. Philadelphia: University of Philadelphia Press.

Feld, Steven 2003. A Rainforest Acoustemology. In Michael Bull / Les Back (eds.), *The Auditory Culture Reader*. New York: Berg, 223-239.

Feld, Steven 2005. Places Sensed, Sensed Places: Toward a Sensous Epistemology. In David Howes (ed.), *The Empire of the Senses. The Sensual Culture Reader*. Berg: New York, 179-192.

Feld, Steven / Aaron A. Fox 1994. Music and Language. In *Annual Review of Anthropology*, Vol. 23, 25-53

Fischer, Eberhard / B.N. Goswamy / Dinanath Pathy 2005. *Göttinnen – Indische Bilder aus vier Jahrhunderten* (Goddesses – Indian Images during four Decades). Zürich: Museum Rietberg.

Fox, James J. 1988. To Speak in Pairs. Essays on the Ritual Languages of Eastern Indonesia. Cambridge: Cambridge University Press.

Fürer-Haimendorf Christoph v. / Elizabeth von Fürer-Haimendorf 1979. The Gonds of Andhra Pradesh. Tradition and Change in an Indian Tribe. Delhi: Vikas Publishing House Pvt Ltd.

Gellner, Ernest 1983. *Nations and Nationalism*. Ithaca: Cornell University Press.

Gellner, Ernest 1992. Nationalism Reconsidered and E.H. Carr. In *Review of International Studies,* Vol. 18, No 4 (Oct.), 285-293.

Gellner, Ernest 1997. *Nationalism.* Washington Square, N.Y. : New York University Press.

Gennep, Arnold v. 1986 (1909). *Übergangsriten.* Frankfurt/M.: Campus.

Glasenapp, Heinrich v. 1986. *Indische Geisteswelt. Band I: Glaube und Weisheit der Hindus.* Hanau: Verlag Werner Dausien.

Godelier, Maurice 1996. *L'Enigme du Don.* Paris: Edition Flammarion.

Goody, Jack (ed.) 1968. *Literacy in Traditional Societies.* Cambridge: Cambridge University Press.

Goody, Jack 1986. *The Logic of Writing and the Organization of Society.* Cambridge: Cambridge University Press.

Guibernau, Montserrat / John Rex (ed.) 1997. *The Ethnicity Reader: Nationalism, Multiculturalism and Migration.* Cambridge: Blackwell Publishers.

Guillebaud, Christine 2008. Le Chant des Serpents. Musiciens Itinérants du Kérala. Paris : CNRS Publications.

Gupta, Ramnika 2009. Adivasi Literature: An Emerging Consciousness. In Ganesh N. Devy, / Geoffrey V. Davis / Kalyan K. Chakravarty (eds), *Indigeneity. Culture and Representation.* New Delhi, 191-202.

Guzy, Lidia 1998. Brahma Kumaris – Weibliche Askese und globale Reform: Oder wie aus dem Tod des Weiblichen ein transzendenter Feminismus entsteht. In Manfred Hutter (ed.), *Die Rolle des Weiblichen in der Indischen und Buddhistischen Kulturgeschichte.* Graz: Leykam, 56-74.

Guzy, Lidia 2008. Par e Sur - Sounds of the Goddess from the Boro Sombar Region of Eastern India. Berlin Museum Collection: Wergo Verlag.

Guzy, Lidia 2002. Baba-s und Alekh-s – Askese und Ekstase einer Religion im Werden. Vergleichende Untersuchungen der asketischen Tradition Mahima Dharma in Orissa/östliches Indien. Berlin: Weissensee Verlag (Dissertation).

Guzy, Lidia / Rainer Hatoum / Susan Kamel 2009. Museumislands. On the New Role of Museums / Museumsinseln. Zur Neuen Rolle von Museen. Berlin: Panama Verlag.

Guzy, Lidia / Rainer Hatoum / Susan Kamel (eds.) 2010. *From Imperial Museum to Communication Centre ?* Würzburg: Königshausen & Neumann.

Hann, Chris 2003. Creeds, Cultures and the „witchery of music". In *Royal Anthropological Institute* 9, 2, 223-239.

Hann, Chris 2007. Weder nach dem Revolver noch dem Scheckbuch, sondern nach dem Rotstift greifen: Plädoyer eines Ethnologen für die Abschaffung des Kulturbegriffs. In *Zeitschrift für Kulturwissenschaften*, hrsg. Michael C. Frank / Bettina Gockel / Thomas Hauschild / Dorothee Kimmich / Kirstin Mahlke, Fremde Dinge, 125-134.

Hardenberg, Roland 1998. Die Wiedergeburt der Götter: Ritual und Gesellschaft in Orissa. Hamburg: Verlag Dr. Kovac.

Hardenberg, Roland 2005. *Children of the Earth Goddess: Society, Marriage, and Sacrifice in the Highlands of Orissa*. Habilitationsschrift. Münster: Westfälische Wilhelms-Universität.

Hardenberg, Roland 2008. König ohne Reich Rituale eines Ko□nigtums in Orissa. Berlin: Hans Schiler.

Hauschild, Thomas 2002. *Magie und Macht in Italien*. Gifkendorf: Merlin Verlag.

Hawley, John Stratton / Mark Juergensmeyer 1988. Songs of the Saints of India, New York: Oxford University Press.

Helffer, Mireille 1969a. Fanfares villageoises au Népal. In *Objets et Monde* IX, 1 Printemps, 51-58.

Helffer, Mireille 1969b. *Castes de Musiciens au Népal.* Paris: Éditions de Département d'Ethnomusicologie.

Hertz, Robert 1907. Contribution à une Étude sur la Représentation Collective de la Mort. In *Année Sociologique* 1. Paris.

Hertz, Robert 1970 (1928). *Sociologie religieuse et folklore.* Paris: Presses Universitaires de France. (contains Hertz 1907)

Hertz, Robert 1988 (1922). Le Péché et l'Expiation dans les Sociétés Primitives. Paris: Èditions.

Hobsbawn, Eric / Terence Ranger (eds.) 1983. *The Invention of Tradition*. Cambridge: Cambridge University Press.

Hornbostel, Erich Moritz von / Curt Sachs 1914. Systematik der Musikinstrumente. Ein Versuch. In *Zeitschrift für Ethnologie* 46, Heft 4/5, 1914: 553-590.

Howes, David (ed.) 1991. The Varieties of Sensory Experience: A Sourcebook in the Anthropology of the Senses.

Howes, David (ed.) 2005. The Empire of the Senses. The Sensual Culture Reader. Berg: New York.

Hubert, Henri / Marcel Mauss 1897-8. Essai sur la Nature et la Fonction du Sacrifice. In *L'Année Sociologique* Vol II: 29-138; reprinted and translated in 1964 by

W.D. Halls with foreword by E.E. Evans-Pritchard: Henri Hubert and Marcel Mauss. Sacrifice: its nature and function. London: Cohen and West.

Hyder, Rehan 2004. Brimful of Asia: Negotiating Ethnicity on the UK Music Scene. Burlington, VT: Ashgate.

ICOM News. 2004. Museum and Intangible heritage. No 4.

Ishwaran, Karigoudar (ed.) 1999. Ascetic Culture: Renunciation and Worldly Engagement. In *JAAS – Journal of Asian and African Studies* Vol. XXXIV, (1).

Jacobsen, Knut A. / Helene Basu / Angelika Malinar / Vasudha Narayanan (eds.) 2009. *Brill's Encyclopedia of Hinduism Vol. 1: Regions, Pilgrimage, Deities*. Leiden, Boston, Brill.

Jamous, Raymon 1992. The Brother-married-sister Relationship and Marriage Ceremonies as Sacrificial Rites: A case Study from Northern India. In Daniel de Coppet (ed.), *Understanding Rituals*. London and New York: Routledge, 52-73.

Kamel, Susan 2004. Wege zur Vermittlung von Religionen in Berliner Museen. Black Kaaba Meets White Cube. (Berliner Schriften zur Museumskunde). Wiesbaden: VS Verlag.

Karlsson, Bengt G. 2003. Anthropology and the 'Indigenous Slot'. Claims to and Debates about Indigenous Peoples' Status in India. In *Critique of Anthropology* Vol 23 (4) 403–423.

Kendall, Laurel 1996. Initiating Performance. The Story of Chini, a Korean Shaman. In Carol Laderman / Marina Roseman (eds.), *The Performance of Healing*. New York: Routledge, 17-58.

Kendell, Laurel 1988. The Life and Hard Times of a Korean shaman: Of Tales and the Telling of Tales. Honolulu, Hi: University of Hawaii Press.

Killius, Rolf 2006. *Ritual Music and Hindu Rituals of Kerala*. Delhi: B.R. Rhythms.

Kinsley, David 1985. Hindu Goddesses. Visions of Divine Feminine in the Hindu Religious Traditions. Berkeley: University of California Press.

Klostermaier, Klaus K. 1994. *A Survey of Hinduism*. Albany / New York: Suny Press.

Koch, Anne 2004. Intermediäre Leitern. Religionsästhetische Deutung eines Bildmotivs bei E. Schumacher, M. Beckmann, G. Segal, A. Kiefer. In *Themenheft Ästhetik- Kunst- Religion Münchner Theologische Zeitschrift*. Jahrgang 55 , Heft 4, 330-342.

Koch, Lars-Christian / Maurice Mengel. 2007. From Elementary Thought to Tone Psychology. Bastian's and Stumpf's Discourse on the Mind as a Condition for the Developmnet of Ethnomusicology. In Manuela Fischer / Peter Bolz / Susan Kamel (eds.), *Adolf Bastian and his Universal Archive of Humanity: the Origins of German Anthropology*. Hildesheim; New York: G. Olms: 114-126.

Koch, Lars-Christian. 1995. Zur Bedeutung der Rasa-Lehre für die zeitgenössische nordindische Kunstmusik. Mit einem Vergleich mit der Affektenlehre des 17. und 18. Jahrhunderts (= Ravindra Dhvani, Schriftenreihe des Tagore Instituts zur Kultur des Indischen Subkontinents, hrsg. von Ananda Samir CHOPRA, Bd. 2). Bonn: Holos Verlag.

Köpping, Klaus Peter / Ursula Rao (Hrsg.) (2000). *Im Rausch des Rituals. Gestaltung und Transformation der Wirklichkeit in körperlicher Performanz* (Performanzen. Interkulturelle Studien zu Ritual, Spiel und Theater; Band 1). Münster, Hamburg, London: Lit

Kroeber, Alfred L. / Clyde Kluckhohn 1952. *Culture: A Critical Review of Concepts and Definitions*. Cambridge, Mass: The Museum.

Kulke, Hermann / Dietmar Rothermund 2006 (1998). *Von der Induskultur bis Heute*. München: C.H. Beck.

Kulke, Hermann 2005. *Indische Geschichte bis 1750*. München: Oldenbourg Verlag.

L'Homme. Revue Française d'Anthropologie 2004. *Musique et Anthropologie*. Number 171-172 juil./déc.

Laderman, Carol / Marina Roseman (eds.) 1996. *The Performance of Healing*. London: Routledge.

Laack, Isabel 2007 Religionsästhetik und Religionsmusikologie. Die Behandlung nonverbaler Quellen in der Religionswissenschaft. In Oliver Krüger (Hg), *Nicht alle Wege führen nach Rom. Religionen Rituale und Religionstheorie jenseits des Mainstreams. Festschrift für Karl Hoheisel zum 70. Geburtstag*. Frankfurt: Verlag Otto Lembeck, S. 114-133.

Laack, Isabel 2009. Musik und religiöse Identität in Glastonbury. Ergebnisse eines religionswissenschaftlichen Forschungsprojektes. In *Musik und (ihre) Mission - Im Schnittfeld von Gemeindeentwicklung und empirischer Forschung. epd Dokumentation 47*, Okt., 32-35.

Lanwerd, Susanne (Hg) 2003. *Der Kanon und die Sinne. Religionsästhetik als Akademische Disziplin*. Luxembourg: Études Luxembourgeoises d`Histoire & de Science des Religions.

Lanwerd, Susanne 2002. Religionsästhetik. Studien zum Verhältnis von Symbol und Sinnlichkeit. Würzburg: Königshausen & Neumann

Lavie, Smadar / Narayan Kirin / Renato Rosaldo (eds.) 1993. *Creativity / Anthropology*. Ithaca and London: Cornell University Press.

Leeuw, Gerardus von der 1920-1921. Die do-ut-des-Formel in der Opfertheorie. In *Archiv für Religionswissenschaft*, 241-253.

Leiris, Michel 1958. La Possession et ses Aspects Théâtraux chez les Éthiopiens de Gondar. Paris: Plon.

Lévi-Strauss, Claude 1952. *Race et Histoire*. Paris: Unesco.

Lewis, I.M. 1971. Ecstatic Religion: A Study of Shamanism and Spirit Possession. Harmondsworth: Penguin Books.

Leyshon, Andrew / David Matless / George Revill 1995. The Place of Music. In *Transactions of the Institute of British Geographers,* New Series, vol 20, No. 4, 423-433,

List of Medicinal Plants Deposited in Various Herbaria of the Botanical Survey of India (no author) 1960. In *Bulletin of the Botanical Survey of India*, 2, 1/2, 180-273. Calcutta, Botanical Survey of India.

Malinar, Angelika 2004. Mantra-Recitation as a Religious Institution: Shri Kalpataru Seva Ashrama in Bhubaneshwar. In Angelika Malinar / Johannes Beltz / Heiko Frese (eds.), *Text and Context in the History, Literature and Religion of Orissa*. New Delhi: Manohar, 175-202.

Mallebrein, Cornelia / Heinrich von Stietencron 2008. *The Divine Play on Earth Religious Aesthetics and Ritual in Orissa*. Heidelberg: Synchron Publishers.

Mallebrein, Cornelia 2000. The Vanishing World of Tribal Arts. In Pratabadity Pal (ed.), *Reflections on the Arts in India*. Mumbai: Marg, 48-59.

Mallebrein, Cornelia 2001. Tribal Art: Continuity and Change. In Pratapadity Pal (ed.), *Orissa Revisited.* Mumbai: Marg, 142-161.

Mallebrein, Cornelia 2004. Entering the Realm of Durga. Patkandha - a Hinduised Tribal Deity. In Angelika Malinar / Johannes Beltz / Heiko Frese (eds.), *Text and Context in the History, Literature and Religion in Orissa*. Delhi: Manohar, 273-299.

Mallebrein, Cornelia. 2004. Creating a Kshetra: Goddess Tarini of Ghatgaon and her Development from a Forest Goddess to Pan-Orissan Deity. In *Journal of Social Sciences*, 8 (2): 155-165.

Marriott, Mc Kim 1968. Caste Ranking and Food Transactions. A Matrix Analysis. In Milton Singer and Bernhard Cohn (eds.), *Structure and Change in Indian Society.* Cambridge: Cambridge University Press, 133-172.

Mauss, Marcel 1923/24. Essai sur le Don. Forme et Raison de l'Échange dans les Sociétés Archaïques. In *L'Année Sociologique*, seconde série, 1923-1924. Paris

Mauss, Marcel 1954 (1950). The Gift. Forms and Functions of Exchange in Archaic Societes. London: Cohen West.

Mc Luhan, Marshal 1962. *The Gutenberg Galaxy: The Making of Typographic Man.* Toronto: Universtiy of Toronto Press.

Mc Luhan, Marshal, 1994 (1964). *Understanding Media: the Extensions of Man.* Cambridge, Mass.: MIT Press.

Michaels, Axel 1998. *Der Hinduismus. Geschichte und Gegenwart*, München: C.H. Beck

Mohr, Hubert 2004. Religion in Bewegung – Religionsästhetishe Überlegungen zur Aktivierung und Nutzung menschlicher Motorik. In *Themenheft Ästhetik- Kunst-Religion Münchner Theologische Zeitschrift.* Jahrgang 55 , Heft 4, 310-324

Moutal, Patrick 1991. A Comprehensive Study to selected Hindustani Raga Sangita Based on Contemporary Practice. New Delhi, Munshiram Mancharlal Publishers.

Munda, Ram Dayal. 2002. India's Protection and Promotion of Tribal Rights: Obligations under ILO Convention on Indigenous and Tribal Peoples, 1957 (No. 107). (Paper submitted at Indigenous Rights in the Commonwealth Project South and South Asia Regional Expert Meeting, 11th–13th March 2002).

Münster, Daniel 2001. *Religionsäshtetik und Anthropologie der Sinne.* (Münchner Ethnologische Abhandlungen, 23). München: Akademischer Verlag.

Mukherjee, Prabhat 1986 (1978). Chaitanya in Orissa. In Anncharlotte Eschmann / Hermann Kulke / Gayan Charan Tripathi (eds.), *The Cult of Jagannath and the Regional Tradition of Orissa.* Delhi: Manohar.

Nayak, Prassana K. 1989. Blood, Woman and Territory. An Analysis of Clan Feuds of Donghria Konds. New Delhi: Publishing House.

Narjinari, Esther Sukruti 2009. Weaving Bodo Women's Identity in Traditional folk songs. In *Moving Words. Chotro Adivasi Voices and stories.* Volume 9 Number 1, 84-102.

Needham, Rodney 1967. Percussion and Transition. In *Man* 2: 606-614.

Nijenhuis, Ennie Te 1974. *Indian Music. History and Structure. Sechster Band. Handbuch der Orientalistik.* Abteilung Indien (hrgs. Jan Gonda). Leiden/Köln: E.J. Brill.

Obeysekere, Ganannath 1981. Medusa's Hair: An Essay on Personal Symbols and Religious Experience. Chicago: Chicago University Press.

O'Flaherty, Wendy Doninger (ed.) 1988. *Textual Sources for the Study of Hinduism.* Manchester: Manchester University Press.

O'Flaherty, Wendy Doniger (ed.). 1981. *The Rig Veda. An Anthology: one Hundred and Eight Hymns.* Selected, translated and annotated by Wendy Doniger O'Flaherty. Harmondsworth: Middlesex, England, New York.

O'Malley. L. S. S. 2007 (1909). *Bengal District Gazetteers Sambalpur*. New Delhi: Logos Press.

Ong, Walter J. 1969. World as View and World as Event. In *American Anthropologist* 71, 4, 634-647.

Ong, Walter J. 1991. *Orality and Literacy: the Technologizing of the Word*. London; New York: Routledge.

Otten, Tina. 2006. Heilung durch Rituale. Vom Umgang mit Krankheit bei den Rona im Hochland Orissas. LIT Verlag: Münster, Berlin.

Otten, Tina 2008. People of the Hills: How Rona Deal with Social Change. In Marine Carrin (ed.*), People of the Jangal: Reformulating Identities and Adaptations in Crisis*. Kopenhagen: Curzon Press, 93–118.

Otten, Tina 2010. The Concept of Biba Among the Rona of Highland Orissa. Wedding Rituals to Ensure Health. In Peter Berger, Roland Hardenberg, Ellen Kattner und Michael Prager (eds.), *The Anthropology of Values: Essays in Honour of Georg Pfeffer*. Delhi: Longman. 33–51.

Pantke, Christiane 2004. Kulturelle Identität und folkloristische Klischees. Die Bedeutung des „Museums der afrobrasilianischen Kultur" im gesellschaftlichen und kulturellen Kontext in Salvador da Bahia, Brasilien. In Peter J. Bräunlein (Hg.), *Religion und Museum. Zur visuellen Repräsentation von Religion/en im öffentlichen Raum*. Bielefeld: Transcript Verlag, 195–222.

Parry, Jonathan 1980. Ghosts, Greed, and Sin: the Occupational Identity of the Benares Funeral Priests. In *Man* (N.S.) 15, 88-111.

Patel, Kanji 2009. Come the Village Fair, May such Hunger. In *Moving Words*. Chotro Adivasi Voices and Stories. Volume 9 Number 1, 48-92.

Pattnaik, Direndranath 1971. *Odissi Dance*. Bhubaneshwar: Orissa Sangeet Natak Academi.

Pfeffer, Georg 1994. Music in Context: Ethnography and Meaning. In *Beiträge zur Musikethnologie* 30, 14–20.

Pfeffer, Georg 1997a. Die Haardebatte: Gender, Glatzen und Gewalt der Bondo. In *Zeitschrift für Ethnologie* 122: 183-208.

Pfeffer, Georg 1997b. The Scheduled Tribes of Middle India as a Unit. Problems of Internal and External Comparison. In Georg Pfeffer, Deepak K. Behera (eds.), *Contemporary Society: Tribal Studies Vol I: Structure and Process*. New Delhi 3–27.

Pfeffer, Georg 2001. A Ritual of Revival among the Gadaba of Koraput. In Burkhard Schnepel und Hermann Kulke (eds.), *Jagannath Revisited: Studying Society, Religion and the State in Orissa*. Delhi: Manohar, 123-148.

Poggendorf-Kakar, Katharina / Lidia Guzy / Hartmut Zinser (eds.) 2000. *Tradition im Wandel: Weibliche Religiosität im Hinduismus, Jainismus und Buddhismus.* Tübingen: Medien Köhler Verlag.

Prohl, Inken 2003. Zur sinnlichen Realität religiöser Praxis in der Aum Shinrikyô und ihrer Bedeutung für die Legitimation religiös begründeter Gewaltanwendungen. In *Zeitschrift für Religionswissenschaft*, 11, 259-276.

Prohl, Inken 2004. Zur methodischen Umsetzung religionsästhetischer Fragestellungen am Beispiel zen-buddhistischer Praxis in Deutschland. In *Themenheft Religion – Ästhetik – Kunst, Münchener Theologische Zeitschrift*, 55, 4, 2004, 291-299.

Prévôt, Nicolas 2005. *Jouer avec les Dieux*. Thèse impubliée soutenue le 12/2/2005, Université de Paris/Nanterre.

Prévôt, Nicholas 2008. How Musical is God? A Pantheon and its Music in Bastar. In Lidia Guzy (ed.), *Religion and Music*. Berlin: Weissensee Verlag, 75-88.

Radano, Ronald 2003. *Living up a Nation: Race and Black Music*. Chicago: University of Chicago.

Raheja, Gloria G. 1988. The Poison in the Gift. Ritual Prestation and the Dominant Caste in a North Indian Village. Chicago: the University of Chicago Press.

Ramusack, Barbara 2004. *The Indian Princes and Their States*. (The New Cambridge History of India). Cambridge /London: Cambridge Unversity Press.

Rangacharya, Adya 1982 (1971). *The Indian Theatre*. Delhi: National Book Trust.

Rangacharya, Adya 2003. *Natyasastra*. (English Translation with Critical Notes). Delhi: Munshiram Manoharlal Publishers Pvt. Ltd.

Ray, Sukumar 1985. *Music of Eastern India*. Calcutta: KLM Private Limited.

Roche, David 2000. Music and Trance. In *Garland Encyclopedia of World Music: South Asia*, 288–95.

Rothen-Dubs, Ursula (ed.) 1989. *Allahs Indischer Garten. Ein Lesebuch der Urdu-Literatur*. Frauenfeld: Im Waldgut Verlag.

Rouget, Gilbert 1990 (1980). La Musique et la Transe: Esquisse d'une Théorie Générale des Relations de la Musique et de la Possession. Nouv. éd. rev. et augm. Paris: Gallimard.

Sachs, Curt 1923. *Musikinstrumente Indiens und Indonesiens*, 2. Aufl. Berlin/Leipzig: Vereinigung Wissenschaftlicher Verleger Walter de Gruyter & Co ( Handbücher der Staatlichen Museen zu Berlin).

Sahoo, Bhakta Puran 2007. Borasambar: A Peep in to its origin & Early History. In *Bora Sambar Cup 2007 Souvenir*. Padampur: No Publisher.

Salomon, Rosalind 1984 (1982). *Kumari Puja or Worship of a young Girl as the Goddess*. Photographic Print: No Publisher.

Samaddar, Ranabir 1998. Memory, Identity, Power: Politics in the Jungle Mahals 1890-1950. London: Sangam Books.

Sax, Williams S. (ed.) 1995. *Gods at Play: Lila in South Asia*. New York: Oxford University Press.

Sax, Williams S. 2002. Dancing the Self: Personhood and Performance in the Pandav Lila of Garhwal. Oxford, New York: Oxford University Press.

Schaffer, Murray R. 1977. *The Tuning of the World*. New York: Knopf.

Scheombucher, Elisabeth 1993. *Gods, Ghosts, and Demons: Possession in South Asia*. In Heidrun Brückner, Lothar Lutze, Aditya Malik (eds.), *Flags of Flame. Studies in South Asian Folk Culture*. Delhi: Manohar, 239-267.

Scheombucher, Elisabeth 2006. Wenn Götter durch Menschen sprechen: Besessenheit in Indien. Berlin Reimer Verlag.

Schimmel, Annemarie 1992. *Mystische Dimensionen des Islam. Die Geschichte des Sufismus*. München: Eugen Diederichs Verlag.

Schlaffer, Heinz 1997. Einleitung. In Jack Goody et al. (ed.), *Entstehung und Schrift und Folgen der Schriftkultur*. Frankfurt: Suhrkamp, 7-23.

Schlesier, Renate / Agnes Schwarzmaier 2008. *Dionysos – Verwandlung und Ekstase.*(Ausstellungskatalog Pergamonmuseum Berlin). Schnell & Steiner: Regensburg.

Schnepel, Burkhard 2002. The Jungle Kings, Ethnohistorical Aspects of Politics and Ritual in Orissa. New Delhi: Manohar Publications.

Schnepel, Burkhard 2000. Der Körper im 'Tanz der Strafe' in Orissa. In Klaus-Peter Köpping / Ursula Rao (Hrsg), *Im Rausch des Rituals*. Hamburg: Lit. Verlag, 156-171.

Schnepel, Burkhard 2008. Tanzen für Kali. Ethnographie eines ostindischen Ritualtheaters. Berlin: Reimer.

Schoembucher, Elisabeth / Claus Peter Zoller (eds.) 1999. *Ways of Dying: Death and its Meaning in South Asia*. Delhi: Manohar.

Shukla, Shailesh / James Gardner 2006. Local Knowledge in Community-based Approaches to Medicinal Plant Conservation: Lessons from India. In *Journal of Ethnobiology and Ethnomedicine* 2006, 2:20, accessible online: (http://www.ethnobiomed.com/content/2/1/20)

Sellers, Julie A. 2004. *Merengue and Dominican Identity: Music as National Unifier*. Wyoming: McFarland Company Publishers.

Senapati, N. and B. Mahanti 1971. *Orissa District Gazetteers. Sambalpur*. Cuttack: Orissa Government Press.

Shah, Nila 2009. A Study of Contemporary Adivasi Literature of Jhardkhand. In *Moving Words. Chotro Adivasi Voices and Stories*. Volume 9 Number 1, 130-138.

Simon, Arthur 2000. Musik. In Bernhard Streck (Hg.), *Wörterbuch der Ethnologie*. Wuppertal: Edition Trickster im Peter-Hammer Verlag, 160- 165.

Skoda, Uwe 2005. The Aghria - a Peasant Casteon a Tribal Frontier. Delhi: Manohar.

Slawek, Stephen (ed.) 2000/2001 Asian Music 32: Tribal Music. In *Journal of the Society for Asian Music* Vol. 32/1. Texas, University of Texas at Austin.

Smith, Frederick M. 2006. The Self Possessed. Deity and Spirit Possession South Asian Literature and Civilization. New York: Columbia University Press.

Snodgrass, Jeffrey G. 2001. Beware of charitable souls: contagion, roguish Ghosts and the poisons of Hindu alms. In *Royal Anthropology Insitute* 7, 687-703.

Snodgrass, Jeffrey G. 2006, Casting Kings, Bards and Indian Modernity, Oxford University Press: London; 287-703.

Spradley, James 1979. *The Ethnographic Interview*. Manchester: Holt, Reinhart and Winston.

Stietencron, Heinrich v. 1972. *Ganga and Yamuna: Zur symbolischen Bedeutung der Flussgöttinnen an indischen Tempeln*. (Ganga and Yamuna: The Symbolism of River-Goddesses on Indian Temples). Wiesbaden, Harrassowitz.

Stietencron, Heinrich v. 1991. *Hinduism. On the Proper Use of a Deceptive Term*. In G.D. Sontheimer, H. Kulke (eds.), Hinduism Reconsidered, Delhi: Manohar, 11-28.

Stokes, Martin (ed.) 1994. Ethnicity, Identity and Music: The Musical Construction of Place. Oxford and Providence: Berg.

Stokes, Martin 1996 Music. In Alan Bernard / Jonathan Spencer (ed.), *Encylopedia of Social and Cultural Anthropology*. London: Routledge, 383-386.

Stoller, Paul 1996. Sounds and Things. Pulsations of Power in Songhay. In Carol Laderman and Marina Roseman (eds.), *The Performance of Healing*. New York: Routledge, 165-184.

Subramanian, Lakshmi 1999. The Reinvention of a Tradition: Nationalism, Carnatic music and The Madras Music Academy, 1900-1947. In *The Indian Economic and Social history Review*, 36, 2, 131-163.

Tambs-Lyche, Harald (ed.) 2004 (1999). *The Feminine Sacred in South Asia*. Delhi: Manohar.

Tedlock, Dennis / Bruce Mannheim 1995. *The Dialogic Emergence of Culture*. Illinois: University of Illinois Press.

Tingey, Carol 1994. *Auspicious Music in a Changing Society. The Damai Musicians of Nepal*. London: School of Oriental and African Studies.

Tiwari, Vineet 2009. Ulgulaan. In *Moving Words. Chotro Adivasi Voices and stories*. Volume 9 Number 1, 93-101.

Turner, Victor 1964. Betwixt and Between: The Liminal Period in Rites de Passage. Symposium on New Approaches to the Study of Religion. In *Proceedings of the 1964 Annual Spring Meeting of the American Ethnological Society*, edited by J. Helm. Seattle: American Ethnological Society, 4-20.

Turner, Victor 1969. *Ritual Process: Structure and Anti-structure*. (The Lewis Henry Morgan lectures). London: Routledge & Kegan Paul PLC.

Turner, Victor 1982. *From Ritual to Theatre. The Human Seriousness of Play*. New York City: Performing Arts Journal Publications.

Turner, Victor. 1957. *Schism and Community*. Manchester: Manchester University Press.

Turner, Victor. 1974. *Dramas, Fields, and Metaphors*. lthaca: Cornell University Press.

UNESCO 2004. Museum International. Views and Visions of the Intangible. No 221-222.

Valmiki, retold by Krishna Dharma 1998. *Ramayana: India's Immortal Tale of Adventure, Love, and Wisdom*. Los Angeles, Calif.: Torchlight Pub.

Vatsyayan, Kapila 1980. *Traditional India Theatre: Multiple Streams*. Delhi: National Book Trust.

Vatsyayan, Kapila 1996. *Bharata. Nataya Shastra*. Delhi: Sahitya Akademi.

Vir, Ram Avtar 1999. *Theory of Indian Music*. New Delhi: Pankaj Publications.

Vitebsky, Piers 1993. *Dialogues with the Dead*. New Delhi: Cambridge University Press.

Vitebsky, Piers 2008. Loving and Forgetting: Moments of Inarticulacy in Tribal India. In *Journal of the Royal Anthropological Insitute* 14, *243-261*.

Wade, Bonnie C. 1979. *Music in India. The Classical Traditions*. Eaglewood Cliffs: N.J. Prentice Hall.

Wade, Peter 2000. *Music, Race, and Nation. Música Tropical*. Chicago: The University of Chicago Press.

Wadley, Susan 1975. Shakti. Series in Social, Cultural and Linguistic Anthropology, No 2. Chicago: University of Chicago,

Waltzer, Michael / Edward Kantowicz / John Higham / Mona Harrington 1982. *The Politics of Ethnicity: A Series of Selections from the Harvard Encyclopedia of American Ethnic Groups*. Cambridge, Massachusetts, and London: The Belknap Press (Harvard University Press).

Weber, Max 1980 (1920). *Wirtschaft und Gesellschaft*. 5th rev. (edited by Johannes Winckelmann). Tübingen: J-B.Mohr.

Wegner, Gert-Matthias 1986a. Anruf der alten Götter - Notation und Analyse einer newarischen Trommelkomposition. In Bernhard Kölver (ed.), *Formen kulturellen Wandels und andere Beiträge zur Erforschung des Himalaya*. St. Augustin. VHG Wissenschaftsverlag, 312-340.

Wegner, Gert-Matthias 1986b. The Dhimaybaja of Bhaktapur - Studies in Newar Drumming I. Stuttgart: Franz Steiner.

Wegner, Gert-Matthias 1987. Navadapha of Bhaktapur - Repertoire and Performance of the Ten Drums. In Niels Gutschow and Axel Michaels (eds.), *Nepalica 4/22*. St. Augustin.

Wegner, Gert-Matthias 1988. The Naykhinbaja of the Newar Butchers - Studies in Newar Drumming II. Wiesbaden: Franz Steiner.

Werbner, Pnina / Basu, Helene 1998. Embodying Charisma. Modernity, Locality and the Performance of Emotion in Sufi Cults. London: Routledge.

Widdess, Richard 1995. The Ragas of Early India. Music, Modes, Melodies and Musical Notation from the Gupta Period to c. 1250.New York: Oxford University Press.

Wilke, Annette / Axel Michaels / Cornelia Vogelsanger (eds) 1994. *Wild Goddesses in India and Nepal. Proceedings of an International Symposium*. Bern and Zürich: Bern: Lang (Studia Religiosa Helvetica 2).

Wilke, Annette 2008. Sound and Sense. Sonic Perception in Hindu India. In Lidia Guzy (ed.), *Religion and Music*. Berlin: Weissensee Verlag: 15-60.

Wilke, Annette / Oliver Moebus (2012) Sound and Communication. An Aesthetic Cultural History of Sanskrit Hinduism. Berlin: de Gruyter.

Wulf, Christoph (Hrsg.) 1993. Das Ohr als Erkenntnisorgan. *Paragrana. Internationale Zeitschrift für Historische Anthropologie*. Band 2 (Heft 1).

Yang, Mina 2008. *California Polyphony: Ethnic Voices, Musical Crossroads*. Urbana: University of Illinois Press.

Zinser, Hartmut 1990. Ekstase. In Handbuch der Religionswissenschaftlichen Grundbegriffe (HrwG) 2, 253–258.

Zinser, Hartmut 1997. *Der Markt der Religionen.* München: Wilhelm Fink Verlag.

Zinser, Hartmut 2010. *Grundfrage der Religionswissenschaft.* Paderborn /München / Wien / Zürich: Ferdinand Schöningh.

Zuckerkandl, Victor 1958. *Sound and Symbol. Music as the external World.* Bollingen Series. Princeton: Princeton University Press.

# *Appendix: Oral Texts*

In the course of my sustainable documentation of the music of the Bora Sambar region, I discovered a highly sophisticated oral culture, whose sounds of words, poetry and music reveal indigenous theories of human life, the world and the cosmos. The narrative and poetic creations disclose a polyphonic synchronicity between both the world of hegemonial Hindu values and the indigenous world views - inseparably intertwined with each other. These cultural creations express themselves through the sounds of instruments and through the verbal metaphors of the local songs performed by musicians, singers and story tellers.

The oral texts rendered here do not represent "authoritative" versions. They are examples of the variations and modifications of a cultural memory and of culturally relevant themes, in terms of cultural *leitmotifs*. In a society dominated by orality, the cultural texts are fluid, and always individually re-enacted or modified, thus shaped by the inventive creativity of the artists. They thus on the one hand disclose an individual poetic and narrative creativity of the performer, singer, story teller and musician, as my interlocutors always explained to me that "*no story is retold exactly the same way*". On the other hand, they however do not represent totally individual inventions, but personal interpretations of the cultural *leitmotifs* of a local memory.

The selected oral texts are meant to manifest the richness of the oral culture of the Bora Sambar region, mediated and transmitted through instrumental and vocal sounds, through rituals and narrations. They are also meant to manifest the oral cultural heritage of this region which interrelates persistently with hegemonic Hindu narratives to *re*create and *re*tell local values, ideas and memories. I deliberately leave these texts largely uncommented to let them speak for themselves – in their own metaphorical language.

All relvant recordings can be found in CD-publication: Lidia Guzy 2008, *Par e Sur – Sounds of the Goddess, Bora Sambar Region / Eastern India.* ©2008 WERGO, SCHOTT MUSIC & MEDIA GmbH, Mainz, Germany. Museum Collection Berlin, ed. Lars-Christian Koch.

**Dhunkel bandana - the story of the dhunkel**

Transcription of a *dhunkel* song on the origin of the *dalkhai* dance "***dalkhai bandana***" (myth of *dalkhai*) [150] accompanied by the dhunkel instrument

**Prelude**

*Rama Rama Sri hari Rama* [repeated 2 times]
Rama [the name of God]-) is the Sri Hari [term for the supreme God])

*Srimukhe bahanaje Rama Kausalya nandana.*
I uttered the name Ram who is the son of queen Kausalya.

*Rama pada mor kara hela, Krishna pada mor kara hela.*
The name Rama has become my main direction, the name Krishna also became my main direction.

*Sunye baandha bhelaa je Rama pade baandha bhelaa.*
Make a raft foundation in the blank space, make a raft foundation in the name of Rama.

*Kuilli Kuilli batisa raga chhaasathi (nai) raaga halu.*
The cuckoo has 32 secondary musical tunes, She could tell 66 raagas [musical "tastes" = melodic and rhythmic musical lines in north Indian music] also.

*Pada debu bhaagaje kuilli pada debu bhaaga.*
And you will give is a portion of your tunes.

*Kaau kala kuilli kala je* [repeated 2 times]
The crow is black, the cuckoo also black.

*Aaur kala kiyelo kuilli* [repeated 2 times]
And oh cuckoo, who is even more black than you?

*Aaur kala maa Krishna kala ken* [repeated 2 times]
The most black is Krishna.

*Naame Chakaadola re* [repeated 2 times]
He, who is named Chakadola.

*Kaau bale rnor Rama Rama maa.*
The crow uttered the name of Rama.

*Gaai bole mor Raama Raam.*
The cow also uttered the name Rama.

---

[150] The recording was made on 25th September 2003 when visiting the village Duduki Jharia. The musician playing the *dhunkel* instrument is Ranjit Bag, from the Mali community. The transliterations of Oriya into English letters are locally common transliterations, realised by Surendra Kumar Sahu.

*Rakha Naarayana je prabhu garuda baahana.*
Oh God, take care of us, your vehicle is Garuda [the mythological king of birds].

*Aadya sira dasharaa maasen maa* [repeated 2 times] *Aadya sira dashami dina.*
In the beginning of the festive month dusshara and in the 10th lunar day of dusshara month.

*Naba khanda mor pruthibi re jagnya aarabhibe je prabhu.*
The sacrifice will start in the Nabakhanda [mythical place of the 9 lands of the world]

*Chauda (nai) bramhaanda re mataa mor jagya aarambhibe.* And, oh mother, this will be observed in the 14th universe [mythical place in the universe] also.

**1.**

*Gindel balm sahara thilaa maa.*
There was a city named Gindel.

*Se saharen Saadhaba thilaa.*
A merchant lived there.

*Satasaha panchaasa barsa banjhaa hoithilaa.*
He was childless for 750 years.

*Mane mane bhaabana kalaa, mane mane kalpanaa kalaa.*
He thought a lot about this [=he was depressed].

*Raatra suihaghadi ujaagaren maa sadhaba basilaa.*
Night after night he was sleepless.

*Saadhabani ku sange nei se aranye gamilaa je mata* [repeated 2 times]
And lastly he went to the forest with his wife for a whole day and a night

*Kete dura mor desanara hoigalaa saten se paara.*
They crossed many remote lands.

*Kapilasha kandaren jaai hoilaa haajara.*
And reached the Kapilash forest [mythically holy forest].

*Purba diga ku mukha kalaa, paschima ku se pachha kalaa.*
He sat there, looking forward to the east and back to the west.

*Maala ki japilaare se Shivanku janaana kalaa.*
He sang invocations to Shiva and incanted him.

*Saata dine mor saata raatin santusta hoile Shiva.*
After 7 days and 7 nights Shiva calmed down his please

*Jaachina kanyaa ratna ku pradana karile re Shiva*
and blessed a little girl to him.

**2.**

*Eka mukha hoi saadhaba gharaku gamilaa* [repeated 2 times]
Then the merchant left his home without looking backward [without remembering the bad times].

*Nija raajyare aasikari prabesha hoilaa re saadhaba* [repeated 2 times]
And he entered his own kingdom.

*Ehipari ketedina galaa, saadhabaani garbhabaasa helaa.*
After many days passed, the merchant's wife became pregnant.

*Taapare saadhabaaninka garbha sanchaara helaa.*
Then she had an abortion

*Saatabarsen mor saata kanyaa ratnajanarna hele segharen.*
but in between seven years, she gave birth to seven girl children [the *sato bhoni*= the seven mythical sisters]:

*Chanchalaa ,Bimalaa, Kansalaa, Pramilaa, Subhrataraa, mor Subhrakeshi* [repeated 2 times]
*Sana jhiara naama ate se naama ti Ahalya je.* [repeated 2 times]
The seven sisters are Chanchalaa, Bimalaa, Kansalaa, Pramilaa, Subhrataraa, Subhrakeshi and the last one is Ahalya

*Sadhaba bhaabilaa mane ho kalapana kala.*
The merchant thought that,

*Sivar thaanu bara anithili mui.*
"I had got the great favor of Shiva.

*Saata kanyaa je janma hele devi atanki manabi.*
Are the seven children celestial beings or humans?

*Napaarili jaani tanku napaarili chinhi.*
I cannot know, I cannot think."

*Tahi utaaru ketedina galaa, mane mane saadhaba chintaa kalaa*
After some days the merchant thought

*Saata kanyaa ratana nei aranyen garnilaa saadhaba* [repeated 2 times]
to leave the children in the forest.

*Jaaun jaaun deshaantara paara ratnagiriparbate jai hoila haajara*
After crossing many lands they reached the forest Ratnagiri [mythical forest].

*Tadu suryadeva asta hoigale paschima meru giridanda tale.*
The sunset started in the west.

*Chhai kanya ratna ku nein gachha mule bichhaai delaa.*
And the merchant left six girls beneath a tree.

*Khali Ahalyaa ku dhari saadhaba gamana karilaa re* [repeating 2 times]
The merchant only went away with the last one Ahalyaa.

*Ahalyaa kunein saadhaba Siaala bandha re baandhilaa.*
He tied her then to a siala bush. [common bush]

*Eka mukha hoi se raajyejai mililaa.*
Then he went back home without looking backwards for a single moment.

*Siaala bhanaare padina se mahaasati je jaana*
The abandoned Ahalya laid down in the Siala bush.

*Bikalare kare se rodana maa akulare kare se rodana*
And wept there.

*Ekamra banare shiba paarbati rahithile.*
At that time Shiva and Parvati were in the forest.

*Aranya bhramana pain baahara hoile.*
And they started a wandering tour.

*Buli buli mor kete dura hoigale paara.*
After moving a long way

*Giri parbate jai kari hoile haajara*
they reached the forest Ratnagiri.

*Tenu kari mor Mahaasati maa tenu kari mor Parbati*
This is why the great chaste Parvati

*Krandana dhwani karnare sunanti*[repeated 2 times]
listened to the weeping sounds of Ahalya.

*Sehi diga ku gamile maaje* [repeated 2 times]
Then Parvati moved towards the place

*Siala bhana rejai prabesha hoile*
And approached the siala bush

*Eka kanyaa ratna boli siala bhana ru anile*
She brought a little girl from the bush

*Kolaku karile re sati* [repeated 2 times]
And kept her in her lap.

*Aamar ghare tajhia nain ke Sibar gharen ta jhia ham*
Shiva and Parvati thought that they had no girl child

*Dhararam jhia re sina mor kola kth mor nei gale*
They accepted her as their adopted daughter

*Kapilashe prabesha hoile*
And they went back to Kapilash [holy forest].

**3.**

*Ehipari kete se dina ho chaligala tajaana.*
Like this – remember it – many days passed.

*Ekkus dina hoi aasilaa se ekkus dma hoina gala.*
21 days passed for the special day.

*Siva tenu mane bhabile chaara maananku pathaaile*
Then Shiva planned to send his spies/messengers.

*Purba paschima uttra dakshina gamana karile re se chaara gamana karile.*
They went to the four corners of east, west, north and south

*Rusi mathe jaai kahile ho, rusi mathe jaai baarataa dele.*
to give the message in the saint's hut.

*Mahi mandale Shiva Kanya naama karana debaa bhaie*
The girl was named as Shiva Kanya! - This was spread in the world.

*Chaara maananka baartaa paai chaari diga ku Raaja aasai.*
When getting the message from the messenger, all kings came there [to the Kailash forest].

*Raajya maananku Raaja aasi mathare mililere*
The kings met Shiva.

*Subarna aasthana dei je sammana rakhile re Shiva aadare rakhile*
Shiva gave them the honoring golden seats.

*Chaara mananka baarta paai risi mane gamai tahi*
The saints also came there after getting the news from the spy.

*Shiva mathe jai prabesha hoilere rusi.*
They entered Shiva's temple.

*Bhrugu, Angira, Durbasha, Poulastya, Maricha rusi Basista sahita misi hele sapta rusire maa mora hele sapta rusi.*
Bhrugu, Angira, Durbasha, Poulastya, Maricha and Basista are seven saints [of one mother]

*Shivanku dakilere risi paakhe daaki pachaari dele.*
The saints called Shiva and asked him

*Chhuaara keeun diga ku munda thilaa ho? keun diga ku pinda thilaa?*
On which side the head of the child was laid? And on which side the body of the child was?

*Keun parbate janmi kari baalika kaanduthilaa?*
In which forest the girl took birth and in which forest she was weeping?

*Shiva setharu kahileere maata shiva setharu uttara dele*
Shiva said and answered that:

*Giri parbate janma taara ho* [repeated 2 times]
"She took birth in the Giri forest.

*Purva diga ku munda kari paschima ku pachha kari*
She rested her head towards the east and back to the west

*Bikale krandana je sati mora akule krandana* On my chest she wept there."
*Rusi maane bichaara kale ho sapta aanguli gaara kaati naama dele taara re naama dele taara*
Then the saint considered to give the name to the child and drew a line of sapta anguli [local measure: the length of seven fingers]

*Aahalyaa boile maataanku Aahalyaa boile*
And said her to Aahlyaa.

*Rusi mane naamati dei*
The saints gave the name.

*Raajaa mane aasirbaada dei*
The king blessed her

*Nija raajye gamana kale se mathe*
They left their own kingdom and their huts

*Paalile ati jatane ho badhilaa dina ku dina*
Shiva brought her up with proper care and she grew day by day.

*Abhinaba ni jaubana maa ehipari kete je dina*
Like this after many days,

*Se jhia ku baara barasa je purana helare satinku* [repeated 2 times]
The youthful girl arrived in her twelfths years.

*Matanka pakhaku jai baraje maagilare jhia paada tale padilaa*
She went near her mother [Parvati] and took refuge at her feet to bless her. [= to prostrate is a local gesture of great respect, of adoration and loving humility]

*Jeun jagya jagate nahin diya bara sina go maataa*
Bless me with a gift of observation which is not known in the world

*Tenu kari mahaasati mor bhasile bachana*
Then the great chaste Parvati said that:

*Tirijaati abhela jaati najaanai kichhire muin najaanai kichhi*
"The female community is very negligent, they don't know anything.

*Tora pita kapilasha kandare maa joga dhyana re basichhanti*
Your father is mediating at the Kapilash forest [the abode of Shiva].

*Se thaabaku kanya ratna chala tu jhatati*
You set your journey there - be quick my dear child."

*Maata agyan re pai kari Ahalyaa chalilaa*
Ahalya went there after getting the order from Parvati.

*Saata samudra suladhaara tera nai ke bela paara*
She crossed the seven oceans, sixteen mountains and thirteen rivers.

*Kapilasha kandare jaai hoilaa haajara*
Then she reached the mountain top of Kapilash.

*Jogadhyana re basithile tenu ho shiva hojaanile*
Shiva sat there in his meditation position and knew that.

*Ahalyaa ra antara sabu jaanije shiva samasta jaanile*
He knew what Ahalyaa's heart is telling

*Joga dhyana ku bhaangidei maa* [repeated 2 times]
He broke his meditation

*Ahalyaa paasaku jai kolare basai je shiva gela e karile*
He kept Ahalya in his lap [he embraced her]

**4.**

*Keun kathaa maa ghati achhi keun bipada ghati achhi*
"What happended my dear child?

*Raajya ku chhadichhu je maata aranye gamichhu*
You have left the kingdom and came to the forest.

*Shiva katha maa sunikari Ahalyaa paadare padilaa*
After listening that from Shiva, Ahalya took refuge at Shiva's feet

*Jeun bara jagate nahin se bara dia boilaa*
She said: "bless me with a vow which is not existing in the world"

*Shiva kale bachana je (maata) bachana bhaasile*
Then Shiva said:

*Bhaai jagyan jagate nahin, kara sinaa bhale re maa* [repeating 2 times]
"The Bhai jagyan [the religious vow / adoration for the welfare of brothers] is not in the world, observe it from now on my daughter.

*Niama re chalile tuin brata demi muin re maa inor* [repeating 2 times]
Obey the rules I give to you

*Tini bela nain parajante ange tela na bolile, bhai rakta makhaa boile*
Until tinibela [tini — three, bela — half of the day) don't smear oil on your body. If you break this rule this equals to smear the blood of your brother.

*Tini bela parajante mukhe ama na bhunjile bhair maansa khia re jhia* [repeated 2 times]
Until tinibela don' take rice. If you take rice that is similar to eat the meet of your brother's flesh.

*Tini bala nain parajante haste kathi bhaangile, bhair haadabhanga* [repeated 2 times]
Until tinibela don't wash anything in your hand. If you are unable to observe this, it is like brushing your brother's bone."

*Sabu niama maanibi boli Ahalyaa sapatha kale*
Ahalya promised to obey all the rules

*Saata samudra tera nai paara hele re maataa raajyare milile*
After crossing seven oceans, thirteen rivers she reached her own kingdom

*Nagranaari maananku dakaai brata bujhaaile re maataa* [repeated 2 times]
She gathered together all the women of the town and instructed them about the rules of their [new religious] vow.

*Paahilaa rajani ante udey hele mor dina mani*
After dawn the night came and then the sun raised.

*Prabhaata samaya ru jaani, nara naari maananku gheni*
From the morning along with all men and women

*Samudraa re puni ja maa mane* [repeated 2 times]
They went to the ocean.

*Sehithaaru suna ho suna purva diga ku mukha kale*
There they listened, there they looked towards the east.

*Paschima ku pachhaje kari snahana karile*
And back to the west they took their bath.

*Sapta naari jejaaikari saata changhuri baali aani*
Seven women bring seven baskets of sand

*Prathame linga ku thaapilere maataa* [repeated 2 times]
First, they established the lingam [the phallic symbol of Shiva]

*Balukaa linga sthaapana kale*
They established the sand-phallus image.

*Dwitiya re agra pujaa Ganesha*
Second, they started the worship of Ganesha

*Trutiya re je adimaataa, chartutha re tini digara debataa*
Third, they worshiped Adimaataa [the first mother] and fourth they worshipped three deities of the three corners

*Panchama re BanDurga je maataa*
Fifth, they worshiped mother Bandurga [the forest Durga]

*Sastha re arambhilere maataa sargapura saaralaanku*
Sixth, the goddess Saaralaa of heaven

*Saptama re baais koti devataa tettis koti chaachuri naa koti katyaayaani*
Seventh, they worshipped 22 scores of deities, 33 scores of divine messengers and 9 scores demons.

*Naba kalasha saja kale naba kanya ratna je bahi*
Nine girls prepared to carry nine pitchers

*Dui batiaa baate aasi kalasha sthaapile*
On the cross roads they put the nine pitchers [the cross roads are an apotropaic symbol]

*Pujaa bidhi mor saari dei nrutya aarambhile*
After completing their worship they started to dance.

*Baajilaa ho bira baadya, baajilaa ho sankha naada*
The ritual music is played there and the shell's sounds resonate there

*Raajadaanda mor purigalaa baadya sabadare*
The king's street is filled with the sound of music

*Keun naari mor aanandare nrutya aarambhile sethaare*
Some of the women start to dance with pleasure.

*Naanaajaati mor geeta gaai dma bitaaile sethaare*
They passed the whole day singing various songs.

*Jui, jaai mor maalati, kiaa, ketaki, naageswara, arka, duduraa, swetachampaa ken mandaara*
Like the flowers of jasmine, screw pine, mesuaferra, naageswara, arka, duduraa, swetachampaa.

*Naba kalashe rakhi kari hoile bahara je maa mane* [repeated 2 times]
Kept in the nine pitchers they [=the goddesses] set out their journey

*Baajigala bira baadya aagho aagho chaalile bajaara*
The ritual music played and they went in front of the musical procession.

*Saata samudra mor sula dhaara tera nai ken hele paara*
They crossed seven oceans, sixteen fountains and thirteen rivers

*Chantiaa nagare milile re maa maane* [repeating 2 times]
And all the women reached Chantia town.

**5.**

*Tenu kari Ahalyaa naari Biswakarmaanku mane sumari*
Then Ahalya remembered Biswakama [Hindu god of instruments]

*Baikuntha pura ne Biswakarmaa je thilaa rahi*
Biswakarma was in heaven.

*Ahalya sumarina maatrake chhaamure milile re maataa* [repeated 2 times]
He met her after her calling [remembering].

*Biswakarmaanku dekhikari sundari bhase bachana*
After seeing Biswakarma she said him that:

*Sapta nadira tirare eka mandira tiaaribu*
"You will make a temple in the bank of Saptanadi river

*Ganga, Jamunaa, Saraswati anukhyane bahi jauchhanti*
The rivers Ganges, Jamuna and Saraswati have always flown there

*Semadhyare eka mandira tolibure jhatati*
Be quick to build a temple there."

*Ahalyaa agayaan paai Biswakarmaa jaai mandira tolilaa*
After getting the order from Ahalyaa, Bishwakarme constructed a temple

*Purva diga ku muha kalaa, paschima ku pachha kari mandira tolilaa*
He built the temple looking forward to the east and in the back to the west.

*Chha maasara se mandira chha dinare se tolidela*
He completed the temple within six days which normally takes six months

*Baikuntha pura ku jaai Biswakarmaa re mililaa*
Then Biswakarmaa went to heaven.

*Adbhuta naamaje eka nagra je thila rahi*
There was a village named Adbhuta

*Manikyapaatanaa desa se nagra atayi*
That village belonged to the Manikpatna kingdom

*Sei graamare maharanaa baasakari jr rahu thilaa*
In that village a potter lived

*Ahalyaanka sumaranaa chhamure mililaa*
He met Ahalyaa when Ahalyaa called him

*Jaa tume ho maharanaa samudra ne tirtha ku*
Oh potter man, go to the bank of the river

*Se mandira bhitaren toli deba debataa naama*
And make the images of the gods and goddesses.

*Maharanaaje aagyan paai mandire gamilaa*
Then the potter man went to the temple

*Baais koti debataa tettis koti ken chachuri chitraje aankilaa*
He drew the pictures of 22 scores of deities and 33 scores of messengers.

*Sesare Durgaa pinda aararnbha kalaa ken* [repeated 2 times]
Lastly he drew the image of Durga

*Saata thara katilaa aaur saata thara metailaa*
He drew all that for seven times and then for seven times consequently he erased it.

*Durgaa sira bankaa re maa maane saata dma bitije galaa*
Oh mothers, like this seven days passed but Durga's head remained awry.

*Jagyan dma ku mor aasi kari prabesha hoilaa*
The day of ritual observation arrived.

*Tenu kari Ahalyaa maata beda bramhaanku sumarile*
This is why Ahalya remembered Bramha [the creator]

*Sumaranaa maatrake Bramha ken ubhaa je hoile*
After remembering him, he appeared.

*Mandira bhitaren jai darashana dele*
And he entered the temple

*Bramha kamandalu paani aani sarba mahosodhi aanikari jala madhyare misaaile*
Bramha brought the kamandalu water and the sarbamahosodhi water [holy waters] to mix them

*Mrutyu sanjibani mantra padhi paani jhiti dde je Bramha* [repeating 2 times]
He chanted the mrutyusanjibani mantra [a holy verse] and sprinkled the sacred water.

*Baais koti debataa tettis koti chachuri jibanyasha paaikari atahaasya kale*
Then the 22 scores of deities and 33 scores of messengers became alive making a huge noise.

*Samastanka sira chhaata maa Durgaa sira je ache baanka*
All of the heads were straight but Durga's head was awry.

*Tenu kari debataa maane karataali dele*
So, the deities made jokes about her.

*Durgaa sira ki baanka kari atahaasya kale*
Then Durga got angry for her awry head.

*Tenu kari maa Durgaa devi maharanaanku dakaaile*
This is why Durga called the Maharanaa

*Samastanka sira chhaataje kintu mor bankaa ke helaaje?*
"All of heads are straight, but why is my head awry?"

*Boll pachaarile maata puchha kale*
Said the mother Durga

*Sehikshyani jagatara maataa Mahaaranaanku bhakhile re maataa* [repeating 2 times]
Immediately she killed the Maharanaa and sucked his blood.

*Sehi dinu jagatara maata sarba bhakhi naama tor sarbabhakhi*
From that day you mothers named her as sarbabhaki [this, who takes all].

### *Ghugia song*

Sung by Kageshwar Bag from Sakti village, the ghugia for the Gour and the Soara, accompanied on the *brahma veena*[151]

1. *Sri satya Jugpre mago helu purnomasi*
In the truth era you became most powerful like the day of full moon.

2. *Treta Yugare Mato helu Lankeswari*
O mother, in the third era you became the deity of Lanka [Sri Lanka]

3. *Dwapra jugare mago nama to hela Birabhadri*
In the second era your name was Birabhadri.

4. *Ahi Kalijuge mago nama tora Samley*
In today's Kali area [synonym for the worst area] your name is Samley.

5. *Aahipari debiinku je sarana pasuachi muhin.*
Such like to you, I pray to all goddesses.

6. *Na janile padama nago Salmey tuhi debu khanji.*
Give me the unknown sentences [give me a creative verbal spontaneity] and join new sentences, oh Samley!

7. *Gopala manakankara janmanama je kahiba bujhai.*
I will tell you about the birth name of Krishna's friends.

8: *Sri satya jugare kapila rusinka kapale gopala hoiele janama.*
In the true era the Gopals [name for Krishna's friends ] were born from the Kapila dynasty.

9. *Tahankara namamana kahideba suna*
Listen to their names and respect their titles

10. *Adinanda, Parswananda, Sudamananda, Merasananda, Udamananda*
[Names of Gopals]

11. *Kalijuge Khiranira boli nandankara nama*
In this Kali yuga time, there are two types of milkman (gour) community: the milkman gourd and the waterman gour.

12. *Burabara dine bhai Gopalanka janma.*
On Wednesday the Gopal were born.

13. *Somabara dine gai mananka janma*
On Monday the cows were born

---

151 The recording was made on 20th February 2006, at the village Sakti. The transliterations of Oriya into English letters are locally common transliterations, realised by Surendra Kumar Sahu.

14. *Tini hazara bastri lakhya gainkara nama*
There are three thousands and seventy-two lakhs [amount of 1 lakh= 100 000] of cow's names.

15. *Nila, Baula, Buduni, Bhallukuni, Satyachauri, Gainkara nama. Kapila, Kamadhenu, Boli Je gainkara nama.* [seven varieties of cow's names]

16. *Aahipari satapadma gainka nama kahili bujhai.*
Such like the seven lotus (*satapadma*) cows' name,s I explain you. [*satapadma gai*= the seven lotus cow is the name for a cow who gives more milk than others].

**Birthya's song – Ganga shrada geet (death procession song)**
Sung and composed by Alekh Panigrahi, accompanied on the *damburu* drum[152]

1. *Sahaa naama pitrunkara tate go niti! Abanaama jarajana.*
If you will do worship according to all [ritual] rule regulations, then your forefathers will be happy with you.

2. *Mane maana na kari pitru senge bihari*
Avoid any jealousy and wish the good for the ancestors

3. *Bhakati nirajata paana ho lakshye debaa debi maana*
And devote your life - as a result your personal god and goddess will be pleased with you

4. *Agati kari jiba paari ho jiba lakshye barsha taara*
Then, disasters will not occur for lakhs of years [more then 100 000 of years]

5. *Bhagati dusana se pitru debataa angati naamaku jaahaa*
Have you accumulated guilt, then your forefathers will give a new body [=you will be reborn]

6. *'Gaahaaka' ra dina lakshye ho samaaja pitru pita naama kahi*
The life period of a 'reciter' will be lakhs of days, because he recites the names of his paternal ancestors.

7. *Agati hoile pitru tari gale ayaya sata kahtaa mane*
Those will be released who obey this truth.

8. *Pitru debaa ho lakshye Ganga ku dhari*
And with keeping up the tradition of one lakh community people

9. *Gahagaha mana attire tosana lakshe pitrupitaa tora*
Your lakhs of kindred will be much pleased.

---

[152] The song was recorded on 01.04.2004 in the village Konsor; transliterated and transcribed by Surendra K. Sahu according to the locally common transliteration Oriya-English.

10. *Jagata paalina lakshe piru maana aaja bansata kala nirmaana he lakshe Gangaa je bhaai*The ancestors obeyed the system of the world [= the universe] and created a specific clan and a family.

11. *Aahaa thumbhe Gangaa Gayaa jiba mukta nohibaa dipaku*
You will go to the Ganga Gaya river - this is for your release,

12. *Tume lakshe Gangaa je bhaai*
You are the one lakh community people.

13. *Ghuba ghruta maana Patitapaabana maata pita sagaraku*
The ritualistic materials like ghee are for Patitabaabana [the God who saves the normal man] and for the parents of the Saagaraku [= a sea which symbolises the greatness of all people who believe in God and who worship their parents].

14. *Parama aatamaa chaali jaauthibe sunya sarjanaa maajanare saba gati ta dine.*
The supreme spirit will be going into the creative vacuum space [state of spiritual release] at the obsequies day.

15. *Ganga Gayaa pitrumaane he seva sebaarya dine.*
Oh! All you fathers, you should serve or worship the river Ganga Gaya whenever you have a chance.

16. *Pancha jaba tan a hele Bhaagarathi pita maata muka chare.*
[not understandable] [Bhagarati is the mythological ancestral figure who took the river Ganga from Parvatis head, thus saving the world from draught]

17. *Pitha mukha*
Father's mouth!

18. Brata juga dia Kahi kara naam Dwapare hari ta paana
[not understandable]

19. *Turtia jugare se Dungi Chuaana Harijana naama Kali Jugana*
In the progenitor's era of the world the first progenitor was called Dungi Chuhaan – now in the Kali area [worst world area] he is called Harijan.

20. *Lakhe Ganga bahi kahanti garbar baajuchhi Siva dambaru jana*
One lakh community brothers say proudly that "now the damburu is playing for us only"

21. *Gangaa Gayaa gale mukta kean Labhile ebe pitaaku hasaae je gangaa hau go paari.*
When we go to the river Ganges Gaya your soul will be released because the bones of your father are there, but if not - your father's soul has not found release.

22. *Naama hebaa bhaagirathi upar ho ganga heuje paari*
The name will be renounced as Bhaagirathi. In order to conquer all difficulties, we cross river Ganga.

23. *Aahaa pitaadeba pitruseba debaa debi sraga gati paha puja*
And the paternal ancestors will be at the place of heaven - with gods and goddesses.

24. *Duba Bhruta dipa jail alangana ebe pitru parimana dei je lakshya ganga ku dhari*
You should stick to your community: to your forefathers by offering them sandal, ghee and a lamp.

25. *Bhaitarani nad! ku hoi bu paari je lakhey ganga ku dhari*
You will cross the Baitarani river through the community people.

26. *Tapa japa kari Bhagirathi putra lakshey Ganga jaati tora.*
The one lakh community people are like the "Ganga" through which Bhaagirathi saved his forefathers.

27. *Saraju nadee re panda paari thibu ebe Ganga jalare*
You will observe the obsequies rites in the bank of Sarah river and in the Gaga water.

28. *Bhaai bhauni samasthe jaana ho lakhe Ganga ho puna.*
Oh, brothers and sisters and also all of you [meant are all members of the community], you should know that!

29. *Sebaa karu thibu niti je niyame pita mata mukha chaanhi*
You will obey and observe the rules and regulations everyday respecting always your parents.

30. *Chaauda tepana prusha ganu thibu mukati labhibu barije*
Near about the 14th to 13th ancestry - you will release with all your community people.

31. *Bahgirathi nama bela tari he mukhe Ganga ku dhari.*
Bhagirathi was uttering the name Ganga in his mouth for his forefathers and he was released when he has Ganga from heaven.

32. *Jete deba debi sarba pitrumane swargagati mukti paije lakhe Ganga ku dhari.*
All god and goddesses and the ancestors have their home in heaven and are happy with the one lakh community people.

33. "*Chhatra pati manima – Tora Chhatra pati Manima aatha – Gune Bhamana na Dungi Chhuhan*" – "*Raja Gjapati mahraj bikuntha pure thaan- Lakhe gharke lakhe samaj chhatra pati manima*"
"O emperor! - The eighth fold of the sacred thread wear the Brahmin, but the nine fold of sacred thread wear Dunghichhuan"- "So the king Gajapati knows the place in heaven for one lakh homes and community people".

34. *Haribola daaka padu acchi sarba jaaka jagatare*
The sound of Haribola [name of a local god] is vibrating in every corner of the world.

35. *Naba badya baaju acchi sabu sthane naba khanda mahi tale jiba parama!*
Now the 9 kinds of instruments are sounding it the world!

36. *Ebe Baitarani nadire paari ho pitru debata jete aaja mukati hoiba puna he lakhe ganga jibana.* The unique spirit now crosses the Bhatarani river. All paternal ancestors are crossing the river - lakhs of people's lives will be purified today

37. *Naba gadi dine pitru udhariba saraju nadire jai.*
One day you have to go and save the paternal ancestors at the Saraju river.

38. *Lakhe ghara maana pujaa paau thiba aaju Bhagarathi putra !*
In one lakh homes you will be worshiping from today, Oh son of Bhagarathi!

39. *Baara baara bari barasa pariyante tapashya pari ta purna ho bhaagarathi putra.* Bhagarathi mediated twelve years in order to save his forefather from punishment.

40. *Tebe Ganga Sambhalibe Taanku ho Bhaagarathi putraku.*
So the Ganga will take care of Bhagirathi's sons.

41. *Pita mata baikuntha bahana ho aaja subha ta dina.*
The parents avoid the place Baikunthapura(near God) because of an auspicious day.

42. *Lakhe bhai bandhu kutumba sahi je Gangare kale sarana.*
With one lakh community people, with the whole kindred they observe the obsequies rites at Ganga.

43. *Hari bola daka manima je daka sabada sarita galare aajun helu mukati.*
Through the sound of Haribala and through the sound of Manima [a local god's name] we are released today.

44. *Lakhe gharar saba tara gatigo aaun helu mukati!*
From today the one lakh community of forefather's souls also got salvation. From today on, we got liberation!

45. *Aahaa ghaata daana baata daanaje, dae khana daana deuthiba bhaai.*
The donation at the *ghat* [ghat= place on the sea shore where the hairs during the funeral ceremony are shaved] are expensive and the sacrificial fee must be paid.

46. *Khanda ghaata daana pitrupita maane bakunthe paaibe jaai go lakhe Ganga je bhaa i- o Chhatra pati manima* ![repeated twice]
At the end of the village street where the people stop with the dead body for the last look, they leave some paddy in a winnowing fan. They leave an earthen pot by giving their donations to the paternal ancestors. They will hold the place in heaven. Oh, community people!

47. *Ghee, dhupa, bati, deepa, jalui thiba charana mukati dine.*
They lighted the lamp, the candle of ghee and incense in the day of liberation.

48. *Lakhe ghara maana puja paau thiba chhau bhuji Sansara dine je aaja sarana gali*

In lakh homes all community people will worship you in the four directions of the world. Today I praise you and take refuge at your feet [gesture of devotion and respect]

49. *Ebe Gangaru heli na paari ho aaja sarana gali*

Now, I cross the Ganga river and today I take refuge at you feet!

50. *Ganga re janama Ganga paari jana niti karu thibu pujaa.*

We are born out of the Ganga river- that means that we have grown up with our surrounding, with our community and that we have to cross the Ganga river for the whole of our life. We should daily worship Ganga!

51. *Lakhe ghara pain shibbadya baaja chhau bhuji parama raja go aaja mukati baate.*

Shiva's drum plays today for one lakh houses, for their liberation.